READING STRATEGIES:
Focus on Comprehension

READING STRATEGIES: Focus on Comprehension

second edition

Yetta M. Goodman
University of Arizona

Dorothy J. Watson
University of Missouri

Carolyn L. Burke
Indiana University

Richard C. Owen Publishers, Inc.
Katonah, New York

"The Stonecutter" from *Roads to Everywhere* of THE GINN BASIC READERS by David H. Russell and others. © Copyright, 1966, 1948, by Ginn and Company. Used by permission of Silver Burdett Ginn Inc.

The poem "The Pickety Fence" from *One at a Time* by David McCord. © Copyright 1952 by David McCord. Used by permission of Little, Brown and Company.

Library of Congress Cataloging-in-Publication Data

Goodman, Yetta M., 1931–
    Reading strategies : focus on comprehension / Yetta M. Goodman,
Dorothy J. Watson, Carolyn L. Burke. — 2nd ed.
      p.   cm.
    Includes bibliographical references and index.
    ISBN 1-878450-86-7 (pbk.)
    1. Reading comprehension.   2. Reading.   I. Watson, Dorothy J.
(Dorothy Jo), 1930–   .   II. Burke, Carolyn L.   III. Title.
LB1050.45.G66   1996
428.4'07—dc20   95-49164
                                      CIP

RICHARD C. OWEN PUBLISHERS, INC.
PO Box 585
Katonah, New York 10536

Printed in the United States of America

9 8 7 6 5 4 3 2

Preface

Reading Strategies: Focus on Comprehension applies sociopsycholinguistic concepts to specific reading strategy lessons within a whole language curriculum. It documents how reading lessons are a part of a school reading curriculum that is part of reading in the larger world. This book is written for classroom and resource teachers and those planning to teach who want to keep reading embedded in a whole language context rather than focused on isolated skills. It is particularly well suited to the development of whole language reading programs that make use of a wide range of trade books and authentic reading experiences. It is appropriate for use in graduate and undergraduate courses in reading assessment, informed and authentic assessment, special education, miscue analysis, reading comprehension, and reading instruction.

The concepts behind *Reading Strategies: Focus on Comprehension* started to develop in 1973. It is being revised to take into consideration recent understandings about the reading process, the writing process, authentic assessment, and the development of whole language. We want to reflect the greater focus on authentic reading experiences as well as take into account authentic assessment that is evident in whole language classrooms today.

Reading researchers and theorists have been developing models of the reading process based on insights from linguistics, psychology, anthropology, and the social nature of learning throughout the twentieth century. These models are intended to help answer the questions: How do people read? How do people learn to read? What text features and instructional features affect reading and learning to read? What are the human factors concerned with social, political, linguistic, and pedagogical issues that affect reading and learning to read? What is the nature of literacy in our culture and how does this impact reading and learning to read? Teachers are constructing their knowledge about reading from stimulating dialogue taking place in the field and by actively participating in the debates. Teachers are asking, "How can I take all this new knowledge and put it to use in my classroom? How can I use my knowledge to observe students reading and understand what I hear and see?" We are joining the conversation by addressing many of these questions in this book.

Our research, supported by others, has led us to believe that the reader's focus must always be on constructing meaning, using his or her knowledge in transaction with the published text (K. Goodman 1994; Rosenblatt 1978). The reader's proficiency in constructing meaning occurs as a natural consequence of using written language for real (authentic) purposes. Teachers who understand the importance of how readers become proficient organize a literate environment for students so that the natural reading process is nurtured. Reading instruction in school settings is greatly affected by views of literacy held by members of society at large. It is, therefore, necessary to use the latest knowledge about reading, reading instruction, and the social community to plan and develop reading programs and instruction in schools.

Reading Strategies: Focus on Comprehension has two parts. Part I, "Reading and the Reading Curriculum," places the reading process within a language framework in a sociocultural context. It includes our general rationale and theoretical perspective about the reading process and reading instruction. We explore the process of reading as it relates to the other language processes of listening, speaking, and writing. Language, art, music, dance, and math are among the many alternate sign systems that communicate meaning. The different perspectives which we take as we make use of alternate sign systems in exploring our world become systematized into alternate domains of knowledge (i.e., social studies, biology, humanities). We use knowledge about language, learning, teaching, and curriculum to develop a rationale for a reading curriculum in the sociocultural context of the classroom. We explain why a whole language comprehension-centered transactional reading program is the most effective way to teach and relate such a program to a whole language view of curriculum.

Part II, "Reading Strategy Lessons," specifies instructional experiences that enable readers to become secure in their quest for meaning. The specific strategy lessons grow out of our theoretical framework using a nesting metaphor that places reading instruction in the context of all the curricular experiences in the classroom and places literacy in the learners' world inside and outside of school. The three chapters in Part II are organized by focusing on the language cueing systems: semantic/pragmatic, syntactic, and graphophonic. The reading strategies of sampling, inferring, predicting, confirming, and integrating meaning are highlighted within each language system.

The text for each reading strategy lesson and the procedures for each literacy event are an organized classroom procedure through which individual, group, or class lessons can be presented. In addition, each organized experience explains why the lessons and events are important, describes the students whom the lessons and events will benefit, and provides additional understandings about the relationship of these procedures to sociopsycholinguistic views of language, learning, teaching, and curriculum. In this way we show that each lesson grows out of knowledge and theory.

Reading Strategies: Focus on Comprehension is appropriate for teachers with varying degrees of experience and expertise in the teaching of reading. Therefore, this book may be read in a variety of ways.

For example, preservice and inservice teachers who are new to a comprehension-centered whole language view of the reading process may want to read the first three chapters and the general information that precede the strategy lessons and then select one or more students to work with who will benefit from the lessons. The specific rationale and strategy lesson is most helpful when the teacher is ready to present the lesson to students. After working with some students, the teacher will find it beneficial to read additional information about the reading process, strategy lessons, and miscue analysis listed in the references.

For those familiar with a whole language view of reading, it may be most helpful to review Chapters 1 and 2 and read Chapter 3. Then, the experienced teachers may select students with similar reading profiles, find the strategy lessons written for those students, and plan to research the effectiveness of the strategy lessons with students. Prior to presenting the lessons, these teachers may read the rationale and lesson plan for the appropriate strategies, making appropriate adjustments to their specific situations.

WHO WE ARE

Individually and collectively, we have had considerable experience teaching children, adolescents, and adults in elementary and secondary schools and in teacher education programs in colleges and universities. Our teaching experiences have been enriched by our research and involvement with teachers in curriculum planning and professional development. In association with Ken Goodman, we have been involved in miscue analysis research projects, taping the reading of hundreds of readers of various ages and proficiencies and analyzing their miscues in order to learn about the reading process. Our research also involves studying early literacy development, documenting the ways readers become consciously aware of their own miscues, their personal views of reading, and the effect of these views on their reading. We also are actively involved with teachers/researchers studying literacy learning in their classrooms.

We are always relating research and theory with practice. We believe that what is happening in whole language classrooms influences research as much as research has influenced the development of whole language. We are interested in the experiences and knowledge that support teachers of reading, as well as the experiences and materials needed to support students as they learn to read. Through our work with teachers, we have developed instructional procedures that focus on helping readers develop their strengths. All of our teaching and research experience has led us to view the reader's search for meaning as the primary focus of reading. When reading instruction supports readers' construction of meaning, the natural desire to make sense is legitimatized and readers' energies are expanded productively. The reward for such effort is comprehension: the readers' understanding of the published text. Because we are aware of the social nature of reading, we always think about reading in the broader sociocultural context of the classroom and the community.

We believe that within the school the teacher plays the most significant role in helping students learn to read. No published reading materials or programs can teach students to read; these are only tools. In the hands of a master artist, good tools can be used to produce a great work of art. In the hands of an insecure or weak artist, not even superior tools are very helpful. Teachers are like artists as they construct classrooms that are innovative and conducive to learning. Artists bring to their work knowledge of perspective, color, line, form, space, and theme, as well as techniques implemented with a variety of tools. Outstanding teachers bring to reading instruction a strong knowledge base of language, learning, and teaching, and they know the cultural background and experiential differences of their students.

Reading Strategies: Focus on Comprehension is organized to provide support for this background knowledge and, at the same time, offer suggestions for the selection and construction of reading materials.

Teachers are decision makers. It is not our intention to tell teachers what to do. Rather, this book is an invitation to consider the information; to demonstrate the relationship between theoretical belief, language, knowledge, and practice; and to provide examples of lessons to serve as guidelines or demonstrations for teachers to use in constructing their curriculum. This is meant to serve as a guide so that teachers can use their professional judgment and adapt lessons to meet the needs of the readers in classrooms and school settings. It is often helpful to write lessons with other teachers. It is essential that teachers adapt, modify, and personalize these lessons based on their unique personalities, their knowledge, and their theoretical views.

This work has been modified and developed through the help of many colleagues who have reviewed and critiqued our work throughout the years. We appreciate the benefit of their experience and thoughtful opinions. We are especially grateful to Nancy Browning, Marilyn Carpenter, Debra Jacobson, Ann Marek, Prisca Martens, Marilyn Richardson, Marie Ruiz, Monica Taylor, Mary Weiss, and Kathryn

Whitmore and to the authors of the strategy lessons for students: Valerie Gelfat, Debra Goodman, Charlotte Hazelwood, Barry Sherman, and Irlene Sherman.

Above all, we owe a great debt to the students and their teachers with whom we have worked over the years to research and critique the strategy lessons, the literacy events, and the curriculum we propose.

Yetta M. Goodman
University of Arizona
Education 504
Tucson, AZ 85721

Dorothy J. Watson
University of Missouri
216 Townsend Hall
Columbia, MO 65211

Carolyn L. Burke
Indiana University
Reading Department
Bloomington, IN 47401

Table of Contents

Part I

Reading and the Reading Curriculum

1

Reading and Reading Strategies: The Making of Meaning

THE READING PROCESS

Reading is a problem-solving, meaning-making process. As readers, we consider the meaning the author is making while, at the same time, we are building meaning for ourselves. We use our own language, our own thoughts, and our own view of the world to understand the author's meaning. The language, thoughts, and world views of both the author and the reader are influenced by personal and social histories. Our interpretations are structured and directed by what we know.

Because of the differences between the language, thoughts, and meanings of the author and those of a reader, reading can never be an exact process. Because the language and thought of the reader transact with the language and thought of the author represented in the published text, readers can never be certain that they have discovered the meaning the author intended. The term *transaction* is used to suggest the dynamic change that takes place in readers whenever they have decided to actively engage with a published text. The reader and the text are changed through the transaction (Rosenblatt 1938, 1978). However, since readers are compelled to make sense, they interpret actively while reading in order to build meaning, thus achieving their ultimate goal. The reader is as active in constructing meaning as the writer is in producing written language. Both the author and the reader are powerfully influenced by views of literacy held by their cultural groups. All these layers of complexity are considered in developing a model of the reading process.

The model of reading presented in Figure 1-1 is an attempt to graphically represent the reading process. Reading starts with an inquiry by the reader. To help solve the major problem confronting every reader—*What does what I'm reading mean to me?*—the reader uses a number of complex plans or strategies (K. Goodman 1994). The significant strategies in the reading process involve *sampling, inferring, predicting, confirming,* and *integrating.* Simultaneously, the reader is integrating the new information, ideas, and feelings with the knowledge he or she already has. These strategies are used by all readers with varying degrees of proficiency from the very earliest of reading experiences. In most cases, readers are not consciously aware of the complexity of the reading process as they engage in comprehending what they read.

Sampling, Inferring, and Predicting Strategies

Readers use their purposes, language proficiency, and knowledge about the world to sample the printed material, to infer aspects of the meaning of the text, to answer self-posed questions, and simultaneously to make tentative predictions such as the following:

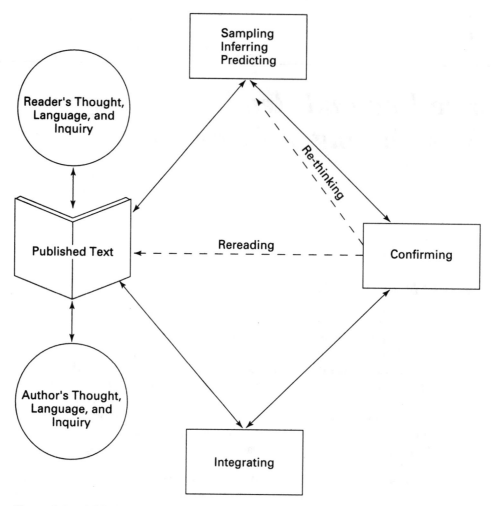

Figure 1-1. A Model of Reading

- Is the printed material fiction, a recipe, a description, song lyrics, traffic directions, or expository text?
- Is the format of the piece narrative, poetry, play, dialogue, or comic book?
- Is the writer's style formal, informal, technical, inviting, or difficult?
- If the piece is fiction, is it romantic, mythological, political, historical, or science fiction?
- Are the events initiating or following in the story going to be happy, sad, perplexing, exciting, depressing, or . . . ?
- Does the phrase "extenuating circumstances" mean "long and drawn out" as in "extended" or . . . ?
- Will the next word be a noun, a verb, an adjective, or . . . ?

(The above questions and predictions are rarely conscious but readers need such knowledge to continue reading.)

When a teacher shows first graders a big book and asks "What will this be about?" the readers might say, "It's going to be about a boy who's going to get into trouble." The children use their knowledge about stories, book handling, and print to *sample* format, illustrations, and print, and to *infer* possibilities. Based on additional information from what they sample from the cover of the book and hear from other children and the teacher, they infer and *predict* from a number of possibilities, all of which seem true at this particular moment. Older readers do the same thing.

When they sample from the sports page of a newspaper, they infer that there will be the language of sports, information about their local team, names of particular sports figures, cities, or sports arenas, for example; and based on their knowledge of the sports world, they make predictions to fit what they expect to find in the text. The more the reader knows about the sport and is experienced in reading about sports, the more likely it is that the predictions will match the sports writer's language and content.

Such hypothesizing involves sampling, inferring, and predicting. Sampling involves selecting information from the available information on the basis of inferences and predictions. In sampling, the proficient reader selects the least amount of print information necessary to make inferences and predictions. Inferring is coming to understandings based on informed predictions, and at the same time informed predictions are based on inferences. Inferring and predicting are not trial and error phenomena; these natural reading strategies are based on knowledge and background experiences. Sampling the text, inferring, and predicting are integral and cyclical. These reading strategies usually occur without conscious awareness.

Consider the following:

> **lag** [lăg] *v.* lagged, lag·ging, lags . . . 1. To fail to keep up a pace; straggle. 2. To proceed or develop with comparative slowness: *The electric current lags behind the voltage.* 3. To fail, weaken, or slacken gradually; lag . . . —*n.* 1. The act, process, or condition of lagging. 2. One that lags. 3. A condition of slowness or retardation . . .
> **la·gniappe** [lăn-yăp', lăn'yăp] *n.* . . . . 1. A small gift presented by a store owner to a customer with the customer's purchase. 2. An extra or unexpected gift or benefit . . . [. . . from American Spanish (*la*) *ñapa...*]
> **laid** [lād] *v.* Past tense and past participle of *lay.*
> **lais·sez faire** Also **lais·ser faire**. [lĕs ā fâr']. *n.* 1. An economic doctrine that opposes governmental regulation of or interference in commerce beyond the minimum necessary for a free enterprise system to operate according to its own economic laws. 2. Noninterference in the affairs of others. [French . . . to let, allow . . . to do]—laissez-faire' *adj.*

(Soukhanov 1992, 1007–1008)

The moment you perceive the example above, you immediately start sampling, inferring, and predicting. You do not see every letter and word. Rather, you tap the knowledge you have constructed through years of experience with written language, in this case, dictionary use. You infer the kind of reading material that is being presented but also begin to predict what purposes you might have in using these dictionary entries. Even though we requested that you read the passage, you may have chosen not to read it all. You probably ignored the pronunciation marks because you knew you would not need to pronounce the words, or if you knew how to pronounce them, you knew you did not need the marks. You may have glanced at the example and read this paragraph first because you didn't want to expend any effort reading it until you believed you could make an inference about the purpose. The decisions to read or not to read and what features of the print to attend to are based on inferences about, and predictions of, what aspects of the material are going to be significant. Did you react differently to unknown words than to familiar ones? Were they all equally familiar? Your reactions to specific words are based on predictions of how much you would know about the words. You were probably not concerned about the incomplete sentences ("Also laisser faire") and lack of parallel grammatical construction ("The act, process, or condition of lagging.") because you expected and, therefore, predicted just these kinds of non-parallel grammatical structures in dictionary entries. If the entry had been the beginning of a novel, such language units would have been jarring because you would have predicted complete sentences. Were you immediately aware of the words that were not common English spellings (*lagniappe, laissez*)? Once again, your years of being an experienced language user provided you with the necessary predicting strategies to quickly perceive non-English or unusual spelling patterns.

When we read, we infer, based on our schema (the organized knowledge we have in our brains about the world), why certain features have been written and what purposes they serve for the author and for us. We know the author intends for us to understand unstated assumptions and ideas. We do not make predictions on the basis of looking at every punctuation mark, letter, word, or sentence. Instead we sample the surface information based on what we have learned over years of being readers (and writers) and what we consider to be the most significant aspects of the available language.

Young beginning readers also make appropriate predictions based on their print experiences as they interact with a variety of environmental settings, are read to, and see people write. They sample cues surrounding the print, such as pictures, nonalphabetic symbols, color, and graphic design, as well as information about the relevant contextual setting, in order to infer and predict what the print might say. For example, preschoolers predict on the basis of the stylized, multicolored letters, shape and design of the carton, and the functional setting that the print is "Crest" or "toothpaste." On the other hand, they do not look at such a carton and say "McDonald's" unless someone has placed golden arches next to the toothpaste logo (Y. Goodman et al. 1989). Beginning readers sample a wide range of relevant cues for inference and prediction; they know that the print "says something," that it communicates. Young children's responses during the reading of patterned, predictable books show their ability to infer and predict.

As readers, we sample, infer, and predict, using all the language systems. We interact with our knowledge about the relationship between the letters and sounds of the language as we predict graphophonic units of language. (We never predict an *ng* as the beginning of an English word unless we have experience with the Vietnamese language.) Our knowledge of the rules of grammar or syntax is brought to bear as we use appropriate linguistic cues to predict the syntactic system of language. (We know when to expect dialogue or questions. We know when to expect male or female pronouns if the language uses pronouns. If it doesn't, we select other cues to predict gender.) Our understanding of the world around us helps us to infer what the author means and helps us to predict the language and meanings of the text as we use the semantic and pragmatic systems of language. (We would hardly expect a robot to be in a chapter about George Washington unless we were reading a science fiction novel.)

Readers sample and infer the most significant graphophonic, syntactic, semantic, and pragmatic cues, and they predict what they believe subsequent graphophonic, syntactic, and semantic structures are going to be. No reader uses all of the available cues. Reading would be too slow and inefficient if this were so. Nor are the cues sampled in any consistent order or sequence. The weight and significance readers give to individual cues vary with the experiences and language information they bring to their reading and depend on the predictions the readers make about the specific purpose and the nature and content of the text. Sampling, inferring, and predicting strategies used by readers to transact with the language cueing systems occur so rapidly as to appear simultaneous.

Confirming Strategies

As inferences and predictions are made, readers test these hypotheses against their linguistic and conceptual knowledge to see if they are meaningful. Such hypothesis testing leads to the confirmation or disconfirmation of the semantics and of the syntax through which the meaning is being constructed.

Readers ask two questions to test their predictions: *Does this sound like language? Does this make sense to me?* If the answer to both questions is yes and if the material is worthwhile, reading continues. However, if the answer is no, optional strategies are available to readers:

- Regress, reread, and pick up additional cues until the text makes sense.
- Stop, consider, and rethink why what is being read doesn't seem to make sense. Adjustments are made without rereading.
- Continue reading in order to build additional context; in so doing, generate enough understanding to decide why things don't make sense.
- Stop reading because the material is too difficult or not relevant.

Consider the following passage[1]:

> Shirley was a beautiful yellow canary. He was loved by his family, but they were all disappointed because he didn't sing very much or very often.
>
> Shirley would welcome the members of the family with tiny tweets whenever they came home. He chattered whenever he heard people talking, but he never sang.
>
> One day the man who gave Shirley to the family came to visit. They told him that they loved Shirley but wished he would sing. He went to the cage and held Shirley in his hand.
>
> He called out, "Shirley is a female canary, not a male. I must have made a mistake when I gave her to you. Female canaries don't usually sing."
>
> The family continued to call the canary Shirley but began to refer to him as "her."

Please reexamine the selection and with a pencil place a check mark at any point in the reading where you regressed for any purpose or where you were puzzled by what you were reading.

Each reader brings a unique background and experience to the written material so we can't possibly predict everyone's unique miscues. There are many places where you might have been aware that you wanted to confirm or disconfirm your predictions.

If you predicted that Shirley was female, it probably surprised you, at least momentarily, that a male pronoun was used to refer to the canary. You might even have read *she* for *he* at the beginning of the second sentence and had to reread to disconfirm your prediction of a female canary. You might have stopped to rethink the relationship between the male pronoun and a name that is not commonly used for males in your experience.

Did you predict that the family in the story was a bird family or a human family? If you predicted a human family, subsequent information confirmed your guess and you had no rethinking to do. However, if you predicted a bird family, you had to reorganize your notions about the story when you got to the third paragraph and had to disconfirm your prediction.

In the third paragraph, there are ambiguous references to "he." Did you get confused and think the paragraph was badly written because of the ambiguity? Did you rethink or reread in order to confirm or disconfirm who was doing what in the story?

You may have knowledge about canaries that helped you predict the reason the bird was not singing. You probably felt good about your prediction when you confirmed it at the end of the story.

---

[1]Our examples are usually short because of the limitations of space and somewhat contrived because of the points we are trying to make. You might try these same strategies with a real article or story.

Did you want to reorganize the last sentence into two sentences? Did you try to create a first sentence that ended with *canary,* and start a second sentence with *Shirley?* If you did, you had to rethink the structure and change it back into a single sentence.

As you examine your check marks, explore why you reacted to the particular language units as you did. Consider how your knowledge of language and the world interacted with the print, the grammatical structure, and your thoughts about what the author was trying to say.

Beginning readers also test their hypotheses while they read. The more information they have available to them as they interact with print, the more appropriate their sampling, inferences, predictions, and confirmations will be. Illustrations accompanying stories or articles are important sources of information that readers utilize in order to test their hypotheses about the content and structure of the story, as are memories of other stories they've listened to or read.

Constructing Meaning

The concern readers have for constructing meaning (making sense of what is being read) influences how readers use the reading strategies. As we read, we are continuously making choices about which chunks of information are to be remembered. These choices are usually related to the purpose we set for reading. We build a meaning for what we are reading by integrating the new information with our existing knowledge and schema.

There are a number of considerations we take into account as we read, depending on our purpose for reading and our knowledge, schema, and beliefs about the world.

1. My purpose for reading:
   a. This is very important for my purposes, so I will add the information I believe I've gained to things I already know.
   b. The information is not exactly what I expected, therefore I have to rethink my reasons for reading and perhaps set some new purposes.
   c. I'm not sure whether it's important for my purposes, so I'll remember what I'm reading until I have enough information to make a better decision about its usefulness.
   d. This is not important for my purposes, so I'll forget it.
2. The relationship of what I am reading to my view of the world:
   a. This information is similar to what I know and fits into my belief system. I will easily accommodate it into my view of the world.
   b. This information is new to me but fits with my belief system and what I know. I will have to think about it for a while, but it will help me expand my view of the world.
   c. This information does not fit into my belief system. If the author makes a strong enough case, I will consider altering my belief system completely.
   d. This information does not fit into my belief system. If the author does not make a strong enough case, I will intuitively reject the information or distort it to fit my own view of the world.

The following sentences are available to explore some of the preceding statements about the strategies we use to construct meaning. Suppose you were to read:

1. "As I approached the corner, the traffic light turned green, so I crossed the street."
2. "As I approached the corner, the traffic light turned purple, so I stopped."
3. "As I approached the corner, the traffic light turned red, so I crossed the street."

The first sentence is easily processed because we understand most information that fits our view of the environment or the schema we have already developed. Even if we skipped this part in the reading or forgot it because it is insignificant, we would nonetheless believe we had read it and be able to discuss the information with others because it is information we bring with us to the reading.

The second sentence, however, poses a different problem. We know that traffic lights are usually red, yellow, or green. A purple traffic light is new information, but we may still be able to relate this to our belief system because we have other knowledge that permits us to accept this information: 1) Purple has red in it; perhaps the author is stretching the truth for some reason that will be disclosed to us as we continue reading; 2) Maybe the author is going to talk about color blindness, and since we do not know much about color blindness, it may be that color-blind people see red as purple; 3) Perhaps we are reading science fiction or a comedy. We also have the option of rejecting or distorting the text information.

If we think of jaywalking as a possible cause for the third example, we may follow a procedure similar to the one described for the second example. However, if all our lives we have stopped for red lights and crossed on green lights, this information may jar our belief system. We may be so comfortable with our belief system that we read *green* for *red* or read *didn't cross* for *crossed.* Another possible option to consider is that the printer has made an error.

If the author of the third example makes a strong enough case for this new system, we may come to accept the notion that there are times when we can safely cross the street on a red light. Our belief system has been changed by reading. We may integrate this into our schema, or we may build new schemas in response to the new information, reasoning that perhaps a scramble system is being described in which all cars must stop on the red light and the pedestrians can cross the street in any direction.

A MODEL OF READING

Sampling, inferring, predicting, confirming, and integrating—always resulting in a personal construction of meaning—are the key operations or natural strategies within the reading process. Now let us observe these operations as they interact within a reading instance.

Read the following paragraph through once and only once. Then, without rereading, write down everything you have read.

> The king called the assembled to order. He stood regally waiting for silence. As the noise ceased, he spoke. "Tomorrow, I invite you all to the place. There we will make the decisions necessary to overcome the enemy."

Look back over your representation of the paragraph and compare it with the versions of other readers. Compare these versions with the original passage. Can you identify, through your observations, the various strategies of the reading process?

Which cues did you sample as significant, and which did you discard? *Regally* is often omitted. Because readers assume that kings are regal, the word becomes redundant. Few people write both *waiting for silence* and *the noise ceased.* These, too, are redundant statements, and a reader needs only one, or some combination of them, to integrate that information into the meaning being constructed.

Can you provide evidence from your written statement that you were sampling, inferring, predicting, and confirming? When you read *assembled* did you realize that you had actually anticipated people, courtiers, or a meeting or assembly? Does your version contain *palace* instead of *place?*

At this and similar points in the published text, you might have felt the need to reread even though you were told not to do so. Some readers disregard the directions and reread. Other readers follow the directions but are frustrated by them. Both cases are instances of the use of confirming strategies. These are places where readers encounter unexpected cues or where they want clarification. Some people ignore directions because confidence in their reading strategies overrides the directions; comprehending takes priority. Others allow their need for clarification to be frustrated because they believe doing what a teacher or author says takes precedence over their personal needs to construct meaning.

Did you notice that the words and sentences of your version of the text were more or less different from the versions of other readers and from the original text than were your *meanings?* There will always be variations in meaning attributable to personal reader experience and background, but at the same time there are similarities because of similar literary experiences and common societal views about what we are reading.

Reading a short paragraph and then writing down what you remember is not like continuous silent reading, but it can provide some insights into the reading strategies that readers use. Reading begins when, based on some purpose, we decide to transact with an author through the medium of printed material. The reading process proceeds continuously, simultaneously, and transactively. This process results in reading comprehension, that is, the construction of meaning. As we read, we continuously add to, alter, or reorganize our meanings and, in doing so, expand the universe of our knowledge.

Language and Its Systems

Children come to school already in possession of a great deal of language knowledge. They are proficient users of the language of their home and their community. They have already begun to make use of written language and are aware that print communicates enticing messages such as McDonald's, Coca-Cola, funny cartoons with speech balloons, reminders on the refrigerator, or exciting titles on TV. Many children have the experience of being read to from books by parents, nursery-school teachers, or librarians and of paging through books themselves, using pictures to tell or retell the story. Many are writers who use pencils and felt-tip markers skillfully. They have a variety of experiences seeing adults in their world read and write for all kinds of purposes or functions. Children have a developing language knowledge to use as they transact with new printed materials. A clear relationship between the language and meaning of the text and the children's own experiences, language, and knowledge makes printed material predictable. The more this reading material reflects the meaningful language children use, the more proficiently they apply their developing language knowledge and world view to the construction of meaning.

This is true for all readers who, in the process of constructing meaning, will make use of the language cueing systems: graphophonic, syntactic, semantic, and pragmatic.

Graphophonic System   In an alphabetic language such as English, the *graphophonic system* refers to the symbol systems of oral and written language and the relationship between them. The system of sounds of oral language are known as the phonological system. The written language system is known as the orthographic system, and the relationship between the two is known as phonics. The phonological system is not only the system of the specific sounds of the language but also includes the intonation system: the stress on syllables and words, the variations in pitch that helps disambiguate meanings, and the juncture relating to breaths in the stream of speech.

The orthographic system is the way in which print is organized in the written language world. Differences in upper and lower case, punctuation, spacing, and the spelling system are all aspects to consider in understanding the orthography of written language. Phonics is not a simplistic relationship between single letters and single sounds. Phonics is not a program to teach reading. Phonics is what readers learn to understand as the complex relationship between how people talk and how language is organized in written texts (K. Goodman 1994).

Contrary to popular opinion, the English spelling system is quite regular and not haphazard. However, there can never be a simple one-to-one correspondence between the orthographic and the phonological systems. There are language features that exist in written language that do not exist in oral language. *Once upon a time,* a phrase frequently found in folk and fairy tales, is seldom used in oral language except in storytelling. Clauses such as *said Mother* or *John laughed* preceded or followed by quotations are common in written language, even in beginning reading material, yet are not features in oral language. There are many other influences that do not permit a simple one-to-one relationship between written and oral language: the complexity of intonation, the personal relationship of speakers and the unfamiliarity of authors and readers, and dialect and language variations.

Because of its long and complex history, as well as influences from other languages, the English spelling system has more than one spelling pattern that relates to the same sound. Examples include *ai* as in *bait* and *a-e* as in *hate.* Although English is to a large extent spelled in a standard way, there are different ways to pronounce the same written words. To some speakers of English *Mary, merry,* and *marry* are homophones—pronounced exactly the same. For other speakers only two of those three are homophones, and for still others all three words are pronounced differently.

People who say *cuz, watchamacallit, jeet,* and *gonna* must learn to recognize their counterparts in written language as *because, what you may call it, did you eat,* and *going to.* The oral forms are not sloppy renditions of the written forms, they are different forms representing the same meanings. *Each reader must learn the set of relationships that exists between his or her oral language and its written counterparts: the phonics of language.* The relationships are not the same for all speakers because of differences in dialects, as well as idiosyncratic differences. In addition, spelling has syntactic and semantic roots as well as sound/letter roots.

In recent years, research on young children's spelling patterns has provided us with evidence that, despite the complexities of the English spelling system, children's understanding of the relationship between the phonological and the orthographic systems of written language develops in a logical and conventional way (Wilde 1992). Beginning readers use their proficiency in the sound system of their language and their developing understanding of the symbolic nature of print to build relationships between oral and written language. Spellings such as *morosiacos* for *motorcycles* (written in a story by a dominant Spanish speaker), *grapa* for *grandpa,* or *frinstance* for *for instance* are not only understandable but help us see how readers build their phonics knowledge.

What's true for young children is true for proficient readers as well. Because the purpose of reading is comprehending—constructing meaning—readers use their syntactic, semantic, and pragmatic systems in order to build the relationship between the sound system of language and written language.

Syntactic System   The phrase *syntactic system* refers to the relationships of words, sentences, and paragraphs. These systematic relationships include word order, tense, number, and gender. *Grammar* is a more common term for *syntax*. All children use the rules of their own grammar[2] rather proficiently by the time they come to school. When English-speaking five-year-olds are asked to complete the sentence: "A boy is sliding down the _____ ," they will always supply an acceptable noun or noun phrase at the end of the sentence. They may not be able to call the word they supply a *noun* or know the definition of the word *noun;* nevertheless, they know where nouns and other parts of speech go in English sentences. When we use the terms *syntax* or *grammar,* we refer not to the rules imposed on the language by grammar books but to the rules people know intuitively by virtue of being language users.

In some dialects of English, people say, "I am going to university" while others say, "I am going to the university." However, both groups of speakers could say "I am going to college" or "I am going to the college," depending on the meaning intended. How do we *know* whether or not to use *the* before *university* and *college?* Grammar books do not provide rules about when we should or should not use the determiner *the* in such sentences because no clear-cut rule system concerning this syntactic phenomenon has been discovered by linguists.

Consider each of the following sentences. In which cases can you use the determiner *the?* Can you say any of the sentences with and without *the?* If so, in what instances will the meaning be changed?

I went to (the) hospital.
I went to (the) school.
I went to (the) town.
I went to (the) library.
I left (the) home.
I left (the) house.

The awareness you, as a speaker of your language, have that a sentence does or does not sound right is your intuitive knowledge of the syntactic system. Children also have a strong intuitive knowledge about the language they speak.

When written material has sentence structure similar to the syntax that is familiar to students, they are better able to predict the language and know whether a particular sentence is acceptable. But, as stated earlier, there are forms of written language that are rarely part of oral language. It is through lots of experience with written language (being read to, for example) that readers become familiar with the syntax of written language. Even before their oral language is understood by adults, two-year-old children have been overheard saying something that sounds like *The End* when they finish turning the last page of their favorite book.

In a list of isolated words with only graphophonic cues available, students may have difficulty remembering how *merry, Mary,* and *marry* are different and often are unable to provide a grammatical function or a meaning for each word. However, as soon as syntax is available, readers use their syntactic knowledge to support their predicting and confirming strategies. Even if many of the other words in a sentence are nonsense, readers usually determine how the word functions in the sentence.

Mary femped to the plurn clumbly.
The lum and the sanin flam to marry.
Jeff blees a merry roun.

The syntax of written material provides significant cues for readers. They are able to ask, *Does this sound like language?* They use syntax to predict and then to confirm the acceptability of their predictions.

---

[2]We refer here to the grammar of their sociocultural dialect.

But in order to comprehend, readers must also have the *semantic* and *pragmatic systems* available.

Semantic and Pragmatic Systems

The *semantic system* is at the heart of language. It includes the relationships between language and its meaning systems. The semantic system includes what words and phrases mean and how they change over time. It includes dictionary definitions but also what kinds of definitions words or phrases have in different contexts. The *pragmatic system* includes the meaning or semantic system, taking into consideration the social, cultural, and historical context of language in use. For example, a *Family Circus* cartoon once showed Billy answering the telephone. The caller said, "Is your mother there?" Billy put down the phone and went into every room of the house, finally spotting his mother. At that point, he returned to the phone and said to the caller, "Yes." The cartoon suggests that children are sometimes more tuned into surface meanings than pragmatic meanings. Speakers of English learn to know that when a caller says, "Is your mother there?" this is really not a yes/no question. In the context of a phone call the sentence means "If your mother is there, please ask her to come to the phone." Examining language, keeping in mind that the pragmatic system is strongly influenced by social and cultural conventions, helps us understand the many times people construct different meanings even though they are in the same language setting. Personal meanings are influenced by the society in which we live and interact, as well as everything that the language user has been learning and thinking about the world.

People who live in apartments, trailers, or box cars that are secure, warm, familiar places have established their various meanings of *house* and *home* through their own living experiences and their use of language in various real-life settings. Regardless of what kind of structure they live in, they say to others, "Come over to my house after school today" or "Take this home to your mother." They may, therefore, have difficulty with school lessons that try to explain an instructional meaning of *house* and *home* or may not understand why a poet would rhapsodize, "It takes a heap of living to make a house a home." Marlene, who travels from New York to Los Angeles in five hours to visit her grandmother and who speaks to her grandmother on the phone a number of times each year, may have difficulty understanding the total break of family ties and the trauma involved during the migrations of the Westward Movement. The closer the content of reading materials is to the life and experiences of students and the closer the concepts of reading materials are to what students already know, the easier it is for them to construct their personal meanings as well as to understand the meanings that the author may have constructed.

At the same time, reading must expand students' knowledge and view of the universe. If the material to be read has many known concepts along with some unknowns, readers can use what they know to better understand the unknown content or concepts. When we comprehend, we connect new information to what we already know. In order to provide opportunities for expansion of experiences and broadening of concepts, teachers encourage students to read material that involves unique experiences or new ideas that are to some degree beyond the students' understandings. However, if too many of the experiences, ideas, or concepts are unfamiliar, a student will have a more difficult time reading. You can explore this yourself. Try to read something about which you know very little. If you are a language person, try reading a physics or chemistry piece. If you are biology-oriented, try to read an article by a linguist. When we explore such experiences, we realize the important relationship between what we know, what we are reading, and the reading process. That is why the selection of reading materials for the purposes of instruction and evaluation needs to be carefully considered.

Only when the semantic and pragmatic cueing systems are accessible to the reader and when these systems are used in concert with the syntactic and graphophonic systems are there the necessary supports for making the most proficient use for the development of the reading strategies. When all the systems of language are in place, readers predict and confirm language using the semantic and pragmatic systems intelligently and at the same time are selective in their use of the graphophonic and syntactic information. Simultaneously, readers integrate what they are reading with what they know in order to comprehend and construct their own meanings.

When we add semantic and pragmatic meanings to the examples of the spelling patterns presented earlier in the chapter (*Mary, merry, marry*), we see the significance of these systems:

Mary ran to the store quickly.
The man and the woman want to marry.
Jeff sees a merry clown.

The more context available to the reader, the more support there is for the reader to use semantics and pragmatics in order to understand and construct meaning.

Mother needed milk for dinner. She asked Mary to go to the store for her, but Mary was playing with her friend and did not want to go. "If you go to the store, you don't have to do dishes tonight," Mother told her. Mary ran to the store quickly.

In this paragraph there is more information about Mary than in the preceding sections on graphophonics and syntax or even in the sentences introducing semantic and pragmatic meaning. These systems help the reader support the development of the most important of all reading strategies: **"Reading is supposed to make sense to *me*! Not just to my teacher, my father, or my classmate, but to *me*!"**

It is important to keep in mind that language systems and reading strategies operate in an interrelated fashion. When readers are concerned with any one of the individual strategies or focusing on any one of the language systems, all the other strategies and systems are still operating. Although proficient readers balance their use of reading strategies and language cueing systems successfully, beginning readers may need some extra support in order to achieve this ability. They may need to be directed away from overreliance on a single language cueing system and underutilization of one of the reading strategies. With experience, with reading and writing, and with appropriate guidance by knowledgeable teachers and parents, beginning readers learn to integrate all the strategies and language cueing systems effectively and efficiently.

The reading strategies and language systems introduced in this chapter are discussed in greater detail in appropriate sections of the specific reading strategy lessons. The bibliography lists sources that supplement the information provided here.

2

A Reading Curriculum: Focus on Comprehension

In Chapter 1, we described reading as a language process. In the model of reading we examined the relationship between author, text, and reader—that is, the processing of the language cueing systems and the reading strategies that readers apply to any written text to achieve their purpose for building meaning.

In this chapter, we examine ways to merge our model of reading with a philosophy of education that places teaching and learning within a socio-cultural view of literacy. As we examine the relationship between reading in the world and reading in school, we address the issues of teaching and learning, specifically reading instruction. We propose ways for teachers to determine their roles in supporting the development of reading proficiency and ways to create instructional settings and materials that support such development. As we consider these matters, we propose a reading curriculum that includes the functions of reading and the relationship between personal and social reading.

INVENTION AND CONVENTION—PERSONAL AND SOCIAL LEARNING

In order to consider issues related to the development of a reading curriculum, we first explore considerations about learning. We believe that students assume a great deal of control over their own learning, but personal learning is always influenced and constrained by the knowledge presented to them in their social world. Babies are immersed in the language of their social community. As their language develops through risk taking and exploration, they come to implicitly understand the reasons people use speech, how language works, and how it is organized. Such personal influences on language development can be viewed as the child's *invention* of language. There is constant tension between personal invention and social *convention* because all invention occurs within the constraints of the social conventions of language that affect development and learning within the social community. Although social conventions are relatively stable, they do change because life itself is dynamic and evolving.

Children resist social conventions that conflict with their conceptualizations. A person can, we believe, *learn* to read but cannot be *taught* to read if teaching is characterized by directly teaching letters, sounds, words, or language rules. Consider "you can lead a horse to water, but you can't make him drink." Both the horse and the person leading the horse must be active in their specified endeavors. When the horse will not drink, its behavior is fairly obvious, and we are immediately aware of the situation, if not the solution. Sometimes students' responses to a learning situation are just as direct. They will not do homework or they refuse to answer questions or they fail to participate in discussions. But at other times behavior is more circumspect. Students memorize a list of words and pass the spelling test based on that list but never use the words in speaking or writing; they successfully complete the computation of fractions, but are unable to adjust a recipe to accommodate a varying number of guests; or they read assigned stories with a minimal number of oral miscues and with some retention of facts, but develop no facility for applying the information to similar situations or show no interest in being critical of the ideas or seeking solutions to problems through reading. The role students play in their own learning has an impact on the quality of that learning. At the same time, by providing meaningful reading experiences, teachers season the water with all kinds of good tastes and smells so the learners will want to drink. In some ways, then, children invent who they are becoming as readers and learners, and the role of teachers and parents is to provide the social settings (conventions) in which such learning inventions occur.

Active Involvement

Personal involvement in learning leads to invention or construction of meaning in school when learning and teaching are considered a collaborative venture among the teacher, the student, and other students. The teacher's role becomes one of facilitating learning rather than one of imparting knowledge. Decisions concerning the concepts, content, and focus of reading instruction come from three interrelated and equally important factors: 1) the students' interests and concerns, including their cultural background; 2) the teacher's knowledge of language and thought processes, including the reading process; and 3) the teacher's knowledge of the students' instructional strategy needs informed by kidwatching (Y. Goodman 1985, 1991), miscue analysis, and other kinds of evaluation.

As active participants in the teaching-learning process, readers need to be aware of their own strengths and weaknesses. They need to develop the ability to evaluate their personal reading needs. The teacher becomes responsible not only for helping students develop as readers but also for organizing the instructional environment so that pupils will develop a conscious awareness of and responsibility for their personal involvement in the process.

The learners' conscious awareness must not be confused with superficial verbalization. It is not memorizing the geometry theorem: The measure of an inscribed angle is one half the measure of its intersected arc; or stating a grammatical definition: Nouns are the names of persons, places, or things; or being able to respond correctly to a comprehension question: What is the theme of this story? Rather, it is being able to make purposeful use of relationships underlying the processes in use. Conscious awareness is evident when a seven-year-old reader correcting *rooshed* (rhymes with bushed) for *rushed* in the sentence:

©
$rooshed
I rushed up the front stairs.[1]

reasons: "As soon as I saw *stairs* I knew it had to be *rushed.*" Another example of awareness is an eight-year-old reading *lose* (producing the long *o* and long *e* sounds as marked) for *lose* in the context:

---

[1] $ indicates the reader substituted a nonword that sounded something like *rooshed* for *rushed.*
© indicates the reader reread the underlined section, self-correcting the miscue.

His mother said, "You'll lose your ticket!"[2]

but reading it appropriately minutes later in a new context after references to losing and finding things:

He was careful not to lose his money,

and exclaiming, "Hey, that's the word I didn't know before." Both of these readers are developing an awareness of the role that context plays in reading. As students consider the sense of what they are reading, they return to the text, paying closer attention to language units, how they look and sound, and the place they hold in the sentence and the story. Because readers discover these relationships and know they can make their own self-corrections when they deem necessary, they are able to take control of the reading process.

To Err Is Human

Readers must be in an environment in which the process of miscueing is valued and understood. Every reader must have the right to make miscues for two reasons:

- Reading is not an exact process and always, for all readers, involves miscalculations and approximations.
- Learners develop an understanding for the parameters of a process by exploring them.

If reading were a mere parroting of memorized items, accuracy would then be the appropriate measure of readers' success. But as the reading model presented in Chapter 1 indicates, we are dealing with a much more complex process. Readers screen the language and thoughts of another person through their own language and thought processes. They must expect to vary from the author's intentions. Readers' willingness and ability to risk such variations thus become of central importance.

A concern for accuracy can actually lead to a true breakdown in the reading process. A focus on correctness causes readers to concentrate on individual words and on the surface structure of the text, rather than on the language and meaning of the text as a whole. The accuracy focus is on "handling" or "attacking" each item—producing an appropriate sound or word. The different ways in which one thirteen-year-old reader, Gary, handled *contented* and *tassels* within the context of one story demonstrates this point.

In the story, the stonecutter wanted to be the most powerful in the universe. Each time he saw something powerful, he thought that it was stronger than himself and, therefore, wanted to become that thing. A wizard always gave him his wish. With each wish the stonecutter was sure that the change would bring contentment. But each time he would see something more powerful, grow discontented, and wish to become that new thing.

The first powerful thing the stonecutter becomes is the king. In reading about the king's servants holding a sunshade over him, Gary came to the sentence *"The sunshade was turquoise with golden tassels hanging from it."* He paused after *golden*, mumbled *tissels* (rhymes with *thistles*) under his breath, and finally produced a word that sounded like *tessels* (rhymes with *wrestles*). The word *contented* also appears in the story. On the first occurrence in the text, Gary pronounced *contented* conventionally, but in two later encounters he produced nonwords such as *conted* or *contented* (with

---

[2] $ indicates the reader substituted a nonword that sounded something like *lowsee* for *lose* and continued to read.

the accent on the first syllable). If the ability to pronounce accurately and the ability to gain meaning are synonymous in reading, then we can assume that Gary understood the feelings of the stonecutter only in one instance and did not know what was hanging from the canopy of the king's sunshade.

When asked to retell the story in his own words after reading the whole story aloud, Gary was able to recount the sequence of demands that the stonecutter made, but he did not seem able to assign a state of mind to the stonecutter. Though he had accurately produced the word *contented* at one point in the text, he had apparently assigned it no meaning.

Following the retelling, Gary was asked if there were any words he was aware of that had given him trouble. He responded, "Oh yeah, those goldlike fringes on the sunshade." In this case, saying *tessels* instead of *tassels* did not prevent him from coming up with a functional definition.

Expecting the reader to miscue indicates an acceptance of learning by doing, an acceptance of learners as experimenters constantly involved in making hypotheses. An active learning environment is possible when teachers plan open-ended learning experiences, encourage real discussion, integrate students' contributions into the curriculum, and commit classroom time to exploration. Gary was able to work through his own reading problems with *contented*. His substitutions for *contented* show his ability to recognize when his strategies are not working. Gary's miscues provided him and his teacher with specific information about his reading strengths and needs. For instance, Gary was able to use graphophonic relationships to produce expected or near-expected oral language for unknown text items. In the case of *tassels,* where sufficient context was provided, Gary produced a functional definition.

Observation of uninterrupted reading situations provided Gary's teacher with information about the material he was reading. When this one instance of reading is combined with other experiences, Gary's strengths and weaknesses as a reader emerge. The fact that Gary was able to develop a meaning for *tassels* but not for *contented* not only shows how Gary operated as a reader but also illuminates how the structure of the published material influenced his reading. An examination of the story (see Chapter 3) indicates that tassels were described by the author, but the stonecutter's desire to be contented was never explained. Gary's background and experience with fringes on umbrellas, curtains, and scarfs aided his understanding of the concept of tassels.

Both Gary and his teacher must be active and alert, but patient within the teaching-learning partnership. Gary must be willing to apply reading strategies and to continue reading. He must have the patience to hold some of his problems in abeyance and allow his understanding to develop as the text supplies additional clues. He must be willing to build what he can from previous reading experiences and to add his new, budding knowledge to a developing schema.

Gary's teacher must be alert to ways of evaluating Gary's successes, intentions, and interests. She must be active in determining what instructional experiences will offer the most immediate benefits, and she must have the patience to allow Gary his own discoveries and inventions without immediately imposing her knowledge and experience. Gary's teacher must understand that a definition is seldom fully developed the first time a new idea is encountered in any context; rather, it grows over a period of time through a variety of encounters with the same idea in different settings. (Gary will be discussed more thoroughly in Chapter 3.)

Encouraging students to explore, to take risks, and to make miscues involves a respect for learners' intellectual capacity and for their investment in the learning process. As a result of such encouragement students become committed to taking responsibility for their own decision making, for evaluating the effectiveness of the alternative paths they have explored, and for formulating tentative conclusions. In such an environment both student and teacher become focused on finding workable solutions and progressively discover more satisfying ones. Their focus is not on determining single correct answers to simplistic questions.

THE READING PROGRAM IN WHOLE LANGUAGE CLASSROOMS

Attention in publications about whole language research and classroom practice has focused on the success of process writing, writing workshop, and literature study. These programs are successful because they provide relatively clear paths for teachers to make changes from skill-based philosophies and practices to more holistic ones with straightforward methodological directions and goals, based on sound theory. They support teachers as they make changes, they provide teachers with opportunities to observe how students learn holistically, and they are enjoyable for students and parents.

The whole language movement is growing from a strong tradition of research about the reading process (K. Goodman 1989; Y. Goodman 1989; Rhodes & Shanklin 1989; Stephens 1990). Given the popularity of writing process and literature study, it is both timely and necessary to re-emphasize the reading process in whole language programs. Teachers can enrich all learning experiences, including the process writing and literature study components of their whole language programs, by becoming more knowledgeable about how reading works and how that knowledge can best be incorporated into a rich and engaging curriculum.

Whole language teachers want kids to become lifelong readers and to use reading as a central means for lifelong learning, but they are sometimes uncertain about how to reach these goals. As a result, some whole language classrooms, particularly during the process of change, have strong writing programs while the reading program remains more skills-oriented, perhaps even unchanged with the continued use of basals and other packaged programs and materials. This section is intended to provide specific information about the reading curriculum in whole language programs; that is, to provide teachers with practical ideas for designing, organizing, and evaluating whole language reading experiences.

Nesting Metaphor

In order to discuss a reading curriculum within the school setting and to suggest a reading instructional program for students and teachers, it is necessary to consider how any such program is embedded in its ecological setting within the sociocultural views of literacy in the world. This includes taking into consideration issues about literacy both inside and outside of school.

Ultimately the focus in this book is on exemplar reading lessons that teachers *choose* to adapt or use with particular kids in specific classroom settings. However, in keeping with a whole language view of teaching and learning, we use a nesting metaphor to show the role of reading strategy lessons within the world of literacy itself.

The nesting metaphor is represented by the accompanying diagram (see Figure 2-1). It shows the *Reading Strategy Lessons* (RSL) to be presented in Chapter 3, nested within the teacher's *Reading Instructional Program*. The *Reading Instructional Program* is nested in the *Reading Curriculum* that includes the language and literacy policies of the nation, the state, the province, or the district, as well as locally established policies that are agreed upon by principals, school staffs, parents, and students. The *Reading Curriculum,* if it is reflective of what is now known about literacy and literacy learning, takes into consideration *Reading in the World* influenced by the society and culture in which each reader lives. We'll examine each literacy nest before we explore further issues of the *Reading Instructional Program.*

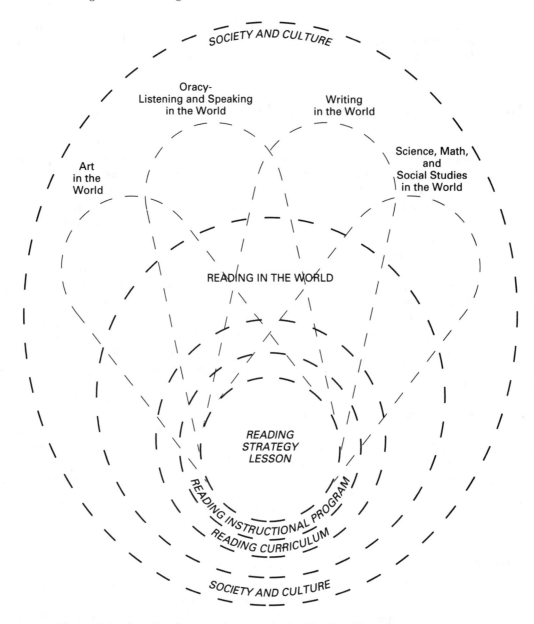

Figure 2-1. Reading Strategy Lessons in the Nesting Metaphor

Reading in the World

Reading in the World represents the literacy events in which people use reading and writing as they go about the business and pleasure of their daily lives. Reading in the world includes the attitudes and values people have about literacy and literacy materials. We borrow from Paulo Freire and Donald Macedo's concept of *Reading the World* and *Reading the Word:*

> Reading does not consist of merely decoding the written word or language; rather, it is preceded by and intertwined with knowledge of the world. Language and reality are dynamically interconnected (Freire & Macedo 1987, 29).

The more we understand how literacy works and the attitudes and values people have about the literacy events in their daily lives, the more likely we are to develop reading curricula that connect to the lives of our students and enhance the power of literacy for them. Freire describes his early literacy experiences with his teacher:

> With her, reading the word, the phrase, and the sentence never entailed a break with reading the *world*. With her, reading the word meant reading the *word-world* (Freire & Macedo 1987, 32).

In order to understand any specific aspect of reading itself it is necessary to see how all aspects of reading are embedded in the family and in the community. Attitudes about literacy that parents hold influence how children respond to reading and writing. The functions or reasons that families and community members have to use literacy have an impact on how school children view what reading and writing are all about. Recent studies by anthropologists, psychologists, and educationists show that in North America social groups are literate in different ways (Heath 1983; Moll et al. 1992; Taylor & Dorsey-Gaines 1988). Not all members of a literate society are enamored by great books and novels. Many people use literacy mostly to transact business in their world of work. Others use literacy to receive or distribute goods and services necessary for daily survival. This world of literacy must be taken into account in the design and development of a reading instructional program in schools. Early readers have been influenced by real world literacy, and, therefore, it is necessary to embed instruction in the child's view of the literacy in his or her world. Literacy learning should build on and make connections with the literacy learning that has already taken place in the home, the preschool, and the community. If more than one language is used, the biliterate nature of the community is an important resource for reading instruction. So we keep in mind that the home and community are the children's first teachers, and as such they continue to be influential and cannot be ignored in the school setting without negatively affecting the students' view of literacy and themselves as readers.

As shown in Figure 2-1, there are other important aspects of the world to be considered as we plan reading strategy lessons. A major influence on *Reading in the World* is, of course, *Writing in the World*. Because writing and reading influence each other so much, and often occur simultaneously, we address issues of real world writing as we examine reading instruction and reading strategy lessons in school. *Oracy in the World* strongly supports the reading/writing connections. Readers and writers listen and speak as they participate in literacy events. Strategy lessons and reading instruction are planned to include a great deal of speaking and listening.

We also establish the importance of various knowledge domains, such as science, math, and social studies, that are integral to curriculum development. Reading and writing are not ends in themselves. Rather they are tools we use to explore, understand, and enjoy the content or subject matter that occurs in our daily lives. We have therefore sketched into our model *Science in the World, Math in the World, Social Studies in the World,* and *Art in the World.* You might add your own nests or areas to the diagram to personalize the aspects of the world that have a significant impact on the development of literacy learning and reading instruction in your world.

The significance of *Reading in the World* relates to the continuous relationship between home and school that is central to building a strong reading program. There is a strong impact on the student's literacy development when school and home collaborate with each other.

The Reading Curriculum

Although teachers may decide to close their doors and do what they think is best for kids regardless of mandates from outside influences, in reality, classrooms do not function well apart from the entire school system. Teaching practice in isolation does little to promote lasting change in schools. It is necessary to consider the mandates that have bearing on what happens in the classroom because policies that interfere with a professional teacher's instructional practices seriously limit the learning-teaching process. Teachers expend a great deal of valuable energy getting around inflexible policies in order to use their best professional judgments about planning for literacy and literacy learning. Such energy is best spent planning for those experiences that teachers believe are most facilitating for their students' learning.

Teachers incorporate aspects of districtwide policies to support the planning they do with their students. For example, if a school district recognizes the importance of a wide range of reading while at the same time mandating a basal text, teachers can ask for support to provide a range of reading materials and the time needed to achieve the district goal of extensive reading within their instructional program. Teachers often believe there are mandates from their districts, only to learn when they look more closely that the mandates are suggestions open to negotiation which may or may not be incorporated into the instructional program.

Teachers can collaborate with other teachers to take a critical stance about school policies and curriculum, to take leadership roles, and to be involved in changing policies to reflect the latest knowledge about literacy development and its influence on reading instruction in classrooms.

In the development of a curriculum that is in keeping with the latest knowledge about literacy learning, a great deal of dynamic energy is generated. School district policies can support and encourage teachers' goals to build exciting curriculum within the school and the classroom and to strengthen relationships with parents and the community while building new programs. District policies can support teacher selection of reading materials and schoolwide units or themes, recognize the importance of the relationship between a literacy program and the city or district library, appreciate the significance of school librarians working collaboratively with teachers, encourage principals and teachers to plan professional development that focuses on in-depth understandings of the reading process and reading instruction, and so on. When school and district policies support the kind of literacy curriculum we are suggesting, they provide a framework in which each teacher can work to enhance the literacy development of every student.

When schools value the importance of a rich literacy environment and dynamic literacy experiences and send consistent messages to parents and other citizens about the power of literacy in the school building as well as in the classroom, these messages have a strong impact on students' views of literacy. If welcome signs, forms, and flyers that go home represent all the languages in the school community and not just English, an unwritten and unstated message is sent to parents, students, and the community about the power and value of literacy in all languages. When parents are invited to respond to and make suggestions about their children's reading and writing instruction, when they are included in making policies about homework and discussing the kinds of reading and writing that take place in school and at home, the message is clear that the school curriculum reflects respect for literacy, for languages, for parents, and for the community.

THE READING INSTRUCTIONAL PROGRAM
with Kathryn F. Whitmore

In the context of the nesting metaphor, reading instruction in school takes on a new appearance and purpose. The *Reading Curriculum* is built upon the reading done outside of school by valuing home and community literacy as important and expanding it to include new functions and purposes integrated with instruction and evaluation.

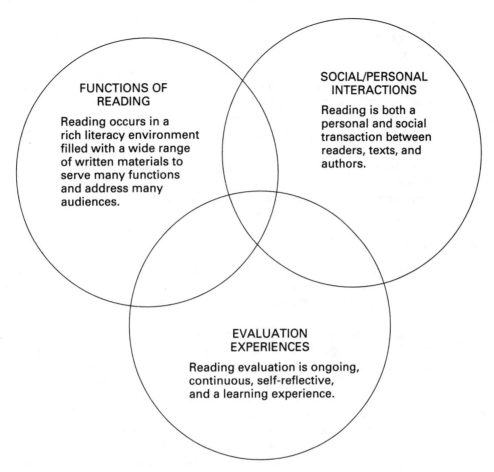

Figure 2-2. Function/Personal-Social/Evaluation Circles in the Reading Instructional Program

An effective whole language reading instructional program includes three interactive components: functions for reading, social/personal interactions, and the evaluation of reading experiences, as represented by Figure 2-2. All three are necessary for the development and planning of a complete reading curriculum, including the reading instructional program. These three frequently overlap when they are actualized in classroom experiences. The first two circles are discussed in this chapter, and evaluation is discussed in Chapter 3. Although the discussion in this section focuses specifically on reading instruction, we apply the ideas equally to writing—functional writing, personal and social writing, and writing evaluation—to parallel the reading experiences discussed here.

Reading is characterized as a personal, ongoing, long-distance discussion between the reader and the author. The author has the major responsibility for introducing and elaborating ideas, and the reader has the major responsibility for considering and making meaning of them. By no means is meaning construction a one-way street. The reader and the author communicate with each other through the processes of writing and reading. Ideas are fed into the discussion by both participants, and meaning making is the responsibility of both. When reading is personal and individual, there is no need for a non-participant (such as the teacher) to direct that discussion or focus its interpretation.

But reading is also social. The social aspects of reading occur as readers share their personal meanings about a text, such as a McDonald's sign or a classic novel, and build a meaning of the text together. Sometimes readers try to explain their interpretations of the author's meaning to each other, sometimes they want to share the joy of a piece of writing with others, sometimes they want to argue or reject what is written and get other readers' validation about their views, or sometimes they want others to help them understand the impact a piece of writing has on their daily lives. Sometimes readers need communication with other readers to understand a text. Teachers are an active part of this process.

Both social and personal reading must be functional to be authentic, however. Whole texts, real audiences, and real materials used for real purposes are some of the ingredients required to develop authentic literacy events. We use *real* and *authentic* to contrast with some packaged reading programs that develop contrived settings and materials. We begin by discussing function, as it is essential for a whole language reading curriculum and reading instruction. We then turn to the personal and social components of reading.

Meeting Function with Form

The discussion that places reading curriculum in the nests of the real world clearly demonstrates that reading and writing are used in daily life for a variety of purposes and with a range of intended audiences. Authentic literacy and other language experiences occur both in and out of classrooms when the purposes, functions, and audiences for literacy are relevant and meaningful. Four functions for reading in daily life (see Figure 2-3) include: 1) environmental—to survive in the world; 2) recreational—for pleasure; 3) occupational—job related; and 4) informational—to gain information (K. Goodman 1994). In whole language classrooms, just as in life outside the classroom, reading is used to accomplish real purposes; the purpose of reading is not limited to practice or instruction isolated from active, functional use. Therefore, reading in school is as much like reading in the real world as it can be.

Any language event—discussing rules for playing blindman's bluff, writing an article on the latest sports event in town, relating the symptoms of a malfunctioning

	Books, Magazines, Newspapers	Research/Problem-Solving Sources	Alphabetic & Nonalphabetic Symbols	Primary Sources
Environmental	coupons advertisements book jackets	telephone book recipes directories	labels, signs daily schedules menus, posters t-shirts, graffiti	messages lists bills price tags
Recreational	literature genres cartoons, comics poetry movie critiques book reviews	Guinness books "how-to" pamphlets video game guides model-building instructions	musical notation word puzzles/games jokes & riddles computer games	tickets scrapbooks theatre/sports programs
Occupational	want ads stock reports job-related articles job-improvement articles	professional literature bibliographies portfolios webs	blueprints graphs manuals eye chart computer keyboards	memos autobiographies prescriptions checks written reports
Informational	weather/health/ sports reports biographies nonfiction news stories	definitions encyclopedias dictionaries medical charts guide books	maps, diagrams toy boxes photo albums computer menus calendars clocks	birth announcements receipts invitations

Figure 2-3.   Materials/Functions Grid

engine to a mechanic, or ordering a meal from a menu—is the result of one's facility with language, one's grasp of the context of a particular situation, and one's ability to mobilize thought and language forces. Language users involved in the event have a meaning-making need—learning the rules of the game, understanding how the public responds to sports events, repairing the motor, eating the food—and they satisfy their need through the use of available language and information resources. Each language event serves a different function for the language user and the function shapes the form of the language.

A rich and interesting variety of forms develops in response to the varied functions for reading and writing in everyday life. The Materials/Functions Grid in Figure 2-3 summarizes many of the forms that are present in the print environment of the world. Depending on the purpose and function of the materials for the reader, many of these examples could be placed in other categories. Many examples meet multiple functions of written language. The grid may be used to assure that the classroom is rich in a wide range of literacy materials so students can easily engage in *Reading in the World.*

The *environmental function* of reading is encountered daily by all children. It is reading that is necessary in order to move about on the streets, to find the right bus or subway, or to buy food at the Circle K mini-market. It's also the reading used to select one's favorite breakfast cereal, to read what time to go to bed, and to find the right channel on TV. The environmental function of reading in the world can be brought easily into school. A "What We Can Read" bulletin board in the hallway outside of a classroom shares children's reading with others and also helps individual children become conscious of themselves as readers. A record of what children read in their home environment helps parents realize how important literacy is to their family and how to make it more obvious to their children. Children become active, critical consumers by reading the labels on grocery items as well as on toy packages and price tags. They keep clips of such items in a notebook called "Questioning What We Read."

The environmental function of reading in the classroom includes making it purposeful as well as decorative. Reading the schedule to determine what activity to do next and reading friends' names on cubbies or mailboxes to deliver notes is environmental reading. So too is reading a thermometer to record the daily temperature on a graph, and reading a note from the teacher or a time schedule reminding a student about an upcoming writing conference. These activities are prevalent in whole language classrooms and can be capitalized on by calling attention to them as real reading. Similarly, labels placed functionally in the classroom, so that their actual purpose rather than quantity of appearance is the guiding principle for their use, foster environmental reading. For example, placing the gerbils' names and how to care for them on a card next to the cage serves a functional purpose. Putting the word *wall* on the wall or *chair* on a chair doesn't usually serve an authentic purpose.

Recreational reading is often associated with reading at home, perhaps as a bedtime ritual or a weekend pleasure. However, recreational reading is equally important at school. Each student could have at least three books in their cubby or desk at one time: one that is self-selected for personal reading, one that is suggested by the teacher, and one that is being read for a literature study (Y. Goodman & Watson 1977). The self-selection of recreational reading materials as discussed below provides an opportunity to build choice and negotiation into the curriculum.

To encourage recreational reading, students self-select and read a wide variety of materials that *they* enjoy. Comic books, romances, sports magazines, and even babysitting club novels all have a place in classrooms within the function category of recreational reading. A wide range of recreational reading materials is essential in order to please students with a range of reading interests and to build sufficient experiences to become critical readers capable of determining the literary quality of what they read.

Occupational reading concerns the literacy associated with work. People are involved in a range of reading at their work. Mechanics read information about parts and ordering, car magazines, and diagrams. Secretaries read and write letters, memos, and schedules. Homemakers read recipes, coupons, and package labels. Numerous occupations require writing and reading of reports. Professional positions include reading professional literature. Computer networks and faxes have stimulated new occupational functions of reading. Some researchers (Moll et al. 1992) contend that reading associated with work is a strong indicator of literacy development in homes and communities.

There are many jobs in classrooms that require reading. Filling in forms required for attendance, field trips, and food; keeping track of classroom supplies; and following directions for taking care of animals, plants, the library, and art centers are all necessary to keep the classroom working smoothly. Students are capable of assuming responsibilities for most of these activities that include occupational reading.

Informational reading happens continuously in daily life. Newspapers are a common source of information, not only for daily national, international, and local news, but also for sales and coupons, horoscopes, weather predictions, financial and sports reports, want ads, and religious and recreational activities. As people read the newspaper and other informational sources, they often seek answers to questions. Manuals and directions are followed when specific questions are raised about how to build something or accomplish a task. Maps are read when directions are necessary for planning a route or finding a location. Dictionaries are read when searching for a correct spelling or for understanding a word. Nonfiction literature in addition to fiction is a significant resource for students involved in critical inquiry projects or themes.

Informational reading occurs easily and purposefully at school as students dig for answers to their questions about the world. Students who are involved in thematically organized curriculum need a rich variety of materials to help them search for the information they need to solve the problems posed by their personal inquiry, by science experiments, or by mathematical equations. In addition to encyclopedias and textbooks, maps, pamphlets, informational books, and posters are valuable. So are the genres of historical fiction, biography, and autobiography. Real purposes for reading informational materials grow from opportunities to be involved in questioning, researching, and solving problems. Students can search for uses of informational reading in their homes—as family members read recipes, use the phone book, and study computer or repair manuals. These uses of reading for information can then be validated by students, parents, and teachers as important functions for written language.

Students as ethnographers in their classrooms and in their homes can develop records and lists of how adults and other children use literacy to search for information: mechanical and technical manuals, professional journals, business records, schedules and calendars, computer printouts, and so on. These types of reading materials can be incorporated into dramatic play areas in early childhood classrooms and used for their authentic purposes in theme studies and for self-selected reading.

Teachers can enrich the functional uses of reading in their classrooms by exploring the literacy in their daily lives. It is helpful to list every reading and writing experience that occurs throughout one or two days. The list can be shared and compared with the lists of other teachers. Then the many functions for reading can be listed and considered for incorporation into the reading curriculum. Students participate in a similar procedure by interviewing the significant people in their lives in order to create a list of how people use literacy every day. A long list of real uses of reading will develop quickly. This list helps teachers and students be more aware of the reading going on around them. Each of these functional uses of written language can then be validated as real reading and accepted for classroom as well as family use. Students become aware of how pervasive literacy is in their lives. Beginning there, students' uses of reading at school can expand to include all functions of reading as they build upon their successes and interests.

Personal and Social Reading Experiences

Figure 2-4 lists selected aspects of both personal and social reading experiences in classroom settings. The lists are meant to serve as possibilities that teachers will consider and expand on in planning their reading instructional program.

The reading program must include a strong personal component that gives students the time and opportunity to develop individual reading preferences and histories. To begin, students must be allowed self-selection of their reading materials. A minimum of five books for each student in a classroom is an appropriate goal to provide readers with adequate numbers of books for selection. Good school libraries and librarians who work collaboratively with the classroom teacher are vitally important to strong reading programs. Whole language librarians develop research inquiries with kids, work with individual teachers on thematic curriculum development, help students learn to select materials, and keep teachers and students informed about the latest books and materials.

Personal reading also includes adequate time and ample opportunity for browsing and selecting reading materials, for uninterrupted reading at a variety of paces, and for reflecting on personal reading experiences. Many programs are already well-established for personal reading, such as SSR (*Sustained Silent Reading*) or DEAR

to be individually expanded?

PERSONAL READING EXPERIENCES	SOCIAL READING EXPERIENCES
Self-selection of functional reading materials • environmental • informational • occupational • recreational	**Social uses of functional reading materials** • environmental • informational • occupational • recreational
Building personal expertise • develop knowledge about authors, illustrators, and genre • expand on personal interests to become experts • explore new topics and ideas • silent reading	**Organization of shared reading** • book buddies—sharing reading with a friend • text sets in groups • literature circles • big books, poetry, and song charts • current events • thematic inquiries • reading aloud
Self-reflection • literature logs • individual demonstrations/projects including a range of symbol systems • personal literacy histories • personal responses to literature	**Reader response** • compare and contrast • critique • construct social meanings • dramatic presentations • social histories • dialogue journals
	Reading Strategy Instruction (See Part II) • reader-selected miscues • retrospective miscue analysis • reading strategy lessons • reading process discussions
Personal evaluation (See Chapter 3)	**Social evaluation** (See Chapter 3)

Figure 2-4. Personal and Social Reading Experiences

(*Drop Everything And Read*). Extended personal reading periods often begin with shorter periods of time for younger children, but by the intermediate grades at least a half hour daily of continuous reading is necessary.

Readers have both the need and the right to personally choose a significant portion of their own reading material. Self-selection allows commitment and involvement. Since they are investing time and effort, individuals will have a stake in the process and in the outcome. But the ability for self-selection is not a natural gift. Readers need to learn how to judge their own needs, interests, and abilities; where to seek reading material; and how to judge the intents and abilities of authors. Efforts at helping proficient readers will go to waste if they are taught in an atmosphere in which the teacher usually selects the readers' materials. Many people with the facility to learn through reading fail to make use of self-selection because they are insecure about how to do it. Perhaps these people are part of the population who can read but won't.

As students develop their personal reading interests, a range of materials that supports the functions we have discussed and are listed in the Materials/Functions Grid (Figure 2-3) is necessary. Classroom content and experiences for all components of the curriculum, including reading, must take into consideration the personal interests and inquiries of the students. Through personal reading, students discover their areas of expertise that can be nurtured at home as well as supported at school. Collections, hobbies, knowledge about specific topics, and special talents are just a few of the ways that personal interests manifest themselves. Students and families have rich funds of knowledge at home (Moll et al. 1992). Teachers will discover information about their students they might otherwise never know as they encourage students to uncover and develop their areas of expertise. These interests can be celebrated at school with an expert's day, a scholar's fair, or a class-organized conference. Areas of expertise are especially important for students in special classrooms who may never have felt like experts before. The recognition of students with expertise removes the teacher from responsibility as the single expert in a class.

Expertise can also be developed in areas that deal specifically with reading. Students can develop interests in favorite authors or illustrators, for example. In addition to reading many of the authors' or illustrators' published works, students can learn biographical information and become familiar with the range of the authors' writing or the illustrators' art as they compare their work to the writing or art of others. They can also correspond with the author or illustrator. Such knowledge and expertise from reading will undoubtedly cross over into the writing program. Students cannot learn specific abilities, skills, or attitudes if they don't have the opportunity to participate in meaningful activities that allow these attributes to develop.

In addition to having personal time for reading, students need personal time to respond to their reading. Readers need time to wonder, daydream, and ideate (K. Goodman et al. 1987) about their reading inside their own heads. An overt response may come at some later date, perhaps far beyond the end of the school year. Having time to reflect on what they are reading provides opportunities for readers to expand on the meanings they are building. Keeping literature logs is one method for personal response. In a personal literature log, students may make open-ended responses in any number of ways, or they respond by following a format suggested by the teacher or planned by a group of students reading together. Literature logs need not look the same over the course of a year or from year to year. They should reflect the growth and changes of teachers and students as they learn.

Response may occur in a variety of other ways, too. Requiring students to respond to personal reading through book report after book report, particularly with narrowly conceived formats, is a limiting technique when so many personally as well as socially meaningful responses are available. Students may lead a discussion about their reading with others. They may create a dramatic presentation of the materials they've read or write a song or poem in response. Art work provides appropriate ways to respond, including drawing, sculpting, carving, or sewing, for example. Students who are uncomfortable reading out loud might like to practice reading and make a recording of a book for their class to add to their tape library or to share with other classes. Puppetry and woodworking are additional possibilities. Since reading involves the use of the written language system, the incorporation of the other symbol systems in response is very appropriate and leads to a greater internalization of meaning. There should be many times, however, when no overt response is necessary. Books and other reading materials need to be read, enjoyed, and lived with.

Students spend more time reading silently than orally in whole language classrooms. Readers read silently for several reasons; chief among them is that it is economical. They process the information much more rapidly than oral reading allows. This additional speed saves time and permits a greater retention and use of linguistic cues.

Silent reading also encourages self-pacing. There are no intermediaries—no referees, no listeners—whom readers must consider. They need simply to please themselves. They can speed up, slow down, reread, or pause to think, all in an effort to make sense. They do not have the added burden of attempting to present the message meaningfully to a third party or to concern themselves with another's meaning.

Although silent reading is most often appropriate, oral reading is useful in a number of situations. For diagnostic purposes readers read aloud to the teacher to establish insights into the nature of the students' miscues. Students enjoy reading with each other to extend their social learning from the accompanying discussion. Students often read aloud to a class to share information from the newspaper or to prove a point being discussed or debated. Oral reading is pursued as dramatic art as students are encouraged to read aloud radio broadcasts, stories, plays, and so on. For most purposes, however, reading is a silent, receptive, but active experience; oral reading leads to social reading experiences.

Over the last fifteen years, we have begun to understand that a social component is essential to literacy development. In fact, researchers who examine literacy in the social context of families and communities have broadened both our definition of literacy and our knowledge about the functions of written language in the world. Ethnographers such as Shirley Brice Heath (1983), Denny Taylor (1983), Taylor and Catherine Dorsey-Gaines (1988) find that reading is a shared experience both at home and in the community. As families and neighbors receive mail, and read the newspaper, advertisements, and announcements, the information is often shared and interpreted together. Heath (1983) describes such an event as Lillie Mae, a parent in the community, shares a letter about a local day care with the neighbors gathered on her front porch. Lillie Mae and her friends construct a group meaning of the text, each contributing his or her own knowledge of the system, the school, the requirements, and so on. As Heath explains:

> Conversation on various parts of the letter continued for nearly an hour, while neighbors and Lillie Mae pooled their knowledge of the pros and cons of such programs. . . . Lillie Mae, reading aloud, decoded the written text, but her friends and neighbors interpreted the text's meaning through their own experiences (Heath 1983, 157).

The benefits of social interaction in school are evident when groups of two or more children come together to read, listen to stories, discuss their reading, share interpretations, and make meaning together. Caryl Crowell, a third-grade bilingual teacher, believes reading aloud to her students is one of the most important things she does to help build a sense of community in the classroom. It not only sets the stage for literacy and responding to literature but also provides the students and teacher with a shared history as readers. In Caryl's classroom, by the end of the year there are at least 250 stories that she and her students have all heard *together* (Whitmore & Crowell 1994).

Opportunities for social reading are important through all grades. Reading aloud, literature study groups, and book-buddy reading create avenues for kids to read socially with each other and provide opportunities for adults to act as participants and more experienced readers in the group. Teachers can read with very young children in their laps or in one-on-one settings, or they can read big books and poetry and song charts with the whole class.

An example serves to highlight the social nature of reading in classrooms. A small group of students from a sixth-grade classroom were all reading the same story. The plot revolved around a herd of sheep in danger of attack by coyotes. In the course of the story, the coyotes were identified as being bigger than the sheep dog, having long sharp teeth, being able to climb over high rocky places, making loud howling noises, and having coats of long fur. When the readers talked about the coyote, their comments included, "It's like a wolf," and "It's like a wild goat."

The students were aware that their conclusions were tentative, for they prefaced their definitions with such phrases as "I think." They all had use of the same information supplied by the author. But their personal experiences—TV westerns, trips to the zoo, hikes in the desert, animal stories—varied. As the relationship between readers and author varies, so will the information derived from the reading vary. The outcomes of any reading experience are not totally predictable, nor should anyone want to make them so.

Readers come to their own conclusions; they are independent in their meaning making. Each student in the class described above developed as much of a concept of coyotes as their personal experiences and the information they gained from the story permitted. These concepts were sufficient for their immediate reading purposes.

As soon as another person is involved in the reading event, it expands from a personal experience to a social one, and learning continues as readers transact with each other and with their interpretations of the written text. In discussion with others, readers modify or expand their own reading interpretations depending on how they view the status of the teacher, other readers, or members of a discussion group who offer alternate interpretations. This happens even if the other views are no more fully developed than those developed through the initial reading of the story. When the students in our example looked up more information about coyotes in the dictionary, they found one popular pocket dictionary describing coyotes as "wolflike animals common in North America" (Davis 1970, 167). This definition is hardly more sophisticated than their own.

Within a group, more fully developed concepts are formed about coyotes, for example, and there is greater consistency in those concepts than in those developed by individual readers. In the group above, one student said he discussed wolves and coyotes with his father and his father said coyotes were not wolflike. This led the class to search for newspaper articles and to contact the local museum to gain more accurate information. This learning became the result of a number of social reading experiences expanding on and extending beyond the personal reading. The students in this case did not gain new information or develop new concepts through a single reading experience. They did not limit their knowledge search to a single reading experience or single text but continued to build their knowledge through further discussion, a movie, and a trip to the zoo. Less experienced readers, in particular, need such diverse engagements to promote concept development. Involving inexperienced readers and young children in varied, interesting, firsthand experiences will prepare them to cope more successfully with new ideas and concepts they encounter in print.

In another example, a group of eight- and nine-year-olds gathered in a literature circle to study William Steig's life and work (Whitmore & Crowell 1994). Over the course of their membership in the group the students read many of Steig's books, learned biographical information about him, studied his political cartoons, and compared the work he had done over his lifetime. The group began by reading *Sylvester and the Magic Pebble* (Steig 1988), a story about a donkey who was transformed into a rock and back to himself by the power of a magic pebble. The students and teacher talked together following their independent reading and reflection in literature logs. The teacher initiated the discussion with an open-ended question. Notice the variety of responses elicited by her question:

Teacher:	*Sylvester and the Magic Pebble.* What did you guys think about this story?
Rita:	I think they cared a lot for him.
Teacher:	Who do you mean? You mean his parents?
Rita:	Yes.
Teacher:	What made you think that when you read the story?
Rita:	'Cause they really worried about him.
Teacher:	Who else wants to share something? I'd like to hear everybody's ideas . . . Sarah?
Sarah:	I think he got the idea of it when he was little or maybe one of his friends got lost or something.
Teacher:	What do you mean, he got the idea?
Sarah:	He got the idea for his parents to think that Sylvester got lost.
Teacher:	You're talking about where William Steig might have gotten his ideas?
Sarah:	Yes.
Teacher:	That maybe something like this happened to him or someone he knew? A lot of times authors get their ideas from real life things, don't they? Jon, what did you think about this story?
Jon:	It was like a, um, moral story. It's like you can't wish for everything. But in a sense, everything happened to him when he was panicking.

Jon's comment began a conversation about how Sylvester may have reacted if he hadn't panicked. Then Richard shared that he had read the book several times before.

Teacher:	Richard, since this was not the first time you read the story, how did you think differently about it this time?
Richard:	I don't know.
Teacher:	What did you say in your log about the story when you wrote in your log yesterday?
Richard:	That it was a good book?
Teacher:	I guess what I want is for kids to know why they think something is a good story.
Rita:	I said it was a good story because they love their son very much.
Sarah:	I think I know why I was thinking differently. Instead of thinking about what the book said, I was thinking about what the author was thinking when he wrote it.
Jon:	I thought more about what was going on.
Teacher:	Well, that's okay. The first time you read a story you're going to react in a lot of different ways. Look at all the different kinds of things you had to say. Rita talked about the characters in the story and what they must have been feeling. Sarah took the author's point of view. And you saw it as a particular kind of story, Jon. As a moral story.
Jon:	As a fable.

(Whitmore & Crowell 1994, 145)

As the group progressed, they discussed the significant elements in the plot, moving toward a plot analysis they negotiated as their group project. In the midst of their discussion, Sarah (whose turns in the following transcript are emphasized in bold) raised an issue about an event in the plot and asked for help in understanding it. Notice that she was silent during the conversation that followed her question, but she demonstrated her involvement as a listener when she reentered. At the end of this segment, Sarah returned to the text to finalize her response, and put the issue to rest for herself.

Sarah:	**I was thinking, at the end, I always get mixed up, because when they have the rock on him, does Sylvester wish himself back, or does his parents?**
Richard:	Sylvester does!
Rita:	No, they do!
Richard:	Sylvester does! Sylvester does!
Teacher:	Can you find in the book where . . .
Richard:	It's right here, it's right here!
Teacher:	Wait a second. And Richard, if you will . . .
Richard:	It says, "I wish I were myself again. I wish I were my real self again," thought Sylvester.
Jon:	Yes.
Rita:	But his parents did that too.
Richard:	But he said . . .
Rita:	They found the pebble and they . . .
Richard:	Put it on him.
Teacher:	Do you remember how the magic had to work?
Jon:	It would have to be on Sylvester.
Teacher:	What was the only way the pebble had to work?
Richard:	If it was on the person.
Teacher:	If you had it in your hand, right?
Richard:	Or on you.
Teacher:	So if he's a rock, he can't hold the pebble.
Jon:	But he could support it.
Sarah:	**Yeah, he wished himself back.**

(Whitmore & Crowell 1994, 145)

This transcript of a literature discussion demonstrates the social construction of meaning that can occur as two or more readers gather to share interpretations. In this example, the readers transacted with each other's personal texts, as well as with the author's written text, to construct meaning. And, in this case, through a literature study group the meaning became mutually agreed-upon through the discussion.

The social component of the classroom is enhanced through a variety of learning experiences in addition to literature study. Discussions during sharing time, show and tell, and current events also involve reading responses at a social level. Newspapers and news magazines provide ready access for sharing reading, building shared meaning, discussing various interpretations, and becoming knowledgeable about the significant issues and opinions on world and local events. Reading both fiction and nonfiction expands upon the range of possible ways to interpret text. As teachers provide avenues for students to explore various literacy materials socially, they create opportunities for, and knowledge about, participation in a democratic society. During the Gulf War, for example, a group of intermediate grade students shared thoughts, questions, and ideas daily in their classroom. The newspaper, especially captions under photos, provided rich opportunities for dialogue. Rich literacy-embedded discussions were the impetus for more in-depth study that involved the group of readers in the classroom who were the most captivated by the topic in related fiction and nonfiction materials organized in text sets of conceptually related materials.

Response to literature and other social reading happens in a variety of ways, depending upon the group, the materials, and the issues confronted during reading. Sometimes the discussion following reading is presentation enough—it confronts issues, demonstrates individual progress and involvement, and serves sufficiently as an opportunity for response. At other times, however, more involved projects represent shared learning. Comparison webs and charts are effective ways to present learning, particularly with sets of related texts (Short & Pierce 1990). Dialogue journals between group members or buddy readers can be insightful. Writing in the style of a particular author or a specific genre integrates writing and reading. Writing about the desert in poetry like Byrd Baylor's to present an author study about her is such an example. Dramatizing reading material in a variety of ways is also valuable, both in terms of choral reading events and acting out stories.

Through reflection, especially in discussion with others, students are encouraged to be critical readers. The variety of individual student's personal literacy histories can merge to develop a critical social history as a classroom community. Through critical reading, authors' ideas and images are challenged and expanded, the reader's consciousness is raised, and issues of political significance often come to the forefront. In the process, reading materials are critiqued for social issues such as sexist or racist perspectives. Reading in a group, interacting about reading material, then, helps students expand their world views. The group of readers who developed a literature circle based on their concerns about the Gulf War changed their perspectives on war dramatically, deciding, based on their social reading experience, never again to play war games or use war toys.

The *Reading Curriculum* as well as the *Reading Instructional Program* reflect both the personal and the social aspects of reading listed in Figure 2-4.

In Chapter 3 and in Part II, we focus on organizing for *Reading Strategy Instruction,* including authentic evaluation for both personal and social reading experiences.

3

Reading Strategy Instruction: Focus on Evaluation

The *Reading Instructional Program* presented in Chapter 2 includes the learning experiences in school that involve reading and writing. In this chapter, we focus on the organization of *Reading Strategy Instruction,* one aspect of reading instruction within the curriculum.

Reading instruction is most relevant when it is based on careful observation and understanding of the reading needs of the student. We, therefore, begin with reading evaluation. Ongoing evaluation is a major component of the *Reading Instructional Program.*

EVALUATION OF READING DEVELOPMENT

Evaluation procedures assess readers' uses of the language cueing systems and reading strategies, as well as the relationships of the cueing systems and strategies as they operate within the reading process.

Reading permeates the whole language classroom just as it permeates society. Whenever we engage in reading, it is a means of communication: the daily schedule is written on the board, a morning message is posted, a reference book is consulted, a bake sale is advertised, the words of a new song are distributed, or a penpal letter is read.

Although *reading* as a process and *reading instruction* are considered separately in planning curriculum, they actually occur simultaneously and continuously throughout the school experience. The teacher is engaged in ongoing planning and evaluation to make sure that reading development is occurring; that students are constructing meaning from both their reading and their reading instruction. Learners' responses to reading experiences embedded in the curriculum are opportunities for them to demonstrate their knowledge. As readers orally retell, write about their reading, or present their responses in other ways, such as creating a play or a collage, conducting research by working in a small group, or following directions for building, cooking, or experimenting, they reveal their ability to:

- construct a general theme for what they are reading;
- incorporate or relate the information to what they already know;
- develop meanings for concepts presented by the material;
- relate the theme, concepts, or information gained to other situations or circumstances; and
- perceive any patterns or relationships involving the events, concepts, information, or themes.

Such revelations provide many opportunities for evaluation. If, however, there is evidence that students are not reading for meaning, the teacher needs to set up opportunities for students to become more engaged in reading by:

- using authentic reading materials (such as real articles and stories, newspapers, or magazines);
- providing experiential support for the reading (such as participating in a relevant science experiment, group discussion, or field trip);
- altering or expanding on the materials to be read (such as providing concept-related books written in another genre or more accessible style); and/or
- providing reading-strategy instruction.

Detail and perspective become important in planning reading instruction. Teachers document and appreciate the reading strengths of each student, and students need to appreciate their own capabilities. This allows teachers to focus on the needs of readers and support the strategies they use to construct meaning. Through planning and evaluation, teachers examine the strengths readers have and the strategies they use to read complex text. In this way, teachers determine whether readers' difficulties are repeatedly experienced in reading, limited to specific kinds of reading material, and disruptive to constructing meaning. The teacher then decides on the instruction that will resolve the readers' difficulties and support their strengths without disrupting the reading process.

Whole language teachers understand that in-process evaluation means assessing growth, not measuring an end product. In reading, as in all areas of the curriculum, teachers who are kidwatchers (Y. Goodman 1985, 1991) look for strengths and signs of growth and increased understanding, rather than for perfection. For example, kidwatchers understand the development that occurs as children represent the word *the* with a variety of spellings, such as *h, teh, tha,* and *da.* Each spelling reflects the writer's knowledge about how written language works. Miscue research shows that proficient readers are those who construct meaning from the published text, who comprehend, and who read efficiently. They sample the text, make inferences and predictions based on new information and prior knowledge, confirm predictions, and self-correct when necessary. They know that proficient reading is not pronouncing each word perfectly or reading long pieces of text or reading fast. Whole language teachers are constantly watching and listening as students read in order to assess the development of their natural reading strategies.

Teachers, therefore, make reading evaluation integral to the reading program. Reading evaluation occurs all day every day as kids experience written language both personally and socially. Much of reading evaluation occurs through formal and informal miscue analysis and print awareness tasks as students read throughout the day. Ongoing evaluation permeates the *Reading Instructional Program.*

Sampling Oral Reading

We have described reading as a discussion between reader and author. Both contributors bring their language, their knowledge, and their thought processes to this discussion. As in any discussion, there are points where the two participants do not share a common experience—times when perspective or knowledge differ. At these points readers do not always respond in an expected manner with the material the author has prepared, and consequently they do not anticipate what the author planned to write.

Because readers are making use of the available cueing systems based on their personal knowledge and background, they may misinterpret the author's intentions. They produce unexpected responses because they are predicting alternative possibilities and constructing their own text. These unexpected responses are called *miscues* (K. Goodman 1964, 1994). Because proficient readers are concerned with meaning, not accuracy, and because no author and reader ever have exactly the same experiences, knowledge, schema, or perspectives, miscues are natural to the reading process. All readers make miscues. These miscues result from the same process readers use when they make no miscues. Therefore, we evaluate readers' uses of strategies and knowledge of the cueing systems by examining their miscues.

Miscues are collected as readers read orally under the following authentic reading conditions:

- The reading material is new to the readers. Evaluation documents what readers do as they transact with new material as if they were reading silently. The miscues indicate the readers' ability to anticipate the author and reveal information concerning the readers' knowledge about language and content. The material is challenging but most of the language structures and concepts are familiar to the readers.
- The reading is uninterrupted so as not to interfere with the readers' construction of meaning. Help supplied by the teacher reflects what the teacher knows, not what the readers know.
- Readers are encouraged to view the construction of meaning as the purpose of reading. Readers are told to focus on understanding the information and enjoying the reading, not to focus on surface reproduction. There is no concern with performing for an audience or with producing an exact rendition.

These conditions are met when readers are given an unfamiliar but complete story or article to read and are informed that they will be totally dependent upon their own resources, that they must continue reading past any problems, and that after the reading they will be responsible for a retelling of the material. The whole process is preserved for evaluation by tape-recording. Readers' miscues are then available for analysis by replaying the tape and comparing the reading with the printed text (Y. Goodman et al. 1987).

Evaluating Reading Miscues

Evaluation, as an integral part of the reading curriculum, must reflect both the model of the reading process and the instructional procedures being used. Only when the components of personal and social reading, reading evaluation, and reading-strategy instruction are synchronized will evaluation techniques indicate whether students are profiting from the instructional procedures and whether those procedures actually encourage the development of successful reading strategies.

The view of reading and instruction presented in this text is informed by research in miscue analysis. Miscue analysis provides insights into how people learn and develop as language users. It indicates the ways in which the individual reader makes use of the language cues in a text and maintains the integrity of the integrated language systems. Miscue analysis is also useful in examining the relative complexity and predictability of reading materials.

In miscue analysis significance is not attached to any one miscue or the quantity of miscues, but to the general pattern of miscues made consecutively throughout a text. Proficient readers who are constructing meaning will produce a large percentage of sentences that remain syntactically and semantically acceptable regardless of the number of miscues in the sentence. (A syntactically acceptable sentence fits grammatically within the text. A semantically acceptable sentence makes sense within the text.) Insight into the most significant aspects of miscue analysis is gained by asking questions following one of the alternative miscue procedures.

These procedures are discussed in depth in *Reading Miscue Inventory: Alternative Procedures* (RMI) (Y. Goodman et al. 1987). In order to show how evaluation and curriculum planning go together, we provide an overview of one procedure, Procedure III, and show our miscue analysis of Gary's reading of "The Stonecutter."

Miscue Analysis: Procedure III

In RMI Procedure III the teacher asks four questions concerning syntax, semantics, meaning change, and graphic similarity to examine each sentence read by the student. The marking, coding, and analysis are done directly on the typescript of the story, eliminating the need for additional forms as used for the other procedures. The answers to the four questions (see below) provide teachers with valuable insights into the language cues and reading strategies the reader is using to construct meaning.

Procedure III entails the following steps within the context of the reading conditions for miscue analysis discussed earlier. It may be helpful to examine Gary's transcript below first and then attend to this list of procedures:

1. Select the student.
2. Select the material. Selection of material is important. The story selected should have sufficient theme and plot; informational pieces should provide a complete concept or event. The story line or concepts must be of interest to the prospective reader and be at least 600 words in length. The material must be at a level of difficulty that will cause some reading challenges but will not cause frustration.
3. Prepare the typescript of the story by first numbering each sentence and then drawing and numbering a corresponding line in the right margin at the end of each sentence (see Gary's typescript).
4. Prepare a retelling guide, noting characters and major events in the story or listing the major concepts in an article.
5. Obtain a tape recorder to audiotape the reading session.
6. Inform the reader of the purposes and procedures of the taping session, including that no aid will be forthcoming during the session and that when the reading is completed he or she will be asked to retell the story or article.
7. Ask the reader to read the story aloud and then retell it.
8. Listen to the tape later in a quiet setting, checking to see that the miscues are appropriately marked on the typescript. Complete a retelling summary and/or transcribe the retelling.

At this point you may want to read Gary's typescript and retelling and examine the questions. You also may consider taping your own reader following steps 1–8. Steps 9–11 will make more sense as you connect them to your experiences.

9. Code each sentence asking Questions 1–3 (pages 44–45). Codings for Questions 1–3 are written on the line drawn in the typescript margin at the right of each sentence.
10. Code only word-level first-occurrence substitutions for graphic similarity. Graphic similarity (Question 4, page 45) is indicated by writing H (High), S (Some), or N (None) in a circle next to word-for-word substitutions in the text.
11. Compute statistics and produce a reader profile. To compute the percentages, for Questions 1 and 2 divide the number of Y's by the total number of coded sentences. Follow the same procedure for the N's. For Question 3 (meaning change) divide the number of N's only by the total number of

sentences coded for meaning change. Follow the same procedure for the P's and Y's. For Question 4 (graphic similarity), divide the number of H's by the total number of word-for-word substitutions coded, excluding repeated miscues (miscues on nouns, pronouns, verbs, adjectives, or adverbs that are the exact same grammatical substitution after their first occurence). Follow the same procedure for the S's and N's.

This statistical analysis sounds complicated in this written form. It becomes clearer by examining the statistics at the end of Gary's transcript (Figure 3-1). More information is available in *Reading Miscue Inventory: Alternative Procedures* referenced earlier.

In Chapter 2, we discussed Gary reading the story about the stonecutter and documented how his ability to accurately read words was not a prerequisite or guarantee of comprehension. Gary, a sixth grader, was recommended to us because he was considered to be the poorest reader in his school. He had been in remedial reading since first grade, and his standardized reading test score placed him at grade 2.2. Gary did not hesitate to read "The Stonecutter," which was taken from a fourth-grade basal series not used in his school. To understand the application of Procedure III and its illumination of a student's reading strengths and strategies, we now examine Gary's entire reading and retelling of "The Stonecutter."

The Stonecutter

1.   Once upon a time there was a stonecutter[1] who

2. worked hard all day long, cutting stones with

3. hammer and chisel. These[2] he made into blocks   (1) YYN

4. for building houses and[3] roads. It was hard work   (2) YYN

5. but the stonecutter was contented until one day

6. when he saw the king ride by.   (3) YYN

7. The king was sitting in a fine carriage, and

8. servants[4] held a sunshade of turquoise silk with

9. golden tassels[5] over him.   (4) YN-

---

[1]cutter—split syllable enunciated

[2]Ⓡ—rereading expected response

[3]Ⓒ—self-correction

[4]—part of a word is read; partials

[5]$—nonword

ⓊⒸ—unsuccessful attempt to correct

10. "Oh," breathed the stonecutter, "if only I were

(markings above line 10: ⓤⓒ, Ⓡ, Ⓢ; $ breathed, bright; Ⓗ; Ⓒ -cutter / stonecarver / carve / stonecarved)

11. the king, and servants held a silken sunshade over

(marking: Ⓒ s- / sil-)

12. me!   ⑤   YN–

13. Now inside the mountain where the stonecutter

(markings: ⑥; Ⓒ; Ⓗ were)

14. was working, there lived an old wizard who heard

15. his wish and gave it to him.   ⑥   YYN

---

16. In the next minute the stonecutter was himself

(marking: ⑦)

17. the King. He was sitting comfortably in the   ⑦   YYN

(markings: ⑧; Ⓗ comfortable)

18. carriage. Servants were holding over his head the   ⑧   YYN

(markings: ⑨; Ⓒ; Ⓗ him; Ⓒ)

19. turquoise sunshade.   ⑨   YYN

(marking: turquo-)

20. "Oh," he breathed[6] happily. "Now I am the   ⑩   YN–

(markings: ⑩; RM $ breathed; Ⓒ hap-; ⑪)   ⑪   YYN

21. greatest of all people alive. I am the King. I shall   ⑫   YYN

(markings: ⑫; ⑬)   ⑬   YYN

22. wear a crown. I shall sit on a throne.   ⑭   YYN

(marking: ⑭)

23. But one day when he was about to go on a

(marking: ⑮)

24. journey, the servants forgot the sunshade, and

(markings: Ⓒ s- / servant; Ⓗ)

25. the king had to wait in his carriage under the   ⑮   YYN

(markings: Ⓒ until; Ⓢ)

26. hot sun. And he was very uncomfortable.   ⑯   YYN

(marking: ⑯)

27. "I am not, after all, the greatest

(markings: Ⓡ ⑰)

28. thing in the world," he said.   ⑰   YYN

29. "The sun is great enough to

(markings: ⑱; Ⓡ)

---

[6]*RM*—Repeated Miscue. Repeated miscues are not coded for graphic similarity.

         ⑲

30. make me uncomfortable. He   ⑱ YYN

        ⑳

31. is greater than I. How I wish   ⑲ YYN

32. I were the sun!"   ⑳ YYN

  ㉑   Ⓒw- Ⓡ

33.   Again the old wizard gave him

      ㉒

34. his wish. The stonecutter became   ㉑ YYN

      ⓇⒸ   Ⓒstrum Ⓢ stroe- strail-

      ㉓ sho-

35. the sun. He shone down strongly over   ㉒ YYN

36. the land, burning the grasses and drying up the

                 ⒽⒸbeam Ⓗ fires bea-

  ㉔

37. rivers. And the people hid from his fierce beams,   ㉓ YYN

38. and he was happy in his power.   ㉔ NN-

  ㉕

39.   But one day a cloud drifted between him and

         Ⓒsh-

40. the earth, and he could not shine through it.   ㉕ YYN

  ㉖

41.   "The cloud is greater than the sun," said the

          ㉗

42. stonecutter, who was now the sun. "Oh, if only   ㉖ YYN

43. I could be that cloud!"   ㉗ YYN

  ㉘   Ⓡ

44.   The old wizard in the mountain heard his wish,

Ⓡ ⒸⒽate   ㉙

45. and he at once became the cloud. Now he had   ㉘ YYN

          Ⓒup-

46. the power to send down water upon the earth.   ㉙ YYN

  ㉚   Ⓡ

47. And this he did with such might that soon the

ⓊⒸ washed ⒽⒸban- Ⓗits

48. river rushed over its banks, carrying with it sheep

Ⓡ ⓊⒸ(k) Ⓗ $celves

49. and calves, donkeys and horses, and even people.   ㉚ NN-

  ㉛

50.   But one thing the water could not overcome.   ㉛ YYN

  ㉜   Ⓡ

51. That one thing was a great rock which stood fast,

52. and the water had to break and go around it.   ㉜ YYN

  ㉝   Ⓒcarv- Ⓡ

53.   "What!" cried the stonecutter, who was now

54. the cloud. "Is there something more powerful ③④   ㉝ YYN
                                                                                                       ㉞ YYN
55. than I? Oh, if only I could be that rock!" ㉟   ㉟ YYN

_____

56.   In the next second the stonecutter became the ㊱

57. rock. He held himself proudly and looked far ㊲ *looking* *f.* Ⓗ Ⓡ Ⓒ   ㊱ YYN

58. down upon the people moving below him. Rain Ⓡ ㊳   ㊲ NN—

                                                                                    Ⓗ
                                                              $ conted
                                                              con-
                                                              $ conted
                                           Ⓒ Ⓗ   Ⓤ Ⓒ con-t-t-
                                           $wesh   con-ten-
59. could not wash him away, and he was contented. ㊳   ㊳ YN—

60.   ㊴ "Now," he said, "I can watch the days and years

61. come and go."   ㊴ YYN

                                        Ⓡ Ⓒ $ shevery Ⓗ
                                           shev-
62.   ㊵ But one day a shivery feeling went all through

                                                  Ⓝ
                                        Ⓒ a ro-
                                           a
63. him. ㊶ A man was hitting the rock with hammer   ㊵ YYN

64. and chisel, and pieces of the rock were being Ⓡ

65. broken off and falling upon the ground.   ㊶ YYN

66.   ㊷ And the stonecutter, who was now the rock,

67. said, "Is there something more powerful than the   ㊷ YYN

68. rock? Oh, if only I could be that man!" ㊸   ㊸ YYN

69.   ㊹ At once the stonecutter became that man and

70. found himself where he had been at the beginning, Ⓡ

71. breaking the rock with hammer and chisel.   ㊹ YYN

72.   ㊺ "There is nothing greater than man and the

                    in his   Ⓒ
73. work he is[7] best able to do," said the stonecutter.   *abil-*   ㊺ NN—

_____

[7]When it is not possible to determine word-for-word relationships, a bracket is placed above the text sequence to show the complexity.

(H)

$ con-nen-ted

continent

(46)

74. Once again he was contented. (46) *YN*

"The Stonecutter" from *Roads to Everywhere* of **The Ginn Basic Readers** by David H. Russell and others, © Copyright 1966, 1948, by Ginn and Company. Used by permission of Silver Burdett Ginn Inc.

Gary's Statistical Profile

Question 1: No. of Y $^{42}/46$ 91 %; No. of N $^{4}/46$ 9 %

Question 2: No. of Y $^{37}/46$ 80 %; No. of N $^{9}/46$ 20 %

Question 3: No. of N $^{37}/37$ 100 %; No. of P   0   0 %;

         No. of Y   0   0 %

Question 4: No. of H $^{20}/24$ 83 %; No. of S $^{2}/24$ 8 %;

         No. of N $^{2}/24$ 8 %

Holistic Retelling Score $^{4}/5$

Figure 3-1. Gary's statistical profile

Gary's Retelling

R: Okay, Gary, why don't you close the book and tell me what this story was all about.

Gary: It was about this stonecutter. He always cut rocks into big squares, to build things . . . to build houses and roads. And once he seen a King that had servants with a sunsheet over him to stop the rays of the sun. And he wished he could be the King. And this wizard in the mountains heard him and so he was the King. And then one day the servants forgot to bring the sunshade and the sun was real hot that day and then he wished that he . . . how he could . . . how he wished he could be the sun. And the wizard heard him, in the mountains, and he was . . . so he was the sun. And he sent down hot rays on the sun, burning up the grass. And the people ran from its . . . from his fiery rays. And one day a cloud got in between him and the earth and he couldn't shine his rays through it. And he said that he wished he could be the cloud. And then the wizard again heard him and he was the cloud. And he threw storms to overflow the rivers on the earth. And there was rock that was in the water's way that wouldn't move, that couldn't be moved. And he wished that he could be the rock and he was. And one day he felt that . . . he felt a person with a hammer and chisel, hitting him and he wished he could be that man. And then . . . and then he became to be his own self again . . . where he began.

R: What do you think this story is trying to tell us?

Gary: Well, never . . . well, you can't be anything else without trying to be whatever you want to be.

R: Why did the stonecutter first want to be the sun, or the King?

Gary: Well, he wanted to be the powerfulest on the earth.

R: And what happened to him when he was the King? Was he the most powerful?

Gary: No, he thought the sun was. And then . . . then he thought the cloud was, then he thought the rock was. Then he became a man again and then he found out that the man is most powerful.

R:	Okay. Is he going to always be the most powerful?
Gary:	No, because other men can be.
R:	Anything else besides men that can be powerful?
Gary:	I don't really know.
R:	Can you remember one word that you had trouble with? Does one word stick in your mind?
Gary:	About little goldlike fringes on the sunshade.

After Gary read and retold this story, his miscues were marked on the typescript and his retelling was transcribed, following the steps listed above. Each sentence was then coded for Questions 1–3 on its corresponding line in the margin of the typescript. Question 3 is coded only if Questions 1 and 2 are coded YY. Sentences with no miscues are coded YYN. Gary's word-level substitutions were coded for Question 4.

Question 1: *Syntactic Acceptability*

Is the sentence syntactically acceptable in the reader's dialect and within the
    context of the entire selection?

Y—The sentence, as finally produced by the reader, is syntactically acceptable.

N—The sentence, as finally produced by the reader, is not syntactically
    acceptable.

(Every sentence is coded either fully acceptable or unacceptable; partial ac-
    ceptability is not considered in this procedure.)

Question 1 considers how much the reader is concerned that what he or she reads sounds like his or her language and dialect, and how well the reader controls both sentence structure and the relationship of sentences to the entire text. It also evaluates the proficiency with which the reader uses strategies (sampling, inferring, predicting, confirming) to construct syntactically acceptable language.

To read for syntactic acceptability, consider each sentence as the reader finally produced it. All corrected miscues or attempts at correction are read as the reader resolved them. When no attempts at correction are made, miscues are read as produced.

An examination of Gary's typescript indicates his strength in producing syntactically acceptable sentences. Only on four occasions (Sentences 24, 30, 37, and 45) did Gary produce sentences that resulted in syntactically unacceptable structures. Generally, when he realized his syntactic predictions were unacceptable (Sentences 2, 6, and 15 are examples), he self-corrected to create a syntactically acceptable sentence. Even his uncorrected nonword substitutions ($tessels for *tassels* in Sentence 4, $brĕathed for *breathed* in Sentences 5 and 10, $celves for *calves* in Sentence 30, $conted for *contented* in Sentence 38, and $connented for *contented* in Sentence 46) retain the syntactic structure of the sentence. (Intonation reveals the syntactic patterns Gary uses.)

Question 2: *Semantic Acceptability*

Is the sentence semantically acceptable in the reader's dialect and within the
    context of the entire selection? (Question 2 cannot be coded Y if Question
    1 has been coded N.)

Y—The sentence, as finally produced by the reader, is semantically acceptable.

N—The sentence, as finally produced by the reader, is not semantically
    acceptable.

(Every sentence is coded either fully acceptable or unacceptable; partial ac-
    ceptability is not considered in Procedure III.)

Semantic acceptability focuses on the reader's success in producing sentences that make sense within the context of the entire story. The semantic system is the most significant language cueing system because it cues the meaning relationships. Because syntax creates structures that support meaning, semantic acceptability is dependent on and limited by syntactic acceptability. Thus, semantic acceptability is coded *after* syntactic acceptability and cannot be coded Y if the sentence is syntactically unacceptable. (For example, see Gary's Sentences 24, 30, 37, and 45.)

After Gary's sentences are coded for syntactic acceptability they are then read and coded for semantic acceptability. Again, the sentence is read as he finally produced it, including corrections, attempts at correction, or miscues with no attempts at correction. Gary's uncorrected nonword substitutions in Sentences 4, 5, 10, 38, and 46 make those sentences semantically unacceptable even though they are syntactically acceptable. Gary has no reason to correct miscues that make sense (*comfortable* for *comfortably* in Sentence 8 and *washed* for *rushed* in Sentence 30) and thus he does not.

Gary's predicting strategies are visible in his reading *horses of . . .* in Sentence 2 and *until the hot sun . . .* in Sentence 15. When he realizes these potentially appropriate predictions do not work, he self-corrects.

Additional insight is gained into a reader's focus on comprehension by asking Question 3 concerning the degree of meaning change.

Question 3: *Meaning Change*
Does the sentence, as finally produced by the reader, change the meaning of the selection? (Question 3 is coded *only* if Questions 1 and 2 are both coded Y.)
N—There is no change in the meaning of the selection.
P—There is inconsistency, loss, or change of a *minor* idea, incident, character, fact, sequence, or concept in the selection.
Y—There is inconsistency, loss, or change of a *major* idea, incident, character, fact, sequence, or concept in the selection.

Meaning change is only examined for sentences that are both syntactically and semantically acceptable (YY) because it is not easy to ascertain meaning change if any aspect of the sentence is unacceptable. A dash is used to indicate when meaning change is not considered (NN– or YN–).

None of Gary's miscues in syntactically and semantically acceptable sentences (YY) produced a meaning change. They were all either corrected or were acceptable miscues that did not alter the meaning of the sentence, as in Sentence 8.

Question 4: *Graphic Similarity*
How much does the miscue look like the text item?
H—A high degree of graphic similarity exists between the miscue and the text. (Two out of three parts of the words are similar: the beginning and middle; the beginning and end; or the middle and end.)
S—Some degree of graphic similarity exists between the miscue and the text. (One of the three parts of the words is similar: the beginning, the middle, the end, or the word's general configuration.)
N—No degree of graphic similarity exists between the miscue and the text.

Graphic similarity is only considered in word-for-word substitution miscues. It is not marked for omissions, insertions, repeated miscues (RM), or complex miscues involving more than word-for-word substitutions. Graphic similarity provides information about the degree to which the reader uses graphic information from the word in the text to produce the miscue.

Twenty of Gary's 24 word-for-word miscues reflect a high degree of graphic similarity, for example, *were* for *where* in Sentence 6 and *washed* for *rushed* in Sentence 30. Some graphic similarity is seen in the beginning portion of *until* for *under* in Sentence 15 and *strum* for *strongly* in Sentence 23. Gary's remaining miscues (*of* for *and* in Sentence 2, *a* for *the* in Sentence 41) show no graphic similarity.

The total number of Gary's individual miscues is not as significant as the strategies he uses to construct meaning. While some teachers may be concerned with the quantity of his miscues, his retelling clearly evidences his understanding of the story. He sequences major events and indicates inferencing and interpretation with terms such as "fiery rays" and "storms." Gary even knows what caused him difficulty in his reading and demonstrates some understanding of the story theme.

Gary's statistical profile (See Figure 3-1 above), along with his retelling, provide an indication of his strength in integrating reading strategies. Ninety-one percent of his sentences retain syntactic acceptability and 80 percent retain semantic acceptability, with no meaning change. He usually self-corrects when his miscues are not making sense. Gary demonstrates an overall concern for constructing meaning in his reading of "The Stonecutter." (Remember that this is a quick overview of miscue analysis. For greater detail and understanding see *Reading Miscue Inventory* (Y. Goodman et al. 1987).)

The strategy lessons presented in Part II provide suggestions to support readers like Gary in using and strengthening their constructive reading strategies and in expanding reading experience and reading effectiveness. There are also suggestions for readers who need help in integrating their reading strategy use, with a focus on making sense of reading material.

SELF-EVALUATION IN READING

In addition to teacher evaluation, students are involved in self-evaluation. Readers can evaluate both their personal and social reading independently or with their group. Self-evaluation includes examining Reader-Selected Miscues, Retrospective Miscue Analysis, and written reflections of the reading experience.

Reader-Selected Miscues

Reader-Selected Miscues is both an instructional and an evaluation strategy that calls for participation of readers in the evaluation process (Watson 1978; Watson & Hoge, in press). As students read silently a self-selected piece of material, they mark and later record any segment of the text that was troublesome. These miscues are then available for analysis by informally using the reading miscue questions described in the preceding section.

After the students have read and recorded their miscues they share them with each other. *Reader-Selected Miscues* provides the teacher and students with a way of evaluating reading without interrupting the reading process. This procedure is fully described in the strategy lesson *Identifying Hard-to-Predict Structures* in Chapter 5.

Retrospective Miscue Analysis

Teachers become knowledgeable about the reading process as they use miscue analysis to evaluate their students. Readers of any age can also be involved in considering the role miscues play in their own reading. Self-evaluation of one's reading through miscue analysis is called *Retrospective Miscue Analysis* (RMA) (Y. Goodman & Marek 1989, 1996). The RMA procedure also serves as an instructional and/or research experience. In RMA the reader, with the help of a teacher knowledgeable in miscue analysis, tapes himself or herself reading, following RMI procedures. The teacher and the reader then listen to the tape and stop at perceived miscues. The reader explores the reasons for the miscues and the teacher helps the reader see how miscues support the reading process. Sometimes the teacher preselects the reader's miscues to support the integration of reading strategies. It is best to start by discussing high quality miscues, so that it is easy for students to see their miscues as evidence of their developing proficient strategies. In this way, the reading process is demystified.

Readers become aware that even proficient readers make miscues, that it is beneficial to self-correct only those miscues that disrupt meaning, and that miscues often enhance reading.

Written Reflections about Reading Experiences

In the following self-evaluations, Figure 3-2, third graders were asked to respond in writing to three components of their reading program. They were asked to tell something about the strategies they used while reading, to reflect on reading as part of a group, and to articulate a plan to improve their reading during the rest of the year.

The power of self-evaluation is that it brings children to the forefront of their own learning, enabling them to take control of their goals, to understand their development, and to negotiate their formal assessment, such as grades, with their teachers. As students come to understand the reading process and find ways to discuss their reading strengths they are better able to develop as proficient readers. Self-evaluation is crucial in a whole language reading program.

As teachers build a profile of their students from insights gathered from miscue analysis, kidwatching, reader responses, and self-evaluation, they have the background to select appropriate reading instruction for individuals and small groups of readers.

READING STRATEGY INSTRUCTION

The understandings we have been developing about the personal, social, and evaluative components of reading have contributed to new traditions in education, especially in reading. With whole language teachers, we are establishing a tradition of functional, personalized, and social reading experiences, including effective evaluation, in order to create strong reading programs embedded within whole language curricula. We relate reading and writing in school to literacy events in the home and community so that children and their families know that reading the newspaper is real reading and that filling in mindless workbook pages or reading meaningless strings of words is not.

Evaluation of the reading process determines which of the available cues readers are using. Reading strategy instruction is intended to strengthen the cueing systems already in use, to justify efficient strategies that readers have sometimes been taught to believe are inappropriate, and to develop awareness of those strategies and cueing systems not being used effectively and efficiently by readers. Reading strategy instruction has five basic attributes:

- It is public and takes place in a social setting.
- It highlights one of the language cueing systems within a text that integrates language authentically.
- It focuses on one of the natural strategies within the reading process.
- It encourages talk about reading and the reading process.
- It supports and focuses the responsibilities of the reader.

The process of public and social reading strategy instruction involves the reader, the author, and the teacher. In many instances it includes a number of readers who have similar needs. The teacher is necessary for two reasons. The first we have already discussed: the instructional experience is based on evaluative procedures that a teacher knowledgeable about the reading process conducts and carries out through carefully selected and focused materials. The second reason is concerned with facilitating learning. When a learning experience is shared, conscious awareness of the process is enhanced. Learners evoke insight in one another as they share both their attempts at processing information and their partially

Seacira   Dec. 19. 90

① Wean I get stuk on a hard
Word I said it out Like deviding it

② I read all Cinds of books.
I read fary tats and Chiter
books I realy like Lorey Ingels.
Wilder books.

③ I Scher My ides. and I
Like reaing with a partner.
If I did Not work with a
parnter I would Not have the abelate
to lern show to read with a partner and
for them to under stard me and I wold
Not under ston them if t Was Not
in agrope.

Trevor   12-19-90

When I read.....
I use the way where you
skip it and then try to
fiugure it out. I read hard and
funny books. I read a wide
varitey of books. I read a lot
of kird of things. I participate
very well. I read what I'm sopposd
to. I share lots of ideas. I make
connections to help my group. I
plan to stay a reader by
reading as much as I can. When
I read I'm very connexable to
the book people can run over
me but I won't move.

Figure 3-2. Self-evaluations, Third Graders

formulated ideas. The teacher acts as a sounding board against which ideas are played and both the teacher and students ask immediately appropriate questions. Reading strategy instruction often begins at a critical moment when something occurs spontaneously that affords immediate response from the teacher and the student(s). Reading strategy instruction and specific lessons often grow out of such powerful spontaneous moments.

A significant aspect of knowing is not only acting on ideas—a function that is an essential part of the reading process—but being able to put ideas into language. Once something has been communicated, it is available for examination, for further development, and for future use. Language offers some permanency to thought. Exploratory talk about reading strategies and language cueing systems within the community of students and teachers increases the likelihood that what was thoughtfully conceived during the instructional experience can be remembered and used at another time.

During reading, proficient readers intuitively process available cues. Their focus is on the meaning that emerges from reading, not on the process itself. When all goes well, readers do not concern themselves with how meaning is constructed; they are unaware of which cues are derived from which language system.

When things do not go as planned, readers need to be able to select and consider available cues in determining alternative strategies. They need to focus on or highlight the language cueing systems and the reading strategies they use. They need to ask themselves:

- How important is this word or phrase or concept? (Is the missing information significant enough to the message to expend effort in seeking it or should I read on?)
- What do I know? (From my past experiences with language and life what can help me make sense of the text? Which text cues have I been able to process?)
- How can I find the missing information? (Which language cues are generally available in the text and where will I find those cues?)
- What is my best guess? (What tentative concept or meaning have I constructed?)

These questions may never be consciously asked by the reader, but they are part of the intuitive search for sense in which proficient readers engage. With the answers to these questions readers determine what additional cues are available and whether they are able to make use of them. Even in instances in which readers are unable to process further, they understand more fully the nature of their problems and may salvage some cues for later use. Consider the following sentence:

The *grebe* is a waterfowl, which I have heard about but never seen.

If the italicized word in the sentence is unfamiliar to readers, they can pronounce it by using the letter/sound relationship of the graphophonic system, consider its noun position by perceiving it in structural relationship to other items in the sentence, and give it meaning through information gained from past experience, from other texts, or from the context of the immediate situation.

Some readers will immediately determine that a grebe is a bird. They are likely to explain that they came to their conclusion "because the sentence says so." No overt thought is given to the complexity of cues and strategies involved in making that decision. As long as reading makes sense, there is no need to consider the process consciously; there is only the need to make use of it. It is only when reading does not proceed as expected that readers need to shift the focus from ends to means.

Other readers will know *grebe* is a noun and realize that the sentence structure

The *something* is a *something* . . .

denotes a synonymous relationship between *grebe* and *waterfowl*, even if they have no idea what a waterfowl is. If readers consciously determine which cues are available and then fully utilize those cues, their search for further information will be more focused than if they have only a general feeling that they have not understood the text.

Readers will know, for instance, that what they learn about *waterfowl* can be applied to their developing concept of *grebes* as they read the next section of text:

> The surface of the lake was spotted with waterfowl. All of them were in constant motion, busily diving for food, chattering at each other and preening their feathers.

If waterfowl float on water and have feathers, and grebes are waterfowl, then grebes probably float on water and have feathers. Such information will not be available to readers who do not salvage partial cues from the reading of the first sentence. On the other hand, readers may decide that this reference to grebes is of little importance to comprehending the whole text—a fleeting reference not worth much time or effort.

Reading proficiency is based on readers' ability to proceed at appropriate speed with attention focused on the developing meaning, but with the flexibility to reprocess by shifting focus or jumping ahead when difficulty is encountered. In this respect readers are like drivers who proceed along the highway in automatic, shift into low to make the grade up a mountain, and then shift back into automatic. The car engine will be overworked if it is in low gear all of the time; similarly the reading process will bog down if readers constantly focus on the process of reading or become sidetracked by unimportant details.

Not only must readers become aware of alternate available cues, they must develop flexibility in applying them. Reading strategy instruction supports both the conscious awareness of the cueing systems and the development of flexibility. This support is achieved by focusing and narrowing readers' responsibilities during the learning process when needed. One way this is accomplished is through thoughtful selection of reading material used for instruction. When evaluation procedures indicate a need for specific strategies, reading material is written or selected to highlight the use of that strategy.

The reading strategy lesson is constructed to help readers gain information from a language cueing system that they may not be using adequately or that they may believe they should not use. The instruction makes readers aware of the reading process. The structure of the lesson moves readers back into low gear where they can focus on the process as well as on the meaning. The material must present the highlighted strategy in its most complete and unambiguous form. The strategy is considered within a language context complete with all the cueing systems, including those with which readers are most successful. Therefore readers approach the new learning with all possible cues available and supported by some structures that they already control. The structure of the material allows the readers to discover the significance of the highlighted reading strategy and the language cues being used.

The meaning carried by the selected material usually involves information and concepts familiar to the readers. The material must, as much as possible, support the reader in making sense. When the written text is supportive, readers can afford to focus their attention on an aspect of the reading process without losing sight of the purposes of reading—communication and construction of meaning. Because the highlighted strategy is embedded in a context that has familiar meaning and language structure, readers' responsibilities are both focused and manageable.

Reading Strategy Instruction is a way of organizing language and thought systems for instructional purposes. It offers students an opportunity to move thought into language and to make it manageable and available for implementation and experimentation.

Part II

Reading Strategy Lessons

Part II

Reading Strategy Lessons

Our model of the reading process reflects the relationships of the reader, the author, the language cueing systems, and the reading strategies. Our model of reading curriculum involves the relationship of the extended reading experiences outside the classroom with reading events that occur in school and with the *Reading Instructional Program,* which includes evaluation. The reading strategy lessons make use of these nesting relationships (See Figure 2-1) and the importance of these contexts.

SIGNIFICANCE OF CONTEXT

In well-written texts readers have available the graphophonic, syntactic, and semantic/pragmatic systems that establish the reading context. Only in context is the reader able to make use of the language cueing systems and of knowledge about the world in order to decide on the most appropriate possible meanings. Conversely, there is no transaction between author and reader when isolated bits of information are read. For example, we may be able to assign meaning to some of the following words: *if, myself, for, me, will, I, am, who, be,* and *not.* But we cannot understand until these words have a syntactic and semantic context—If I am not for myself, who will be for me?

When learning takes place in context, learners are able to build on and expand the structures or schema (Neisser 1976) that organize their experiences. These schema structures are built through transactions with the environment; the learner then uses the schema to categorize concepts, to notice similarities between concepts and how they operate differently in different contextual settings, and to relate new knowledge with previously held and developing concepts.

Life provides situational contexts. It is from these natural, ordinary, everyday contexts that infants learn by building schema and making sense of their world. Babies use a variety of strategies to discover relationships about language and thinking. Out of such complex situational contexts infants learn to select those things that are significant from those things that are unimportant. They find ways to distinguish the sounds of language from the sounds of cars, cats, and fire engines. In order to learn they do not have to isolate each of these sounds. Children learn to identify and classify significant life events through years of experience that also involve talking and thinking. From a tone of voice they know when someone they live with is sad or angry. They have used many strategies in learning prior to their first school experiences. As a consequence of using language and thought authentically children have learned to sample, infer, predict, confirm, and integrate new information into their existing linguistic and pragmatic schema.

These same strategies are used by students learning to read if they are permitted to capitalize on them in the classroom and if significant written context is available. A student's own strategies are the strengths on which a reading program must be built.

SELECTING AND WRITING MATERIALS FOR
READING STRATEGY LESSONS

In writing or selecting materials for reading strategy lessons, we carefully consider the reader, the language, and the content of the written material to ensure that the context of the material is as supportive as possible of the reading strategies the student is developing. If teachers choose to write or adapt their own material they need to consider the same criteria that we discuss.

The Reader

Reading strategy lessons are most effective when they are used at a critical teaching moment. When we become aware of a student's problem, question, or concern, we immediately select appropriate material for the strategy lesson that will support that student. With knowledge from miscue analysis and other evaluation techniques we decide what will benefit the student most at a particular time. Not all needs can be met at once.

Materials and discussions should be appropriate to the students' backgrounds and experiences. Learners are often confused when they either "learn" something they already know or are "taught" something beyond their understanding. Many students are quick to apply the strategies they use in oral language activities to reading. As students build confidence in their abilities and revalue themselves as learners, they establish the self-assurance necessary to effectively develop reading strategies.

Language

Initially the language of the strategy lesson is familiar to the learner, using common vocabulary and sentence patterns. Unambiguous syntax provides students with opportunities to use their language strengths in order to infer, predict, and confirm as they read. Authentic written texts have a variety of common sentence patterns, making it necessary for readers to predict a range of sentence structures. As students develop their reading, they expand their use of reading strategies to those structures that are less common and teachers, based on the needs of their students, select materials for lessons with unique language patterns.

The language of the material in the strategy lesson reflects literary quality. Value judgments on the part of both readers and writers make it difficult to set up absolute criteria for literary quality. What should be avoided is the stilted, boring language that often characterizes manipulated reading-instruction materials written according to readability formulas. In addition, such material is avoided because it doesn't help kids become flexible in the use of a wide range of genre used in the literacy community.

Written language that does not provide enough information for the reader can cause the reader to misunderstand. For example, consider the sentence *They were flying planes*. It is ambiguous and can easily be misunderstood. There is not enough redundant information for the reader to know whether there are planes that are flying or people flying the planes. However, provided with additional information, the reader has additional cues to make judgments about the author's intent:

> As John walked into the toy store, some unusual movements caught his attention.
> They were flying planes.

For meaning to be achieved, adding just one sentence still may not provide sufficient cues for the reader. Often a greater amount of context is necessary.

As John walked into the toy store, the movement of silver streaks caught his attention. As he moved closer to look at the streaks moving swiftly through the air, he realized that they were flying planes, although he didn't understand what caused them to fly.

Instructional material must be of sufficient length to minimize ambiguity and to accommodate appropriate redundant information. Comprehension is enhanced when the reader has sufficient context to read and when the message is carried to an appropriate conclusion. Miscue analysis research shows clearly that a story is easier to read than a page, a page is easier to read than a paragraph, a paragraph is easier to read than a sentence, and a sentence is easier to read than a word.

Content

When the content of strategy lesson material is of interest to students, it helps provide them with purpose and motivation to read. To meet this criterion, the teacher needs to know the interests of each student—personal likes and dislikes, values and beliefs, knowledge and understandings. In preparing our selections, we have taken into consideration what we think students might find interesting, but each teacher must accept the responsibility for selecting or adapting the lessons to personalize them for the students.

These strategy lessons serve as demonstrations for developing strategy lessons that include interesting content for developing readers. Keeping track of the kind of written material students select when they read on their own will provide evidence of their interests. Involving kids in discussions about what they prefer to read provides additional information.

The content of material in the strategy lessons is significant to the readers. Significance and interest go hand in hand; each supports the other. Readers prefer reading about issues and events important to their lives, and these are the things in which they tend to be most interested. Material should be relevant to the lives of learners and represent the learners' cultures accurately. Relevancy is often personal, since it relates to important aspects in the personal life of the reader, but relevancy is also concerned with social issues such as family, culture, and community.

ORGANIZATION OF READING STRATEGY LESSONS

Each of the three chapters that follow focuses on the information available through one of the language cueing systems: semantic/pragmatic, syntactic, or graphophonic. In keeping with a *whole* language view, the highlighted system is never in isolation, but rather in concert with the other systems.

Each chapter begins with a "General Rationale" that provides theoretical support for the strategy lessons in that chapter. The "General Rationale" complements information about the language systems (pages 10–14) and the model of reading (pages 4, 9–10) introduced in Chapter 1.

Following the "General Rationale" are specific strategy lessons that have been written to be *representative* of potential lessons. We encourage teachers to modify these lessons specifically for their learners, or use them to serve as prototypes for strategy lessons that teachers and their students write. Obviously, the examples presented do not exhaust the possibilities for reading strategy lessons. We hope that teachers will construct lessons for their students using all they know about their students, language, the reading process, and learning.

Each reading strategy lesson is organized around the evaluated needs of the student; therefore, the first part of each lesson, "Evaluation: Who Will Benefit," focuses directly on the reader(s). This section states the specific needs of the reader that the lesson addresses. Readers' profiles, based on teachers' and self evaluations, that are comparable to the characteristics listed in the "Evaluation: Who Will Benefit" section provide information about which students will benefit from a specific lesson.

Although there are a number of lessons suitable for an entire group, for the most part, most of the lessons are not meant to be used with all students. A strategy lesson is used with readers who demonstrate that they need that particular lesson, and at a time when they will benefit most from it.

The "Specific Rationale" builds on and extends the information presented in the "General Rationale" while focusing on more specific purposes of the strategy lesson.

The "Strategy Lesson Experience" section is the teaching/learning event at the heart of reading instruction. It usually has four phases: *Initiating, Transacting, Applying,* and *Expanding.* These are cyclical in nature and often overlap, encouraging students to integrate reading with other communication systems and to use reading for authentic purposes. The intention of the strategy lesson is to engage the learners' interests, thereby motivating them to participate in the experience.

Initiating a lesson is more than starting a lesson. Initiating means that the teacher understands the students' strengths, needs, and interests. Lessons are usually initiated with a selection for reading or listening or with an artifact for study that engages the readers' attention. Although the teacher takes the role of facilitator and leader, students are respected as learners within the experience. They are invited and helped to express their own perceptions, evaluate their own abilities, and plan their own learning experiences. The teachers' role is to establish connections so that students want to engage in the lesson. Later, when appropriate, students often assume the role of teacher and resource person. They are invited to select materials, suggest instructional procedures, and discuss what they know and believe about their own reading.

Transacting is at the heart of the strategy lesson experience. Transacting has a double emphasis. Primarily, transacting means that students are actively involved in the learning experiences. Many times non-proficient readers have had years of instruction built on a transmission model of learning, in which they passively responded with "the single correct" answer and carefully followed procedures as established by their teachers. Such learners come to believe that if they follow the teacher's rules and do all the prescribed activities, they will master the skills of proficient reading. In contrast, reading strategy lessons invite learners to give as well as to receive, that is, to transact with each other and with their teacher. Students and teachers are engrossed in exploratory talk (Barnes 1992) about content, language, and the reading process. Learning is heightened as students transact with peers in nonthreatening and nonjudgmental settings. Students are invited (motivated, encouraged, facilitated, helped) to learn by sharing their thoughts with each other and their responses are respected. Whether the discussion is about how reading works, about the content and concepts of a text, or about a response to a passage, students examine, question, and hear each other's ideas and opinions.

We have all had the experience of learning something more fully when we taught it to someone else. When students present their ideas to others they have a chance to sort out their own thinking and to get responses to their ideas. This transaction among teachers and students stimulates thought, language, and learning. Teachers are active participants in these transactions, but not the final source for all correct answers. It is the atmosphere of "let's see," "try it out," "how do you know?" and "where can we go to find out?" that makes learning liberating and exciting. Progress is made through investigating all "truths."

The second use of transacting is as a meaning-making experience that involves the reader and the text (or author). Louise Rosenblatt (1978) describes reading as a transactional process. As students who value themselves as readers transact with a published text, they "live through" experiences. They "participate in another's vision—to reap knowledge of the world, to fathom the resources of the human spirit, to gain insights that will make [their] own [lives] more comprehensible" (Rosenblatt 1983, 7). In contrast to readers who work hard at reproducing the printed page, at finding out what the teacher wants, and at complying with little commitment and involvement, these readers are actively transacting with text to construct meaning, supported by the totality of the discourse.

The *Applying* and *Expanding* phases tie reading to other aspects of the language curriculum as well as to other areas of the general curriculum. Teachers provide opportunities for readers to use their developing reading strategies in new genres or content areas. Students *apply* their developing concepts about both language and the reading process to new reading events and experiences. With confidence students are willing to attempt to read materials that earlier they may have been reluctant to read. They explore new sign systems, genres, and knowledge domains or disciplines to *expand* and develop their schema and their knowledge base. (The nesting metaphor presented as Figure 2-1 in Chapter 2 represents the organization of the reading curriculum and shows the relationship of the strategy lessons to the greater curriculum.)

There is an abundance of written material available for students in libraries, in book stores, on book stands, in homes, and in the community. To facilitate the bridging of reading instruction into both personal and social reading experiences, the teacher should be aware of the variety of reading materials which should be accessible to students. The "Materials/Functions Grid" on page 24 of Chapter 2 (see Figure 2-3) is a guide to assure a wealth of reading materials in organizing or enriching a whole language comprehension-centered transactional reading program. The applying and expanding phases of the lessons are usually followed by references to additional reading materials.

4

Focus on the Semantic/Pragmatic Cueing Systems

GENERAL RATIONALE

The semantic/pragmatic cueing systems are at the heart of all communication. Understanding how readers use the semantic cueing system (the meaning-filled relationship of words, phrases, and sentences within a text) and the pragmatic cueing system (how the semantic system is used by members of the social community) are complex. By carefully studying learners as they read, retell, and respond to text, teachers discover the ways readers seek and construct meaning. (In Chapter 1, pages 13–14, the semantic cueing system and its relationship to the pragmatic cueing system are discussed.)

One of the insights into the semantic/pragmatic systems is that the author's intended meaning does not correspond in simple to readers' understandings. Considering the information presented by authors and the ways in which they present it may serve as a basis for understanding why and how readers and authors construct different meanings:

1. *What the author intends to say:*
   a. *Purpose.* An author's purpose is often reflected through an abstraction, usually referred to as a theme. These themes are ethical statements, generalizations of the main ideas, or knowledge that the author hopes to pass on to readers.
   b. *Point of view or motive.* All writing expresses a bias or an opinion that the author holds about the knowledge or ideas being presented. Even writing that is not overtly persuasive reflects the author's bias.
   c. *Areas of content.* The specific information or knowledge the author wants to present emerges from many knowledge domains, such as science, math, architecture, and human relations. Authors may or may not be aware of the most current knowledge, may write from an unbridled bias, and may not grasp their audience's degree of understanding. An author's writing may or may not reflect the multiple perspectives from which a topic or issue can be viewed.
2. *How the author intends to say it:*
   a. *Genre.* Authors select forms they are most successful with or feel will best serve the presentation of their messages. Authors decide whether to express themselves through drama, prose or poetry, journalistic writing, including news articles and editorials, instructional materials, and so on. Authors are also concerned with the specific medium through which the

writing will be presented: books, newspapers, magazines, comics, cereal boxes, electronic mail, and so on.

b. *Organization.* Written material is organized around an overall question, problem, or concept of central concern to the author. In fiction this is often called the plot. The author has a plan of action involving events through which the plot emerges and is possibly resolved. Included in the organization is the setting (the time and place described) and characterization (individuals and their traits and behaviors). The organization of nonfiction is different from fiction and depends on the subject matter. History may be organized chronologically, whereas science may be organized by stating a proposition and then explaining it. The various organizations an author chooses are influenced by the content, the overall question or problem, the author's purposes, and the audience.

c. *Style.* Authors' knowledge of language is reflected in their style and artistry. They make both conscious and intuitive syntactic, semantic, and pragmatic choices. These choices reflect their knowledge of the chosen genre. For example, an author of an article for a teen magazine might use current slang, but a reporter for the financial section of the newspaper would not. Authors' styles become familiar to readers as they continue to read through a whole story or article and read other texts by the same authors.

3. *Contract between author and reader:*

Authors make assumptions about the reader's purposes, viewpoints, knowledge, background, and experience. It is as if the author has a contract signed by the reader stating, "I the reader will make every effort to understand what you are saying and why you are saying it." Writing reflects the author's background, knowledge, language preferences, experiences, values, and opinions—in other words, his or her very particular world view. Readers bring the same individuality to their long-distance discussion with the author. There is no great mystery, therefore, in understanding why interpretations of a text vary from author to reader, and from reader to reader, even with the most proficient readers.

4. *Role of the reader:*

Readers approach written material as language users and thinkers. Their thoughts and language are actively involved in processing what they read. They use the reading strategies of sampling, inferring, predicting, confirming, and integrating information, depending on their reading purposes, point of view, knowledge of content, and awareness of genre, style, and organization of the material.

a. *Purpose.* Readers have their own purposes. They form their own themes or generalizations based on why they are reading a piece and what its importance will be.

b. *Point of view or motive.* Readers' biases affect their recognition of authors' biases. Readers may not consider that the author has presented a point of view or has a motive, especially if the reader agrees with the author's interpretation or considers the author an expert whose work is never questionable. However, if readers disagree with the author's point of view, they often reject the truthfulness of the content regardless of the expertise of the author.

c. *Response to genre, organization, or style.* Readers recognize the genre, organization, and style of fiction and nonfiction based on their experiences with these forms. The more they have read or heard specific genre, the more likely they are to predict the genre and its organization.

Since purpose is so intrinsically involved in the search for meaning, the first strategy lesson below focuses on its significance. The aim of this chapter is to provide lessons that will help readers become aware of their responsibility to participate actively in the long-distance discussions between readers and authors. Readers are encouraged to transact with the authors' concepts, ideas, characters, themes, humor, propaganda, and generalizations in order to construct meaning for themselves.

Many of the lessons are concerned with integrating concepts into the readers' schema. The development and integration of concepts extends and expands the reader's ability to construct meaning. We define a *concept* as an understanding of objects, ideas, generalizations, characteristics, criteria, and so on; *misconceptions* are misunderstandings and they develop in the same way concepts develop. Concepts are as varied as what we know to be the color red, which animals we classify as dogs, and what we consider the number two to be. Humanity, cooperation, and justice, as each of us understands them, are also concepts. Although concepts, concrete or abstract, appear to develop almost instantly, they emerge over time through continuous, real, and vicarious experiences that involve reading and other sign systems.

Concepts that are developed and extended through reading must be related to the reader's schema—to experience and knowledge already developed. For example, if a student is reading about the South American rain forest, she will make connections to forests she has visited or seen in photographs or on television. A student who has never seen a forest will have difficulty understanding the concept. Planned experiences that involve film, video, or photographs in addition to reading and writing will support her emerging concepts.

All reading experiences, fiction or nonfiction, provide opportunities for students to:

- expand, modify, and make connections with concepts that are already integrated into their schema;
- develop new concepts and integrate them into their existing storehouse of knowledge or schema; and
- reject new conceptual information and ideas because these new ideas cannot, for a number of reasons, be integrated into their schema.

Readers must become actively involved in their own learning. As they interact with written materials, they have the responsibility to evaluate and critique what they read. When proficient readers are faced with new concepts they ask questions such as:

1. What is my purpose in learning this concept?
2. Is this particular concept important for my purposes?
3. What evidence do I have that helps me know the concept is accurate and appropriate for my purposes?
4. If it is important, how can I best remember the concept?

With these questions in mind, readers are more able to make use of the semantic/pragmatic cueing systems to support their meaning construction.

STUDENTS WHO NEED TO FOCUS ON THE SEMANTIC/PRAGMATIC CUEING SYSTEMS

All learners benefit from understanding that everything they read needs to make sense. A focus on the reader's active construction of meaning is central to all whole language curricular experiences. The lessons in this chapter serve as reminders to proficient readers that reading is a dynamic experience, but the lessons are particularly critical for readers who believe that reading is an act of recoding print to sound, doing worksheets, memorizing vocabulary words and phonics rules, or getting the "right" answers to questions at the end of the chapter.

Teachers gather information about a reader's focus on the semantic/pragmatic cueing systems in a number of ways. It is important to consider students' concepts and beliefs as revealed during discussions of current events, social studies, or science experiences. Casual conversations with students and students' participation in discussions and interviews concerning projects and reports provide teachers with opportunities to evaluate students' understandings and their focus on meaning as they read. Miscue analysis (See Chapter 3, pages 38–39 and *Reading Miscue Inventory: Alternative Procedures,* Y. Goodman et al. 1987) provides teachers insights about readers' proficiency by asking questions concerning the syntactic, semantic, and graphophonic cueing systems.

The RMI questions (Procedure III) used to determine meaning construction are primarily Questions 2 and 3. Question 2: Is the sentence semantically acceptable in the reader's dialect and within the context of the entire selection? If the answer is yes (which assumes syntactic acceptability), then Question 3 is asked: Does the sentence, as finally produced by the reader, change the meaning of the selection? N indicates no change in the meaning of the selection, P indicates an inconsistency, loss, or change of a minor idea, incident, character, fact, sequence, or concept in the selection; and Y indicates a major inconsistency, loss, or change. In addition, the student's retelling of the selection provides important information about the construction of meaning.

The following two RMI Procedure III profiles represent readers who need to be concerned with constructing meaning by focusing to a greater extent on the semantic/pragmatic cueing systems.

- Jeb, age nine, read the first chapter of *Much Ado About Aldo* (1989) by Johanna Hurwitz. His reading resulted in the following:

Syntactic Acceptability	Y 84%	N 16%	
Semantic Acceptability	Y 70%	N 30%	
Meaning Change	N 68%	P 18%	Y 14%
Graphic Similarity	H 82%	S 12%	N 6%
Retelling	18%		

- Susan, age eight, read *The Quilt Story* (1992) by Tony Johnson. Her reading resulted in the following:

Syntactic Acceptability	Y 44%	N 56%	
Semantic Acceptability	Y 40%	N 60%	
Meaning Change	N 60%	P 33%	Y 7%
Graphic Similarity	H 75%	S 10%	N 15%
Retelling	55%		

The following student characteristics (shown in bold) are representative of students who have profiles similar to Susan's and Jeb's miscue analyses. These characteristics indicate a need for strategy lessons integrating the use of sampling, inferring, predicting, and confirming by focusing on semantic and pragmatic cues.

- **Readers who believe that the major reading strategy involves making use of graphophonic cues or who believe they need to always seek help from resources other than themselves and the text to construct meaning.**

Jeb's responses to the following questions, taken from the Reading Interview in *Reading Miscue Inventory: Alternative Procedures* (Y. Goodman et al. 1987), indicate such dependency:

Teacher: When you are reading and come to something you don't know, what do you do?

Jeb:	I look at the first parts and I sound it out, then I sound out all the words, then that's how I get my word out. You can put your finger over the first part and say that, then move your finger until you get the word.
Teacher:	Do you ever do anything else?
Jeb:	Well, I could go ask someone what the word was.
Teacher:	If someone were having trouble reading how would you help?
Jeb:	I would tell them to look at the first word, I mean letter, and think about the way it sounds.
Teacher:	What do you want to do better as a reader?
Jeb:	I would look at the words, and I would look at that word real close. If I can't figure it out I would just ask a older person.

- **Readers who are unable to retell the story or who select insignificant bits of information about the story to relate.**

In some cases, such as Jeb's, the oral reading results for the most part in syntactic and semantic acceptability. The chapter Jeb read describes Aldo, his two cats, and his two sisters. Two sentences on the last page are about a spelling test. Jeb retells insignificant aspects of the story in an unrelated way.

Jeb:	Well, I liked that story because it, because it is sort of a happy story and that's all.
Teacher:	What happened in the story?
Jeb:	The boy and, and the . . . the boy . . . um . . . in his spelling test he got all . . . he got five . . . or two I think, two of them or five of them wrong on the spelling test. And one of them was potato, and the other one was (pause). I can't remember what the other one was, but potato and something else. (Aldo missed three words.)
Teacher:	All right, can you tell me anything else?
Jeb:	Um, no.
Teacher:	That's what you remember?
Jeb:	Uh, well, he . . . he tried to uh . . . get the chicken . . . well, cut the chicken and uh . . . and he gots a chicken leg in his stomach. And uh . . . he ate some of it and the chicken leg got in his stomach. (Aldo ate a chicken leg.)
Teacher:	Okay. Anything else?
Jeb:	No.
Teacher:	You mentioned a boy. What else do you remember about the boy?
Jeb:	Well, he (long pause). Well, after he got done with the chicken, he washed his hands and dried them. And (pause) . . . he had to recopy the spelling words on his spelling test because he got some wrong. And I guess that's all.

- **Readers who omit entire phrases or lines of text without rereading even though the omission results in syntactically and semantically unacceptable sentences.**

Jeb makes the following line omissions:

In fact, he thought of

them as if they were his brothers. Originally the

two kittens had been gifts to Aldo's big sisters . . .

Aldo pointed to the note on the table. It was

from their mother and said that she had gone

shopping and probably wouldn't be home until four.

- **Readers whose miscue analysis profile shows a major focus on graphophonic cues.**

Jeb overrelies on graphophonics as revealed by his graphic similarity score of 94% when High and Some are combined. Only one of his miscues has no similarity to the expected response. Jeb reads carefully and produces high acceptability scores, but he focuses on surface features to such an extent that he is unable to tell much about the story.

Susan's profile indicates that 75% of her substitution miscues have high graphic similarity, with 10% having some similarity, bringing the total to 85%. She leaves the high graphic similarity nonwords (such as $snook for *snaking*) and other miscues (such as *medals* for *miles*) disruptive to meaning uncorrected, which results in her low semantic and syntactic scores. Susan is relying on graphophonic knowledge at the expense of constructing meaning. At the same time her retelling of important ideas from the story is evidence that she is working hard at constructing some meaning.

- **Readers who make no attempt to self-correct miscues that disrupt meaning.**

Jeb:
            kitchen
He took the chicken leg and sat down with it . . .

Susan:
           finish
One day the little girl's family moved away,

    medals   *medals*
across miles and miles of pavement,

    $snook
and snaking grey highways.

Susan:
        trucks
Then tucked her in.

And (Abigail) felt at home again

    quite
under the quilt.

- **Readers who do not use their background knowledge and other available information to help them predict text.**

Susan's class was involved in a theme cycle in which the students were designing and making a quilt. In an earlier discussion Susan shared that her grandmother made quilts. When the teacher gave Susan *The Quilt Story* (Johnston 1992) the teacher said, "I think you'll like this. It's about something we are doing in class and you know a lot about it." On the cover of the book was a picture of a quilt. Despite these cues, Susan did not trust herself to predict based on immediately accessible information, including her own background experience. She chose not to read the name of the story and the word *quilt* on the first four occurrences. It was only on the sixth page, after many illustrations, that Susan read *quilt*.

Other problems readers have with grasping the author's purpose for writing, understanding noun and pronoun references, recognizing relational words and phrases, determining negative constructions, discerning humor, and so on are discussed in each strategy lesson in the section "Evaluation: Who Will Benefit."

Because of the complexity and length of this chapter, the strategy lessons are divided into four sections: Focus I: Making Belief Systems Visible; Focus II: Text Organization; Focus III: Genre (Language of Discourse); and Focus IV: Word and Phrase Semantic Cues.

FOCUS I: MAKING BELIEF SYSTEMS VISIBLE

STRATEGY LESSON: PURPOSE FOR READING

Evaluation: Who Will Benefit

This strategy lesson will benefit readers who:

- are insecure and want their teachers to set purposes for reading;
- often read to gain only the minimum required information;
- are reluctant to choose their own reading material;
- dislike long books; or
- rarely pick up something to read for themselves.

For these readers the purpose for reading is not to discover, to enjoy, or to construct meaning. They do not think of reading as a form of pleasure or as an activity to gather information to answer their own questions. Often their instructional programs have concentrated on fragmented aspects of language such as sounding out letters and words, recognizing words, filling in worksheets, or answering trivial "comprehension" questions. For such readers, reading is an instructional activity, something that occurs only in school in response to teachers' assignments. If students become dependent on such instruction and define themselves as readers based on this instruction, they may ultimately view themselves as less than successful readers. It is essential to help these students revalue reading as a meaning-making process in which their personal interpretation and investment are critical.

Specific Rationale

Readers' purposes often control the strategies they use to predict and to comprehend what they read. Louise Rosenblatt proposes that readers take cognitive "stances" that are either aesthetic or efferent. An aesthetic stance is one in which the reader attends "to the associations, feelings, attitudes, and ideas that these words and their referents arouse within him" (Rosenblatt 1978, 25). An efferent stance is taken when the reader's purpose is to take away from the reading certain information or to discover a solution to a problem. Readers' stances will shift even within the reading of a single text depending on their purposes. Even when they are not consciously aware they are doing so, proficient readers set their own purposes and take a stance. They make decisions about their reading strategies based on these purposes. For example, reading a movie review differs depending on several factors. If your purpose is to find out whether you want to see the movie, you (based on your values and experiences) read to find answers to your questions: Who is in the film? Is there much sex and violence? Can I take an eight-year-old to see it? What is the theme? If you have already seen the film, you won't pay much attention to information about the actors or the degree of violence; you already know this. Now you read to find out if the critic agrees with your opinion. If you regularly read movie reviews you often predict how the critic will respond to the film. In this case, you read to confirm your predictions.

It is important to:

- allow students to set their own purposes and establish their own stance;
- involve students in discussing the importance of setting their own purposes;
- set purposes for readers *only* when there is an educationally sound reason to do so;

- state a purpose in such a way that there will be a number of appropriate, acceptable responses. For example: "After we've read the 'Cross of Gold' speech, let's talk about how it helps us understand our topics and issues";
- encourage purposes that go beyond reading for facts and surface detail. Avoid: "Read to find out how many ships Columbus brought to the New World and their names";
- select a wide range of reading material that relates to the students' purposes for reading and that relates to themes being developed within the curriculum; and
- discuss texts in which the purpose for reading is enjoyment.

Proficient readers have learned to use their own experiences and knowledge of language to set appropriate purposes and to make predictions about the author's message, how it is likely to be said, and the genre in which it is presented. Proficiency in using these various strategies grows as students read widely.

The strategy lesson that follows is designed to help students consider how predicting and confirming strategies relate to their purpose for reading by focusing on semantic/pragmatic information. (We use verbs in second person not to tell teachers what to do but to share with them the procedures we follow in the lessons. We encourage teachers to adapt all lessons to their specific setting based on their professional insights.)

Strategy Lesson Experience

Initiating: Display a variety of written materials such as television guides, comic books, packages with information on the wrappers, science books, grocery lists, baseball cards, telephone books, report cards, and so on. Invite students to talk about who would read the materials presented and why they would read them. Explore the idea that purposes are different from reader to reader and that from time to time purposes change even for the same reader.

A discussion about the purposes of reading helps learners focus on understanding and constructing a meaningful text. Predicting possible purposes helps students relate reading to their own need to understand.

Transacting: If students understand that the major goal of reading and reading instruction is to construct meaning, then the discussion need not continue at this time. However, even proficient readers sometimes need to be reminded of the importance of purposes, both their own and the authors'. If readers retain the characteristics mentioned in the "Evaluation: Who Will Benefit" section or become uncertain about their purposes for reading, it is helpful to consider the following questions:

- What do you read? Why do you read those things? At first students may focus on school-related reasons for reading in anticipation of answers they think the teacher wants. A student might record on the board or overhead the types of materials read and the various reasons class members have for reading them. As students suggest self-directed reasons for reading such as to build a model, follow a recipe, find a television program, learn about people, locate a restroom, or buy a favorite food, support and extend their answers with examples from your own experiences.
- What do you read outside of school? Why do you read those things? If students do not talk about what they read outside of school, help them focus on things they might read and ask them to consider the variety of materials and reasons for reading (See the Materials/Functions Grid, Figure 2-3, on

page 24). Help them realize that reading must be for their own personal learning and enjoyment.

Applying: Invite students to add to what they learned about their own reading materials and purposes for reading by interviewing family members, neighbors, friends, and teachers. Students may research what and why older and younger people read, including those who read a great deal and those who appear to read very little.

Help students generalize that reading has many purposes: for gaining information, survival, job-related purposes, enjoyment, and self-fulfillment. To achieve these purposes they *must understand* what they are reading. Use the words *purpose* and *reasons* as synonyms where appropriate.

Expanding: It helps students to consider that reading should be personally purposeful if they consider the societal significance of literacy. They might do a "literacy dig" (Taylor 1993) by collecting what they or selected family members read and write and develop a collage or album showing who they are as literate citizens. They might label each artifact with the social or individual purposes for reading.

Books about the power of literacy such as those listed below explore purposes for reading and writing. These may be read to the class to stimulate discussions about literacy or a small group may choose to read a few of these as a text set and lead a discussion in class related to the literacy issues raised in these books.

Students may raise the issue that they do not see a purpose for reading certain assignments. This problem should be considered seriously by helping students learn how to respectfully question teachers when they do not understand the purposes for an assigned reading. They will also benefit from pointers on how to understand assignments. Most importantly, they need to realize that becoming good readers *for their own purposes* will help them handle difficult assignments.

Readings for Expanding This Strategy Lesson

Books for Primary Grades

Browne, Anthony. *I Like Books.* New York, NY: Dragonfly Books, 1988.
 A young chimp declares his love of books, inviting readers to share in the celebration of the wonderful world of books.

Bunting, Eve. *The Wednesday Surprise.* New York, NY: Clarion, 1989.
 Grandma and Anna have been reading together to surprise the family. A touching story about the power of literacy.

Cohen, Miriam. *When Will I Read?* New York, NY: Dell, 1977.
 Jim wants to read more than anything in the world. The teacher promises Jim that his turn will come and soon he will be reading.

Johnston, Tony. *Amber on the Mountain.* New York, NY: Dial, 1994.
 Isolated on her mountain, Amber meets and befriends a girl from the city who gives her the determination to read and write.

Marshall, James. *Wings: A Tale of Two Chickens.* New York, NY: Puffin, 1986.
 Harriet, an avid reader, rescues her foolish friend, Winnie, from the clutches of a wily fox.

McPhail, David. *Santa's Book of Names.* Boston, MA: Little, Brown, 1993.
 A young boy who has trouble reading helps Santa with his yearly rounds and receives a special Christmas present.

Polocco, Patricia. *The Bee Tree.* New York, NY: Philomel, 1993.
 To teach his granddaughter the value of books, a grandfather leads a growing crowd in search of the tree where the bees keep their honey.

Books for Middle Grades

Cleary, Beverly. *Dear Mr. Henshaw.* New York, NY: William Morrow, 1983.

In his letters to his favorite author, ten-year-old Leigh reveals his problems in coping with his parents' divorce, being the new boy in school, and finding his own place in the world.

Speare, Elizabeth George. *The Sign of the Beaver.* New York, NY: Dell, 1983.

Until the day his father returns to their cabin in the Maine wilderness, twelve-year-old Matt survives on his own. Although Matt is brave, he's not prepared for an attack by swarming bees, and he's astonished when he's rescued by a Penobscot Indian chief and the chief's grandson, Attean. Matt and Attean teach each other many ways to survive.

Books for Older Readers

Paulson, Gary. *NightJohn.* New York, NY: Delacorte, 1994.

The importance of being literate to black slaves in the United States is the focus of this novel.

Paterson, Katherine. *Lyddie.* New York, NY: Lodestar Books, 1991.

Lyddie teaches herself to read by engaging with Dickens' *Oliver Twist.* Historical child labor and literacy issues are some of the focuses of this book.

STRATEGY LESSON: MEANING THROUGH CONTEXT

Evaluation: Who Will Benefit

This strategy lesson will benefit readers who:

- focus on the graphophonic or syntactic systems at the expense of the semantic system. When such readers encounter unknown or unfamiliar words, they may sound out words but fail to understand their meanings;
- limit themselves to minimal use of language units within phrases or sentences, not making use of the semantic and syntactic cues within the total text;
- effectively read material related to their own experiential background but have trouble with material that contains new concepts or ideas; or
- have the background to handle new concepts in discussion or in nonverbal settings but do not readily grasp new concepts through reading.

Specific Rationale

Avid readers often select a novel by an author well-known to them even when the ways of developing plot or providing provocative information are new to them. Readers who learn to understand such language complexities learn incidentally even through their recreational reading. The thief in one novel is an engineering genius who outwits an electronic, computer-supervised, burglar-proof system. In another, the foreign spy, posing as a native New Yorker, is exposed because he casually tells a party companion that he waited "in line" for two hours to get tickets for a show. Men who are trapped in a mine cave-in are rescued at the eleventh hour by the daring use of explosives. The reader learns from these stories that interrupting the electrical source of a computer can cause it to dysfunction; New Yorkers stand "on line," not "in line;" and the "fire boss" is the man in a mining crew who places and explodes the dynamite charges.

A person pursuing a hobby, meeting a professional commitment, or following a scholarly investigation may have explicit needs that motivate reading. The search might be for a chemical that can be used to polish semiprecious stones, a list of products that contain parts of the peanut plant, the ratings of stereo equipment, or the cultural and political factors that lead to a revolt against the government.

The prospect of learning about the unknown is one of the most enticing lures of reading and one of its major functions. In describing the unknown, authors often present the reader with unfamiliar words, phrases, and concepts. The degree to which readers are unfamiliar with language and concepts varies greatly.

- The reader may know the word or concept in oral language but not be familiar with the written form because of graphophonic complexities between what the language user says and its representation in print.
    When will our *victuals* /vɪtəlz/ be ready?
    He is the *spit and image* /spitniməĵ/ of his father.
- The reader may know an adequate synonym but not understand the synonym's meaning relationship to the text item.
    He is a *laconic* person.
    A *davenport* was the only thing in the room.
- The reader may be familiar with the use of the item in contexts other than the author's.
    There was a *pregnant* pause when the speaker concluded.
- The reader may be unfamiliar with the word or phrase and its related concept.
    His model of how language works is a *heuristic* tool for linguists.

What happens when the reader meets the unknown? If the word, phrase, or concept is significant, the author will probably make reference to it more than once by providing synonymous information; that is, use appropriate redundancy to provide the reader with opportunities to construct meaning. However, when the author does not give sufficient information about a concept, the reader will have difficulty constructing meaning.

Proficient readers develop meaning for the unknown and the unfamiliar by:

1. Deciding if the concept is significant.
2. Inferring and predicting meaning based on the author's cues and the reader's own background information.
3. Confirming or disconfirming predictions based on additional information gained through continued reading or through rereading.
4. Constructing a meaning that fits the text and the reader's schema.

There are two limitations on the reader. First, the reader may never have heard the words and phrases. This means readers may be unsure of pronunciation even after developing a workable concept. *Dowager, misled, parameter, salmon,* and *boatswain* are a few examples of such words.

Second, the development of an expanded and complex concept proceeds only through cumulative experiences across time. A young child may understand that he has a brother, but may not know the meaning of brother within the context of the entire family; for example, he may not understand that his mother is his brother's mother or that he is his brother's brother even after he knows that he has a brother.

Within the context of a reading experience, readers infer from the available text and confirm or disconfirm predictions based on their combined personal knowledge and their inferences.

In the following lesson, students are asked to read stories that contain *slots* (blanks, unfamiliar words, or nonwords). These slots act as placeholders so readers learn to use them to continue reading to gain information from the syntactic, semantic, and pragmatic information. In order to construct meaning, readers infer and predict from the text and their background experiences, and confirm or disconfirm based on their additional reading. The use of blanks, unfamiliar words, and nonwords for instructional purposes allows readers to focus on meaning construction. The readers must replace the slots with language that fits the structure of the sentence and that makes sense within the story.

As readers infer, predict, and continue reading they discover that their predictions are refined, limited, and confirmed as additional information is available. The process of refining predictions, that is, of making closer and closer semantic approximations to the author's possible meaning, requires rethinking and occasionally rereading.

The following example describes the use of this strategy. An adult reader with a history of reading problems was beginning to develop effective reading strategies when he read the story "Bill Evers and the Tigers" (Bank Street College of Education 1972). In the story the word *baseball* occurs seven times. On the first six occurrences the student read *basketball.* This effective prediction reflected his use of graphophonic cues represented by the similarity between *basketball* and *baseball* and his use of syntactic cues since he maintained the same grammatical function. An examination of the semantic cues in the sentences containing the word *baseball* indicates that there is no information through the sixth occurrence of *baseball* in the text to disconfirm the reader's initial prediction of *basketball.*

The boys on the Tiger baseball team were excited.
Bill Evers, the baseball star, was in town.

They wanted him to write his name on a baseball.
Ben felt funny about calling a baseball star.
I'm on the Tigers' baseball team.
He wanted to show the boys how to play better baseball.

However, following the sixth occurrence of *baseball,* this sentence occurred:

Then, just when Bill Evers was showing Ben the right way to hold his bat, a newspaperman came.

When the reader arrived at *bat,* he paused, turned back to examine previous text, and grudgingly read *bat.* Five sentences further in the text he read without miscue:

Bill Evers wrote his name on the baseball.

There were, in this whole story, only two cues to the game that was being played: the word *baseball* itself and the reference to a bat.

It is important to remember that experienced readers also meet unfamiliar texts. The difference between proficient and less proficient readers is that proficient readers confidently use a variety of strategies to sustain their comprehending.

Context is also used to predict the meaning of unknown concepts. A group of university graduate students read an article that began:

Recently, I spoke with a man twice my age who expressed great faith in the future of American youth: "There's nothing wrong with them that ten years, a family, mortgage and car payments won't be able to cure." He, of course, envisions millions of young troublemakers shaving their beards, dropping their hems, marching across the generation gap and acculturating in a sea of baby food, weed killer and convertible debentures (Rapoport 1970).

After their retellings, they were asked to discuss the meaning of *convertible debentures.* While no one had miscued on this segment of text, their responses included: "I don't know"; "payments on a car"; "some kind of debt"; "adjustable benches"; and "false teeth."

Although the readers were unfamiliar with the concept, they used graphophonic and syntactic cues to produce an expected pronunciation. Most of them, just as the reader in the previous example, made use of individual knowledge and semantic context to predict something meaningful. Because *convertible debentures* is only one of several related examples the author uses to make his point, he gives no additional cues to its meaning. Meaning is constructed even if the reader does not already have, or cannot develop, an appropriate meaning for each concept given.

We can never know exactly, prior to reading, which terms, facts, or concepts a reader will find unfamiliar or unrecognizable or to what degree they are unknown. We can only expect that readers will infer meaning from semantic context through progressively more effective predictions.

Strategy Lesson Experience

Initiating: The qualities that are important in the writing or selecting of the materials for this strategy lesson are the same whether the materials contain a nonword slot (as in "The Blog" on page 72), a blank slot (as in "Something Is Missing" on page 72), or an unfamiliar-term slot (as in "Petoskeys" on page 73). The cues relating to the slots must be carefully selected (see discussion in Chapter 5, *Syntactic Cues*) and occur throughout the text, with more general cues coming before those that are specific and limiting.

This strategy lesson is effective as an oral group experience so that individuals can discover the range of predictions possible and hear the predictions of others. "The Blog" can be presented on an overhead transparency or a copy duplicated for each student. Each of the three selections usually constitutes a separate lesson.

Invite the students to read the selection, substituting or filling in the slots with words or phrases that make sense.

The Blog

As Jack approached the blog, he shivered in anticipation. Sitting down on the edge of the blog, he took off his shoes and socks, and rolled up his pants legs. Then he gingerly put first one foot in the blog, then the other. Brrr: It was cold! Standing up, Jack waded to the center of the blog. His feet squished the mud on the bottom of the blog, and ripples splashed his trousers. Oh, but it was cold!

"There's nothing better on a hot day than the old wading blog," Jack thought.

(Barry Sherman)

The discussions suggested under *transacting, applying,* and *expanding* can be used for each of the selections.

Transacting: Ask the group to read "Something Is Missing" silently. If students have difficulty, you may want to read it to them. Encourage creative but plausible substitutes. Write down all possible suggestions for the blanks. As each additional sentence is read, cross out earlier suggestions that are now disconfirmed and add new predictions. To point out that individual experiences and backgrounds lead to unique predictions, invite students to share the thinking that led to their disconfirming and confirming.

Something Is Missing

I was really mad. All of the _____ was missing.

It had been in the box on my desk. But not one piece of _____ was in the box now.

Who could have taken it? I had baked that _____ myself.

It was whole wheat. I wanted to have a slice of _____ with butter and jelly for a snack.

Present "PETOSKEYS" on an overhead. Show one sentence at a time, taking time to consider all predictions of the meaning of "Petoskeys" each time it appears. It is entirely possible to arrive at the end of the text with more than one useful prediction: rocks, shells, or fossils. Note all the disconfirmed predictions on the board. Discuss how readers made use of the progression of text cues to narrow and refine their predictions.

Help students realize that even if they are not sure of the exact meaning, they have enough information to understand the story. Readers in Michigan and some of the surrounding states respond differently to this selection than those in other English-speaking communities because they are more likely to have experience with Petoskeys.

PETOSKEYS

THE BOY WAS LOOKING FOR PETOSKEYS.

HE WAS WALKING SLOWLY TO MAKE SURE HE WOULDN'T MISS THEM.

EACH TIME HE LOOKED, HE FOUND A NUMBER OF THEM.

PETOSKEYS ARE NOT EASY TO FIND BECAUSE THEY ARE ALMOST THE SAME COLOR AS THE SAND.

THE BOY ENJOYED LOOKING FOR THE PETOSKEYS ON THE BEACH. HIS MOTHER USED THEM IN HER WORK.

SHE WAS AN ARTIST AND MADE JEWELRY WITH THEM.

WHEN THE PETOSKEYS ARE POLISHED THEY TURN DEEP SHADES OF BROWN AND GRAY.

A PATTERN OF SIX-SIDED FIGURES SHOWS UP ON THEM.

PETOSKEYS ARE FOUND ONLY ON THE SHORES OF THE GREAT LAKES.

(YETTA GOODMAN)

("Petoskeys" is presented in capital letters to avoid cueing readers to the kind of noun Petoskeys is.)

Applying: Since the above are prototypes, in the applying phase find longer selections to use. (See "*Strategy Lesson: Cooperative Controlled Cloze*" Chapter 5 for an in-depth discussion regarding the development of materials for selected slotting experiences.)

Students may want to work in teams of two. Each team will need two copies of a slotted story, pencils, and two sheets of paper. Independently of each other, the two students apply the procedures established earlier. They will:

1. silently read each story segment;
2. generate a list of predictions to fit the meaning slot;
3. cross out and add to their prediction list as they read successive segments.

When they have completed the story, they will share their prediction lists with each other, noting:

1. how similar or dissimilar their predictions are;
2. the text cues and personal knowledge that each one is aware of having used in the decision making.

Expanding: Encourage students to try their hand at writing slotted stories. They will need to:

1. select an object familiar to most of their classmates (a squirrel, an ivy plant);
2. give it a made-up name or be prepared to leave a blank for the slot;
3. develop a list of traits ("a good climber," "enjoys the sun," "hardy");
4. place the traits from most general to most specific;
5. write the traits into a complete story or article.

Student-authors may then use their slotted story with a small group or a partner. In either case, observation of the reader's predictions can be used by the author in considering any necessary rewrites.

Two to four students may want to play the game "I Spy." One of the group chooses an object within the view of the total group, selects one identifying trait, and informs the group, "I spy something [name a trait]." The group members take turns asking one question until someone identifies the object. That person selects the next object to be guessed. An optional rule may limit the guesses by time or by number. The game "Animal, Vegetable, or Mineral" is similar to this game. It is helpful to discuss the similarity between the problem solving in such meaning-oriented guessing games and the reading of unfamiliar or unknown words and concepts.

Readings for Expanding This Strategy Lesson

Books for Primary Grades

Brown, Ruth. *A Dark, Dark Tale.* New York, NY: Penguin, 1981. Also available in big book format.
> Mysterious text and illustrations feature easy-to-predict repetitive phrases and spooky illustrations.

Guarino, Deborah. *Is Your Mama A Llama?* New York, NY: Scholastic, 1989. Also available in big book format.
> Lloyd the llama searches for his mama by asking his friends the title question. The answers he receives pose riddles written in predictable language patterns.

Hutchins, Pat. *The Doorbell Rang.* New York, NY: Morrow, 1986. Also available in big book format.
> A brother and sister are about to feast on cookies when the doorbell rings again and again and they have to share. Both predictable language and math solutions engage readers.

Martin, Bill. *Polar Bear, Polar Bear, What Do You Hear?* New York, NY: Holt, 1991. Also available in big book format.
> Bold, vibrant illustrations combine with a rhythmic pattern of questions and answers involving zoo animals.

Roebart, Rose. *The Cake That Mack Ate*. Boston, MA: Little, Brown, 1986.
This cumulative and predictable tale chronicles the steps in making a cake and ends with a surprise.

Rosen, Michael. *We're Going on a Bear Hunt*. New York, NY: Macmillan, 1989.
Four children and their father go on a bear hunt. But then the bear comes after them. The language is rhythmic and predictable.

Wood, Audrey. *The Napping House*. San Diego, CA: Harcourt, Brace, Jovanovich, 1984. Also available in big book format.
A cumulative rhyme describes a snoring granny topped by a dreaming child, a dozing dog, and much more.

Books for Middle Grades

Sleator, William. *Among the Dolls*. New York, NY: Dutton, 1975.
A young girl finds out that if she treats her dolls in a mean way, it has an effect on her own life. High level of suspense makes this a good story to read chapter by chapter, stopping at the end of each chapter to get students' predictions.

Song Books—Helpful for Prediction and Confirmation for All Ages

Carle, Eric (illus.). *Today Is Monday*. New York, NY: Putnam, 1993.

Emberly, Barbara, and Ed Emberly. *One Wide River to Cross*. Englewood Cliffs, NJ: Prentice-Hall, 1966.

Jones, Carol. *This Old Man*. Boston, MA: Houghton Mifflin, 1990.

Langstaff, John. *Climbing Jacob's Ladder: Heroes of the Bible in African-American Spirituals*. Illustrated by Ashley Bryan. New York, NY: McElderry Books, 1991.

Mallet, David. *Inch by Inch: The Garden Song*. New York, NY: Harper, 1995.

McNally, Darcie. *In a Cabin in a Wood*. New York, NY: Dutton, 1991.

Norworth, Jack. *Take Me Out to the Ballgame*. Illustrated by Alec Gillman. New York, NY: Four Winds Press, 1993.

Rae, Mary (illus.). *The Farmer in the Dell*. New York, NY: Penguin, 1990.

Raffi. *Wheels on the Bus*. New York, NY: Crown, 1988.

Rojankovsky, Feodor (illus.). *Frog Went A-Courtin'*. New York, NY: Harcourt, Brace, Jovanovich, 1955.

Rojankovsky, Feodor (illus.). *Over in the Meadow*. New York, NY: Harcourt, Brace, Jovanovich, 1957.

Parker, Nancy Winslow (illus.). *Oh A-Hunting We Will Go*. New York, NY: Atheneum Publishers, 1974.

Pearson, Tracey Campbell (illus.). *Old MacDonald Had a Farm*. New York, NY: Dutton, 1984.

Spier, Peter. *The Fox Went Out on a Chilly Night*. New York, NY: Dell, 1993.

Spier, Peter. *The Erie Canal*. Garden City, NY: Doubleday, 1970.

Staines, Bill. *All God's Critters Got a Place in the Choir*. New York, NY: Penguin, 1989.

Sweet, Melissa. *Fiddle-I-Fee*. New York, NY: Little, Brown, 1992.

Westcott, Nadine (illus.). *There's a Hole in My Bucket*. New York, NY: Harper, 1990.

STRATEGY LESSON: RETHINKING AND REREADING

Evaluation: Who Will Benefit

This strategy lesson will benefit students who:

- read for extrinsic reasons: the teacher sets the task, raises the questions, and offers the rewards;
- are more concerned with "correct" answers to questions than with constructing and confirming meaning;
- can give smooth oral readings of material but are unable to discuss much about what they have read;
- hesitate to pause or regress, placing a value on flawless oral performance above meaning construction; or
- make use of rereading and rethinking strategies, but feel guilty about doing so or believe good readers don't engage in such strategies.

Specific Rationale

As readers transact with the written text, they are continually involved in confirming strategies. Miscue analysis shows that readers confirm their inferences and predictions by continuing to read when they decide there is little or no disruption to their comprehending and their construction of meaning. On the other hand, readers often disconfirm when they realize: *This doesn't make sense.* When this happens readers consider rereading a portion of the text to sample additional semantic/pragmatic cues (also syntactic and graphophonic), confirm inferences, make new or additional predictions, and integrate their new understandings with established meanings. These rethinking and rereading strategies are cyclical and seemingly instantaneous. One does not necessarily always precede the other.

Because reading depends on the continuous use of the reading strategies, it is expected that readers arrive at points in the text where they cannot confirm their inferences and predictions, that is, the meaning being constructed does not fit with the portions already read. Good mystery writers depend on this phenomenon. They present the reader, the guest detective, with all the relevant clues and interim hypotheses, just as they are arrived at by the protagonist. Even with this shared information, the reader can't be sure of the resolution until the end of the story because any set of circumstances can have more than one logical interpretation. The detective and the reader cannot be expected to share the same background knowledge.

Articles on controversial topics help readers explore confirming/disconfirming strategies. For example, a piece on the proposed construction of a nuclear power plant helps readers explore confirming strategies. The author presents both the advantages and the disadvantages of the issue and then argues a position. When this happens, proficient readers reconsider the issue in an attempt to identify pivotal decision-making moments; in this way they are able to confirm the author's position while formulating their own.

As long as the reader believes that the search for meaning is proceeding with some success, the reading continues with more sampling, inferring, predicting, and confirming strategies. When the question *Does this make sense?* is answered with a "No," the reader disconfirms and must decide on an alternative course of action such as:

- *Reread.* Resample semantic/pragmatic, syntactic, or graphophonic cues, depending on what caused the reading not to make sense or not to sound grammatically acceptable.

- *Rethink.* Evaluate the ideas or information already understood for alternate inferences and predictions.
- *Self-correct.* If the rereading and rethinking provide sufficient clues, correct.
- *Continue reading.* If rereading and rethinking do not provide sufficient clues, clarify misunderstandings by continuing to read.
- *Stop reading.* If the content is important enough to pursue, select additional resources such as more predictable written material or engage in a nonreading experience such as consulting an expert. If the content is not critical, a reader may opt not to pursue the topic.

The options readers choose are based on four interrelated factors:

- the value the reader places on the content;
- the reader's language resources;
- the reader's experiential knowledge; and
- the support available in the written text by the author.

Rereading is the most frequent strategy used by learners when they begin to have difficulty confirming meaning. Reprocessing information is a strategy common to both oral and written language. Conversational comments such as "Would you repeat that?" "What did you say?" and "Did I hear you say that . . . ?" are all alternate ways of saying, "Wait a moment, your thinking took a twist that I hadn't anticipated and now I must adjust my thinking." When teachers feel that students are not attending to print, some of them will instruct students to reread in order to look more closely at surface features of the text. They assume that miscues are the basis of the student's problem and that more careful attention to graphophonic cues is the solution for non-proficient reading. This attempt to refocus the student's attention often leads to the teacher reading the word or to an impromptu phonics lesson that diverts attention from meaning. This is counterproductive. The reader's attention should always be directed to making sense.

Rereading, with its accompanying rethinking process, is more productive when its application is related to larger-than-word units, preferably to the entire story or article. One teenager, during the Reading Interview (Y. Goodman et al. 1987), provides some perspective.

> Question: When you are reading and you come to something you don't know, what do you do?
> Answer: Read back over it.
> Question: What is the "it" that you read back over?
> Answer: The sentence that I didn't understand.
> Question: Do you ever do anything else?
> Answer: Then, if I don't really understand that, I usually go back farther.

Rethinking is similar to rereading. In both instances the reader reinvestigates the accumulated cues from the already processed text as well as from appropriate life experiences. The task is to project alternative interpretations by reweighing and realigning the relationships. There is often more than one logical inference and prediction for any portion of text. If the reader generates an alternative that makes sense of the sum of available cues, the reading proceeds. Such processing can often be accomplished during rethinking, without rereading, even with the reader's eyes closed.

Self-correcting whenever the reading does not result in sensible meaning construction is another strategy. In oral reading, self-correction is often overt as students reread with the expected response. In silent reading, readers often rethink and continue the reading.

To *continue reading* provides the reader with opportunities to gain more text information and to establish connections with personal experiences. If lack of understanding results, especially early in the reading, reading on helps readers to discover that the context is just beginning to have substance and texture. The available semantic cues may be sparse, and readers are making early assumptions based on their experiential knowledge or schema. If the reader has focused on meaning there is little to be gained by reprocessing, so continuing with the reading may be the best strategy at this point.

When concepts are far removed from the reader's experience, understanding is often best handled either by continued reading, by focusing on the entire discourse, or by gaining first-hand experiences. These experiences help readers to build necessary connections with personal knowledge over time.

To *stop reading* is a legitimate strategy when meaning construction breaks down. There are points at which the limits of the reader's interests and resources and the limits of the textual support combine to make reading nonproductive. Some readers don't believe they have the right to stop reading in school contexts, especially if their reading is assigned. Some students need help to develop this strategy. Students can be encouraged to read a few pages from materials they have chosen and then to explain what they are thinking and understanding. If they are forming ideas and if their interest is maintained, then they should continue reading, constantly confirming as they make meaning from the total discourse. If, however, the communication function of reading breaks down, the appropriate response is to stop reading. Students should be guided in making this decision themselves, because self-monitoring understanding is a major goal of reading instruction and the major strategy used by proficient readers.

Strategy Lesson Experience

Initiating: After students read the cartoon below (or one you've selected to suit your particular readers), discuss their reading strategies, considering the following discussion under *Transacting*.

Transacting: Invite learners to discuss the ultimate responsibility of a reader. They must ask themselves: *Does this make sense?* Have them explore what they do to make sense. How do they respond to new information? Help readers understand that there will always be miscalculations generated by the reader, but these are reconsidered as the reading continues.

Applying: Prepare "Jim's Adventure" as a three-page booklet. The story is divided so that readers must turn back to the previous page(s) to confirm their inferences and predictions.

Introduce the booklet by telling students that it contains the beginning of an adventure story. Invite them to read it through silently to determine what might cause the adventure.

"The Wizard of Id" by permission of Johnny Hart and Field Enterprises, Inc.

Jim's Adventure

(Page 1)

There were three ways to get from the Robinsons' farm to Sam's cabin. Sam was the Robinsons' nearest neighbor and it was two miles to his place if you took the path that went safely along the edge of the forest. Jim's father always made him take this path to Sam's if he were going alone. The other two ways to Sam's were by river.

The quickest route was by turning off the main stream about half a mile from the landing, shooting twenty feet of narrow rapids, then proceeding on the river's branch until you landed almost at Sam's back door. This route was very dangerous and Jim's father had forbidden him ever to take it. Jim never disobeyed his father.

(Page 2)

The third way to Sam's was also by river and was long but quite safe, especially with two people handling the canoe. This river route simply involved staying to the right bank all the way from the landing to Sam's waterfront dock.

(Page 3)

Jim's heart was pounding as he guided the canoe into the icy water. As he paddled along the dark right bank of the river, his arms began to ache but he did not slow his pace. At the first sound of the rapids, Jim slowly began to edge the canoe toward the left bank. His muscles strained and he felt his heart jump as he aimed the canoe into the rapids.

(DOROTHY WATSON)

Observe the silent reading, noting those students who reread portions of the text from either of the first two pages.

At the close of the reading encourage students to talk about their reading. If students don't mention that they returned to the first or second page ask students who reread to talk about what happened to make them do so. Encourage students to indicate just what information they were seeking and what prompted the search. If students wanted to reread but decided not to, encourage them to tell why they did not do so.

Significant points for discussion include:

• Readers cannot always judge ahead of time the significance of information.
• Not remembering does not necessarily mean that readers are careless. It can indicate that they initially thought something else would be more important.
• Rereading or rethinking can sometimes help make sense of what is read.

Introduce a copy of "A Day at the Zoo" by telling students that this is another story that may make them want to rethink or reread. Ask them to read the story silently and to place a mark on the page at the point where their ideas about the story suddenly change.

A Day at the Zoo

The day was bright and sunny—a good day to be at the zoo. Many animal sounds and shouts of laughter filled the air.

"Look at that funny fellow!" said Ambrose.

"Throw him a peanut, quick, before he turns away!" cried Judy.

"Oh, he caught it and is going to throw it back! Clever fellow. Sometimes they seem fairly bright, don't they?"

"He's scratching his head. They always scratch their heads. Maybe they think it makes them look wise, but they're probably looking for fleas."

"It's feeding time! First one down is a rotten monkey!" Ambrose shouted as he swung himself deftly down from the top of the cage to the floor.

"Oh, Ambrose, wait for me," cried Judy. "Visitors' day at the zoo gives me such an appetite."

(Charlotte Hazelwood)

Discuss clues to meaning and evidence that supports or causes readers to disconfirm. The clues may be listed on the board. An example follows:

The Clues	*The Reader Confirms and Disconfirms*
1. "... animal sounds and shouts filled the air ..."	*It's people talking about monkeys.*
2. The fact that Ambrose and Judy are talking.	
3. "Throw him a peanut ..."	
4. "He's scratching his head!"	
5. "Maybe they think it makes them look smart, but they're probably looking for fleas."	*This doesn't ring quite true.*
6. "It's feeding time! First one down is a rotten monkey!"	*Wait a minute! It's monkeys talking about people.*

Expanding: Invite students to play and then to make game boards that include steps to retrace or to take other circuitous routes. Help students see the relationship between such games and the various reprocessing (rereading and rethinking) that occurs in reading. Invite students to find other metaphors for the reading process and to discuss other activities that cause us to retrace our steps.

Teachers or students knowledgeable about problem solving or brain teasers in sets of cards or on video can use the innovative strategies of the games to realize the predictions and confirmations they use in their game playing and how this is similar in reading. During these discussions students may make a list of the reading strategies they use and add to them or change them over time.

Readings for Expanding This Strategy Lesson

Books for Primary Grades

Branley, Franklin M., and Eleanor K. Vaughan. *Mickey's Magnet.* Illustrated by Crockett Johnson. New York, NY: Scholastic, 1956.

> Mickey explores what things will and will not be picked up by a magnet. His father helps him make a magnet with a needle.

Hoban, Tana. *Look Again!* New York, NY: Macmillan, 1971.

Perception is changed by a square cut in certain pages to reveal only part of an object. Then the whole object is revealed. Helps children explore developing concepts by inviting them to talk about differences in objects caused by differences in perceptions.

Books for Middle Grades

Parish, Peggy. *Amelia Bedelia.* New York, NY: Scholastic, 1963.

Amelia Bedelia always misunderstands her boss's metaphors and follows directions in her own fashion. The misunderstandings provide the reader much opportunity to rethink, reread, and continue to read. Making sense of her world is Amelia Bedelia's problem, too. There are many Amelia Bedelia books.

STRATEGY LESSON: VIEWPOINTS

Evaluation: Who Will Benefit

This strategy lesson will benefit readers who are unaware that:

- authors, including scientists and other authorities, have points of view that are often implicitly rather than explicitly embedded in text;
- readers have the responsibility to discover the author's opinions, prejudices, and viewpoints;
- readers have the right to disagree with or question an author's opinions, but should have reasons for their disagreement; or
- because something appears in print does not mean it is true.

Specific Rationale

Complete objectivity in writing is nonexistent. Writers who believe they are truly objective—completely fair and unbiased—are denying "the existence of their own personalities" (Kelly 1955). Even articles on the front page of a newspaper, where objective reporting is supposed to appear, reflect reporters' viewpoints: reporters emphasize selected information as well as include or omit certain information. Writing that expresses an author's opinions and elicits responses from readers is the stuff of written language. In a democratic society where a goal is to eliminate or at least minimize censorship, developing critical readers is a major goal in every curriculum area. Controlling what an author writes is not necessary if students learn that they are expected to be thoughtfully critical: to reject, disbelieve, or question what they read.

A major purpose of this lesson is to establish the idea that all reading is within the learner's control. Students are encouraged to react to everything they read, both intellectually (based on what they know and believe) and emotionally (based on what they feel). Not only do authors have viewpoints and voices that are reflected in their writing, but readers have opinions and voices that are reflected in their responses to a written text.

Strategy Lesson Experience

Initiating: Support the development of critical reading by helping students become critical listeners. Encourage discussion about the degree to which students believe and respond to advertisements. Ask them to share personal experiences in which they followed the advice they found in a variety of media, including television and radio. Explore both positive and negative results.

Using local television and radio news, including sports reporting, discuss the problems involved in eye-witness reporting. Students should be aware that different people perceive and report the same situation in different ways. If students respond critically to listening experiences, there will be an easy move to developing a critical approach to written texts.

Transacting: Ask students to read two recent advertisements that have been duplicated or made into an overhead transparency (*Zillions*, a *Consumer Reports* magazine for kids, provides good articles for supporting and extending this discussion). If possible, select examples advertising the same item but containing different information. Discuss the ads with students, considering the following questions and suggestions:

- Why was this written? Help students realize that what they read is written for a purpose, often to convince others of a particular point of view. If readers explore why something is written, they can deepen their understanding of any text, including ads, essays, reports, articles, and stories.
- Is the author truthful? Readers should not immediately accept and believe everything they find in print. They should question everything they read.
- Identify at least two things that you believe to be factual. How do you know? Identify two things that are opinions. How do you know?

Help students list questions readers should ask themselves. Once compiled, the list can be made into a permanent chart titled "Questions for Critical Readers" for the classroom, or it may be duplicated for distribution. Students can add to this list as the class explores the topic at various times throughout the year. Since these are questions that students are to ask themselves as they read, they do not have to write the answers. Some possible questions include:

- What is the author's purpose in writing this?
- What ideas or facts do I believe, and why?
- What do I question, and why?
- Would I buy this item or not, and why?
- What language cues help clarify particular points? What language cues confuse me?

After a discussion of the questions, ask the students how they can find more information. They can write these suggestions on a chart called "Finding Information for Critical Readers." They may add to this list as appropriate. The list may include the following ideas:

- Find other ads that have similar claims and decide if both are possible.
- Ask people if they have tried the item and compare answers.
- Try the item yourself and make a decision based on personal experiences.
- Ask an expert in the field to discuss the truth value of the ad. For example, if the ad is about medicine, talk to a doctor or pharmacist about it.

Applying: Invite students to begin a collection of materials about controversial issues by monitoring newspapers and magazines and gathering different viewpoints. Controversy related to their own experiences often motivates students. A collection of such material facilitates the exploration of controversial ideas and differing opinions. It also provides a base for extending inquiry questions and projects.

Before students discuss their collections, review their list of "Questions for Critical Readers" (see above). Ask students which questions they prefer to keep in mind while reading. Add any new questions that they think help them read critically.

In addition to the suggested questions listed earlier, other questions may include:

- Do the authors believe what they are writing?
- What is the author's background? Why is this important to know?
- Why would an author write something he or she does not believe?
- How much do authors know about what they are writing?

Ask students to consider the list "Finding Information for Critical Readers" (see above) and add ways that help readers check on authors' biases, knowledge, and viewpoints, such as:

1. Make a list of the most important ideas, knowledge, or beliefs with which you agree and disagree. Leave space to add other people's points of view.
2. Find a variety of opinions on the topic. In addition to reading other written resources, conduct interviews.
3. Experiment with the ideas; check claims for truth based on your own experiences.
4. Check the author's background to find out what he or she knows about the field and to determine any vested interests.

After the two lists have been revised, invite students to work together in small groups. Using "Questions for Critical Readers," encourage them to discuss the relevant questions. Using "Finding Information for Critical Readers," they might explore their points of view and whether or not they support the author's opinion. Any interested students might write a letter to the authors of the articles, explaining the ways in which they agree or disagree.

Expanding: Highlight sentences in the article that give factual information and highlight in another color sentences that show the author's opinion. In the margin indicate what helped distinguish the factual statements from the opinions.

Select a newspaper article, possibly an editorial, in which the author is trying to persuade readers. If students agree with the author, invite them to write a letter telling what arguments are acceptable and why. If they disagree, they should indicate what arguments do not adequately support the viewpoint and why. Have students share their letters with each other to make sure they've stated their opinions clearly. If students misunderstand each other, they should clarify by rewriting the letter.

Younger students might focus on the claims made in television commercials for children's toys. Students who own these products might bring them to class for examination, testing, and for comparison with advertisers' claims. A chart can be made for each product, for comparison:

Advertiser's Claims	Tests Run	Actual qualities
1.	1.	1.
2.	2.	2.

Students may want to inform the manufacturer of their findings, especially if they discover a discrepancy between the manufacturer's claims and the product's actual quality.

Readings for Expanding This Strategy Lesson

Blume, Judy. *The Pain and the Great One.* New York, NY: Bradbury, 1974.
A brother and sister take turns describing one another from their own perspectives.

Geraldine, as told to Charles L. Blood and Martin Link. *The Goat in the Rug.* New York, NY: The Parents' Magazine Press, 1976.
A picture storybook describing the weaving of a Navajo rug from the shearing of a goat to the removal of the rug from the loom. A goat narrator gives the reader a new perspective.

Hall, Donald. *I Am the Dog: I Am the Cat.* New York, NY: Dial, 1994.
A dog and cat take turns explaining what is unique about each of them.

King-Smith, Dick. *All Pigs Are Beautiful.* Cambridge, MA: Candlewick Press, 1993.
    An appealing introduction to pigs presents a unique perspective.

Rodgers, Mary. *Freaky Friday.* New York, NY: Harper & Row, 1972.
    A daughter takes her mother's place physically for a whole day. Enables the reader to put themselves in other people's shoes.

STRATEGY LESSON: MORALS AND INTENTIONS

Evaluation: Who Will Benefit

This strategy lesson will help students who are not always aware that authors have specific intentions for writing based on their belief system and that as readers they are capable of determining those reasons.

Specific Rationale

Many authors write with a lesson in mind. They want their readers to grasp some overall idea, to gain appreciation, or to value something the author values. Other authors want readers to explore certain principles or rules of conduct.

Some readers, however, consider the author's intention to be something other than developing a principle or gaining a value that is intrinsic to the story (K. Goodman & Y. Goodman 1978). For example, when an inordinate amount of reading in school is focused on instruction, readers often view texts as if they were instructional aids for the teaching of "reading skills."

Teacher:	Why do you think the author wrote this story?
Student:	To teach me words.
Student:	To make me a better reader.
Student:	To build my vocabulary.
Student:	To help me read faster.

Some students may respond by suggesting the author's intention is to teach a specific skill that was mentioned in the story although peripheral to it:

Teacher:	Why do you think the author wrote this story?
Student:	To teach you how to make a flashlight.
Student:	To teach people how to take care of pets.
Student:	To tell you what things to take on a camping trip.

In addition to considering an author's intention, learners must be aware that other readers have purposes different from the author's, based on the readers' knowledge and belief systems.

Teacher:	Why do you think the author wrote this story?
Student:	You can get people to do what you want if you tell them the opposite.
Student:	To teach people that they had better not tell secrets if they promise not to.
Student:	To let kids know that they should be good.

Helping readers become consciously aware of authors' intentions enables them to realize that authors often have specific values, ideas, or lessons in mind.

Strategy Lesson Experience

Initiating: Collect a variety of myths and folktales, some of which end with an explicitly stated moral (consider Arnold Lobel's *Fables*). Ask the students to read one for this lesson. Do not prepare them with any other explanation.

Transacting: Invite the readers to discuss the story by considering the following:

1. Do authors have a lesson in mind when they write?
   Explore a variety of genre and formats, including television shows. Help readers understand that authors often try to teach, explain, or pass on sig-

nificant information, beliefs, or knowledge even if they do not specifically state the lesson (as in folktales) at the end of the story.

2. Why is a moral stated at the end of the story?
   Explore the idea that authors and storytellers hope that their listeners or readers understand their purposes for creating stories.

3. Most stories do not end with a stated moral, lesson, or intention. How does a reader know what the author has in mind?
   Help students understand that even when an author does not state the moral or lesson directly, readers make good guesses about such intentions based on evidence from their reading. Therefore, different readers often come up with different conclusions.

4. Do you think the author could have in mind any lesson other than the one stated at the end of the story? What might it be?

Applying: Ask students to read silently two or three fables, myths, or folktales over a period of a few weeks. Working in teams of two or three the students can list the morals or lessons they find in each story. Ask those who read the same story to work together as a group. Invite them to put their most representative conclusions on the board and discuss the variations. They may decide to agree on a single moral, but also agree that there are alternative ones.

Expanding: Encourage students to interview family members for morals, rules, and old sayings. Share these with the class. Interested students might want to use them as the basis of a story or write a class book categorizing sayings with similar and opposite meanings.

Readings for Expanding This Strategy Lesson

Heins, Ethel. *The Cat and the Cook and Other Fables of Krylov.* New York, NY: Morrow, 1995.
> Twelve little-known Russian fables from the nineteenth century poet have been retold. The morals need to be discovered because they are not explicitly stated.

Jones, Carol. *Town Mouse, Country Mouse.* Boston, MA: Houghton Mifflin, 1995.
> Cleverly placed peep-holes in the illustrations encourage children to predict the next adventure in this familiar favorite of the cousins who visit each other. The full-length story offers opportunities for prediction and discussion about the moral.

Lobel, Arnold. *Fables.* New York, NY: Harper, 1980.
> This award-winning book features droll, original fables with morals. The variety of stories will ignite readers' interest as they try to guess the moral.

Paxton, Tom (reteller). *Birds of a Feather and Other Aesop's Fables.* New York, NY: Morrow, 1993.
> A spirited re-telling in verse of ten of Aesop's fables.

Reiser, Lynn. *Two Mice in Three Fables.* New York, NY: Greenwillow, 1995.
> Three short fables feature a cast of animal characters caught up in humorous incidents ending with witty morals. Clearly stated morals will engage readers with their humor.

Watts, Bernadette (illus.). *The Wind and the Sun.* New York, NY: North-South Books, 1992.
> The sun and the moon test their strength by seeing which one can make a man remove his coat.

Young, Ed. *Seven Blind Mice*. New York, NY: Putnam, 1992.
The ancient fable of the blind men and the elephant sparkles with new life in Young's version featuring mice portrayed in distinctive collages.

FOCUS II: TEXT ORGANIZATION

STRATEGY LESSON: PLOT AND SEQUENCE OF EVENTS

Evaluation: Who Will Benefit

This strategy lesson will benefit students who:

- do not identify a central problem in a story;
- find it difficult to relate features of a story that are important to the plot; or
- do not predict endings.

Specific Rationale

The overall question or the central problem of a story generally determines the author's organizational plan and the sequence of events. In fiction the problem and its solution are usually referred to as the plot. In nonfiction, information and events are organized in specific ways depending on the author's purpose, language conventions, and content; for example, biology and geography articles usually are organized differently.

Non-proficient readers may be able to tell what has happened in the story and who was involved. However, they are not always certain how the events and the characters are related, or that there is a problem to be solved. When readers become aware that there are reasons why the action of a story twists and turns as it does, they are becoming aware of plot, main ideas, and the relationships among events and people.

For many articles and stories sequence is usually unimportant. Sequence of events should only be emphasized when it is significant to the plot. In "The Three Billy Goats Gruff," for example, in which the little billy goat goes across the bridge first, then the middle-sized goat, and last the big billy goat, the order in which the characters are introduced is related to the plot and the sequence is therefore important.

In this lesson students infer information from all available cues, predict events, and identify the problems and the solutions presented through the course of the story.

Strategy Lesson Experience

Initiating: Select a variety of cartoons with simple plots, such as *Peanuts, For Better or for Worse,* and *Garfield.* It is helpful, especially the first time these are used with students, to select a cartoon that has the potential for prediction from frame to frame. Students with reading experiences limited by assigned readings in school may not consider their avid reading of cartoons and comic books as real reading. It is helpful to remind students that all kinds of reading are valuable, depending on the reader's purposes.

Make a copy or an overhead transparency of one of the chosen selections. Look at one frame of the cartoon at a time. Invite students to talk about what they infer from that frame, and then predict the next frame. Continue working with one cartoon frame at a time until the end of the strip. Discuss in general terms the concepts of plot and how proficient readers predict the action of a story by making inferences from the text and by using their prior knowledge.

Transacting: Introduce another cartoon. Ask the following questions if the issues have not been addressed thoroughly in the preceding discussion.

1. What do you think is going to be pictured in the next frame? Why do you think so? Encourage students to make suggestions and encourage different responses.
2. Are there alternatives? Why do you think so? The students may not be able to limit their discussions to the next segment. Do not discourage this. After each response ask why they chose that idea. Accept all suggestions and record them.
3. How do you think the cartoonist will end the story? Encourage variability. If students have not had experience with "the problem" as presented by the author, they may be unable to consider the cartoonist's solution and may not understand why it is a possible solution.
4. Do you think there will be something funny about the ending? Why? Not all cartoons are humorous, and your students' responses will depend on what cartoons they read. It will be evident if students have had little experience with cartoons. Once all the solutions are explored, show the last frame.
5. Which of our solutions do you like as well as, or even better than, the cartoonist's solutions? Why? If the students base appropriate or inappropriate solutions on partial information, they need to understand that this is the way the reading process works. Encourage students to explain and support their opinions.
6. Do you think the cartoonist's solution is funny? Which of our endings were funny and which were not? Do not be surprised if students are amused by things that you did not expect them to find humorous or vice versa.

Applying: Invite students to examine only the title of the following selection, "Jane Accepts a Dare," or of a short story with a discernible plot. Ask them to cover the rest of the story, since it will be read in sections. If you use a short story of your choosing, mark lines at various points so students can stop to predict. Consider the following questions to stimulate thinking:

1. What will the story be about? How can you tell?
2. Will it be fact or fiction? How can you tell?
3. Why would anyone want to read the story?
4. How will we find out which of our predictions prove accurate?

Help students realize that these questions are answered by continuing to construct meaning by using inferring, predicting, and confirming strategies.

Ask students to read the story silently, stopping where a space separates the first section from the section that follows. In light of their additional reading ask the questions above again and add the following:

5. Are your original predictions confirmed?
6. Why do you think you are right?
7. Do you like what the author is doing with the story?
8. If your predictions are not confirmed, why not?
9. How do you think this story will end?
10. What was the conflict or problem that the author had to work out? At what part in the story did you begin wondering how things would be solved? What was a concern or problem for the characters?

Invite students to continue reading each story segment in turn, and then consider selected questions once again. The last section of the following story is labeled, "Conclusion." At this point, ask students to predict how the problem will be solved.

Jane Accepts a Dare

Jane was very sorry that she said yes when the other kids dared her to go into the old house at the end of the road. Everyone in town said that the house was haunted, and some people even said they had seen ghosts. Why did she agree to do it? Was it just to show off to the other kids? Was it to prove that she was as brave as any other girl or boy in town? Or was it to prove to herself that she could go into the house even if she was afraid?

Now it was time to go ahead with it. She was standing in front of the gate to the house. The other kids were waiting halfway down the road. Jane looked at the old rusted iron gate and at the tall grass in front of the yard. It was very strange. Every time she passed this house, she noticed that it was always gloomy, as if the sun didn't shine here. Today it was the same way. Everywhere else it was late afternoon, and the sun was shining. Here it looked dark, as if it were already sunset. Jane decided she had better get moving if she was going to be in and out of the old house before the sun really did set.

Slowly, she pushed the gate in. It was tall and heavy. Jane had to use both hands to push it in. The gate squeaked and groaned as it moved, as if it didn't like being awakened after all these years.

"I bet nobody has come here in years," Jane said to herself. The path to the house was almost covered by grass that no one ever cut anymore. Jane tripped twice as her feet got tangled in the long grass. But finally, she was standing in front of the house. She looked up. The house was three stories high. Many of the windows were broken. Others were boarded up.

Jane wondered if she should go through the front door or if she should look through one of the windows first. Would the kids think she was a coward if she looked through the window first?

No, she decided, she would go straight up to the front door and take her chances. Secretly, she hoped that the door would be locked. She turned to see if the other kids were looking at her. Yes, there they were, waiting at the gate. She could see that they were surprised that she had come this far. Well, she would show them just how far she could go!

Jane took a deep breath and knocked on the door. She could hear the sound of her knocking echoing in the big house. She reached for the door knob and found that it turned. The door was not locked. Jane pushed in on the door and it creaked open slowly. As the door opened, a blast of ice-cold air hit her in the face. Jane felt like running away, but she forced her legs to move forward into the house.

Inside the house it was very dark. Cobwebs covered the walls and furniture. But except for cobwebs and dust, the house looked ready for people to live in it. None of the furniture was covered with sheets, and there were lots of candlesticks in the front hall. Jane kept her hand firmly on the door, holding it open. She was not going to let herself get trapped in that house. It looked like a great place for ghosts.

She was trying to see how far inside she could step without letting go of the door when she heard a noise. It was a creaking sound, as if someone—or something—was stepping on the floor and trying not to make noise. And the creaking sound was coming from the dark hallway in front of her! It was getting closer, but Jane couldn't see anything.

Conclusion

Then Jane made up her mind: she turned and ran out of the house, slamming the door shut behind her. As she jumped off the front porch, she thought she heard the sound of laughing behind her, but she couldn't be sure. She ran through the grass without stopping or tripping until she came to the front gate.

"What happened?" asked the other kids. "Did you see anything? Did you see a ghost?"

"I don't know what was in the house," Jane said. "I didn't see any ghosts or any people, but I sure did hear something. I guess I should have stayed around to see what it was." She felt a little ashamed that she had been afraid.

But the other kids didn't agree. They said she had been very brave to go into the old house alone. They all wondered what had made that noise in the hallway of the old house. But they never found out because that summer the house was hit by lightning during a storm, and it burned to the ground.

That was the end of the old haunted house. But Jane never forgot the time she accepted the dare to go inside the house. She always remembered the ice-cold blast of air and the soft creaking sound from the dark hallway.

(BARRY SHERMAN)

Expanding: Invite students to select stories they want to investigate. Divide learners into groups or in pairs, with one student as recorder. Suggest that they follow the above procedure. Encourage those who are interested to make cartoons using their own ideas. Some may want to write their ideas in story form.

Readings for Expanding This Strategy Lesson

Galdone, Paul. *The Three Billy Goats Gruff.* New York, NY: Clarion, 1973.
> The goat brothers foil the troll and get across the bridge to eat grass. The order in which the characters are introduced is related to the plot so the sequence is important.

Galdone, Paul. *The Three Bears.* New York, NY: Clarion, 1972.
> The engaging illustrations of this familiar tale set it apart because it clearly shows the different sizes of the bears.

Galdone, Paul. *The Three Little Pigs.* New York, NY: Clarion, 1970.
> The resourceful little pig survives an encounter with the wolf who ate his brothers. Other traditional fairy tales may be used to expand this lesson.

Moss, Marisa. *In America.* New York, NY: Dutton, 1994.
> While Walter and his grandfather walk to the post office, Grandfather recounts how he decided to come to America, while his brother, Herschel, stayed in Lithuania.

Numeroff, Laura. *If You Give a Mouse a Cookie.* New York, NY: Harper, 1985.
> A boy offers a mouse a cookie. Then the mouse asks for a glass of milk and then a napkin and then . . .

Williams, Marcia. *The Adventures of Robin Hood.* Cambridge, MA: Candlewick Press, 1995.
> Recounts the life and adventures of Robin Hood in a comic-book format.

Williams, Marcia. *Greek Myths.* Boston, MA: Candlewick Press, 1991.
> A retelling in a comic-book format of eight Greek myths.

STRATEGY LESSON: PLOT EXPLORATION

Evaluation: Who Will Benefit

This strategy lesson will help readers who do not easily:

- grasp the problem within a story;
- explain the plan of action in terms of important ideas and events; or
- suggest options for resolving problems.

Specific Rationale

Reading for meaning can be expanded and enhanced if readers explore aspects of plot and theme. As students explore the concepts of plot and theme they need to be encouraged to express their own opinions. When readers are confident that they have the right to infer meaning based on their transaction with the text and on their own backgrounds, they will construct meaning for themselves and not simply read to fulfill assignments.

Authors set up problems or conflicts involving the characters in a story. The plot includes both the problem and the method of solving the problem. Plot relates action and events and can be stated as a question: Will Little Red Hen make her bread and eat it with the others? Will Little Red Riding Hood get to her grandmother's house safely? These questions lead to events within a plan of action. Stories may have more than one plot.

The purpose of this strategy lesson is to help students construct meaning by inferring problems and their related events and action. Readers will be encouraged to decide for themselves what the major problems in a story are, how they are resolved, what relationships cause problems or resolution, and whether the resolution is appropriate.

Strategy Lesson Experience

Initiating: Select a wordless picture book or a cartoon with a highly predictable plot. Invite learners to talk about all the possibilities there are for plot (problems, events, and action). Consider the following questions:

1. What is the most important thing happening in the story? Why is it the most important?
   Encourage students to focus on main points rather than a sequential retelling. Ask those with differing viewpoints to suggest why they think their opinion is important. Explore the possibility that more than one aspect of a story may be important and that different readers often think differently about what is most important.
2. Which are the most important characters in the story and why do you think so?
   Focus on the major characters and how they carry out the action, rather than focusing on specific details. Use information from illustrations to justify answers.
3. What problems do the major characters have?
4. How do the major characters solve their problems?
5. Are different endings possible?
6. Which of the endings do you like best—the original or one suggested by classmates?

Consider that all versions have merit and that by changing the ending, not only has the story changed but a new story has been created.

Transacting: With the students, collect a group of folktales that have similar plots but different characters. There are many Cinderella tales or folktales about simple folks who overcome more powerful people. Some related tales are listed below. Ask each learner to read silently one folktale from the collection. After their reading of at least one story invite the students to prepare for a group discussion by thinking about the most important events in the story. Was there an important event at the beginning, middle, and end of the story? What are the main ideas that make the stories similar? Or in what ways are they different?

Interested students may want to work together to make a play or cartoon sequence and present their work to others. Students may decide to solve the major problem in a different way. They may write or draw the events and end the story with their own solution. They may find a classmate who has a different solution and compare the endings.

Applying: Ask students to recall fairy tales or folktales heard when they were younger and to draw the main events in the form of a cartoon, filmstrip, television program, or picture book. This can be used as part of a theme cycle on folktales and fairy tales. Students may want to draw a cartoon strip of their favorite story or television show. They will have to select only the most significant aspects of the story to develop a cartoon sequence.

Expanding: Ask students to explore the similarities and differences in the plots of their favorite detective series or television programs. Discuss how the characters solve their problems. Invite students to take on the role of interviewers. They have two minutes of television time to tell each character's problem and how it was solved. Students might compare plots of familiar folktales or stories they remember from earlier reading. This may motivate them to look up picture storybook variants. They may want to do an interpretive reading of one of these tales for their own class or for younger children.

Readings for Expanding This Strategy Lesson

Yagawa, Sumiko. *The Crane's Wife*. New York, NY: Mulberry, 1979.
>   After Yohei tends a wounded crane, a beautiful young woman begs to become his wife and three times weaves for him an exquisite silken fabric.

Bang, Molly. *Dawn*. New York, NY: Mulberry, 1983.
>   A retelling of the Japanese folktale "The Crane's Wife."

Hyman, Tricia Schart. *Little Red Riding Hood*. New York, NY: Holiday House, 1983.
>   On her way to deliver a basket of food to her sick grandmother, Elizabeth encounters a sly wolf. Other versions of this story follow.

Mayer, Mercer. *Liza Lou and the Yeller Belly Swamp*. New York, NY: Four Winds Press, 1976.
>   A retelling of "Little Red Riding Hood." Liza Lou manages to outwit all the haunts, gobblegooks, witches, and devils in the Yeller Belly Swamp.

Young, Ed. *Lon Po Po*. New York, NY: Philomel, 1989.
>   A Chinese twist on "Little Red Riding Hood." Three sisters staying home alone are endangered by a hungry wolf who is disguised as their grandmother.

Lester, Julius. *John Henry*. New York, NY: Dial, 1994.
>   A retelling of the life of a legendary African American hero who raced against a steam drill to cut through a mountain. Another version of this story follows.

Small, Terry. *The Legend of John Henry*. New York, NY: Doubleday, 1994.
A Herculean steel driver on the railroad pits his strength and speed against the new steam hammer which is putting men out of jobs.

McCully, Emily. *Picnic*. New York, NY: Harper, 1984.
A mouse family sets off for a picnic in the country but along the way they lose their youngest.

McCully, Emily. *School*. New York, NY: Harper, 1987.
The youngest mouse is left behind when his brothers and sisters go to school, but he finds his way to school to join them.

O'Brien, Robert C. *Mrs. Frisby and the Rats of NIMH*. New York, NY: Aladdin Books, 1971.
Mrs. Frisby must move her family to their summer quarters immediately or face almost certain death. She is aided by the rats of NIMH, highly intelligent creatures. In turn, she renders them a great service.

Turkle, Brinton. *Deep in the Forest*. New York, NY: Dutton, 1993.
A little bear makes a mess of Goldilocks' house in this clever reversal of "The Three Bears."

Wolff, Ashley. *Stella and Roy*. New York, NY: Dutton, 1993.
In a variation of "The Tortoise and the Hare," a brother and sister race around the park.

STRATEGY LESSON: STORY OR ARTICLE SCHEMA

Evaluation: Who Will Benefit

This strategy lesson will help readers who do not realize that in their experiences with a variety of texts they have developed schema about how articles and stories are organized that help them infer and predict new discourse.

Specific Rationale

In order to construct meaning from written texts, readers build understandings about the overall structure of stories, essays, articles, reports, poems, and so on. In other words, they build schema about how a particular text is organized.

By listening to stories, young children become familiar with story landmarks: beginnings ("Once upon a time . . ."); plot sequences that build to a climax and resolution; principles (good triumphs over evil); and endings (" . . . and they lived happily ever after"). These landmarks are aspects of narrative genre. Such landmarks become familiar, comfortable, and helpful. They allow readers to settle in quickly from author to author, to predict the course of the story, and to monitor their own reading.

In response to adults reading or telling them stories, children begin to develop a sense of story, an organizing structure that becomes more familiar and more useful the more it is called upon. The stories that young children hear provide them with general frames of reference for more conceptually difficult but similarly organized texts. As readers gain experience, they encounter written information in a variety of organizations that are characteristic of other genre. Essays are organized in a different way than newspaper feature articles; sports articles are structured differently from "Advice to the Lovelorn"; biology information is presented in different ways than geography. With experience, readers come to know the differences among a range of narrative and non-narrative genre.

This strategy lesson will focus on the cues that help readers see the differences between story and article schema.

Strategy Lesson Experience

Initiating: A natural introduction to diversity in genre is to read aloud to students from a wide range of written materials (poetry, folktales, songs, math problems, science information, social studies, advertisements, menus, recipes, directions). At appropriate points, ask: What will happen next? Does this remind you of anything else we've read? How is this similar? How is it different? Why is this piece organized in this way?

Select reading material that has identifiable sections, such as beginning, middle, and end. Science, social studies, and math books or relatively short stories are good resources for this lesson. Weekly news magazines or daily newspapers have a variety of usable selections. For readers with limited experience, use straightforward materials dealing with relatively familiar organization and information. For readers with wide experiences use text formats with which they have had less experience. The length of the sections depends on the complexity of the concepts and the ability of the students. Keep in mind that reading material that is too short limits the language and knowledge cues available to the readers. This lesson is best done with small groups.

Cut the text at "predictable points" and give each member of the group one section of the printed material. The readers must be able to predict forward and backward as they listen to each other read their section aloud. They then decide the order of the segments. For younger or less proficient readers, cut the story into three or four sections. As students become more able to predict, cut the story into more sections. Include titles, diagrams, and questions that are part of the text. Each section must be long enough to give students something substantial to read, even though they may be reading from the middle of the selection. Appropriate stories or articles might be cut and placed in a file folder; in this way a collection of short stories is easily and inexpensively available for use with this lesson.

Ask students to read their section of the text silently, thinking about what might have happened before and after that particular excerpt. It works well to have as many readers as there are sections or to pair students.

Transacting: Talk with students about the concept of story structure. Just as there is syntax at the sentence level, there is a grammar at the total text level. The following will help students understand this concept.

1. Who has the beginning of the article? Why do you think so? Ask the student to read the section aloud. If two students respond, ask both to read their sections.
2. Do we agree that this is the beginning? Why do you think so? What cues are there that this is or is not the beginning?
3. Do we agree that we've chosen the first section? Who has the next section? Encourage students to make and test predictions; discuss decisions. Proceed through the text.

Applying: Using copies of the same story, ask a pair of students to reconstruct their text independently. Then ask the group members to compare their reconstructed stories with each other and discuss their similarities and differences.

Using questions similar to those raised above, encourage students to talk about what cues help them decide how stories or articles are structured or organized. It is helpful to use genre designations when appropriate. Terms such as *essay* and *persuasive writing* help students become familiar with the language of literature if they are used naturally and in appropriate context.

Expanding: Experiment with variations of the ideas explored earlier. When students feel comfortable reconstructing single stories, provide two texts on the same subject but written in distinctly different styles. Mix these together and explore the ease or difficulty in first separating the two and then reconstructing. You might use a fiction and a conceptually related nonfiction piece; stylistic differences between authors should emerge. There should always be enough cues or differences to reconstruct the two stories.

Readings for Expanding This Strategy Lesson

Prater, John. *Once Upon a Time.* Cambridge, MA: Candlewick Press, 1993.
    A bored boy's world is suddenly populated by three house-building pigs, a girl wearing a red hood, and other familiar nursery characters.

STRATEGY LESSON: CHARACTERIZATION

Evaluation: Who Will Benefit

This strategy lesson will benefit students who:

- need to focus on making inferences concerning characterization. They have difficulty discussing a character's motivation, values, basis for decisions, and relationships with other characters; or
- may be able to recall information about characters but do not infer how time, place, and plot affect them.

Specific Rationale

Authors tell stories through their characters. They produce a setting to establish the living space, time, mood, and background in which the characters carry forward the action or plot of a story. Proficient readers come to know the place, the time, and the characters significant to the story in an intimate way. When such readers know and love a story, they often believe they could recognize the characters and setting if they ever met them, which explains why readers are sometimes disappointed when their favorite stories are made into movies.

The purpose of this strategy lesson is to develop excitement and the desire to know a story's characters and the time and place in which they live.

As they read, proficient readers sort out what it is that makes one character different from all others and how characters interact with and relate to each other. Such understandings are developed not only through the facts of characters' lives—age, family membership, appearance, language, occupation, social status—but also through the way in which they operate within the settings in which they are placed. For example, an eighty-two-year-old female who lives in a twenty-room, three-story mansion in suburban Connecticut in 1995, and has servants and a chauffeur-driven limousine, evokes different reactions in readers than a young female depicted as living in a one-room farmhouse in rural Appalachia in 1932 with neighbors coming in and out of her house daily to provide food and seek advice.

Readers' own views of the world, including their personal values and attitudes, color their responses to characters and the places and times in which they live. Learners have schema concerning men and women of the 1920s and of the 1990s, of people who drink or are teetotalers, and of people who work in mines or in executive offices. These views are projected onto the characters. Children and adolescents view the world differently than adults and students differently than teachers. Young readers may not be cognizant of abstract characteristics such as greed or jealousy as readily as older readers might. However, young people are often aware that they do not like a particular character because of a specific action taken in a story.

A variety of attitudes toward characters in a story can be found within groups of readers. For example, in a story read by fourth- and fifth-grade students, some of the readers were aware of the officious nature of a television executive described as "a very busy man," and said he was silly. Others allowed that he was a nice person because "he spent time with kids" or "he gave the family some money," while still others said he was hard working because he gave orders to others. A few students thought that one of the story's main characters was a girl. The story is told in the first person by a young male whose name is never mentioned. Except for one picture, however, there are only a few subtle references to the gender of the storyteller. The story opens with the storyteller baby-sitting a younger brother. Baby-sitting experiences continue throughout the story. The view that only females are baby-sitters leads some readers to conclude that the storyteller is a girl. Although this misinformation is not significant to the plot, theme, or basic understanding of the story, it does reveal the influence of information on the development of existing schema and emerging inferences.

Readers should not be expected to have the same views as other readers, including the teacher. Through exploratory discussions, students will find opinions to support or contradict their own points of view. As learners are asked to support inferences from their reading, and as they listen to others' opinions, they gain insights and awareness of the range of possible interpretations. Teachers' opinions are only one of several possibilities, never the last word or "the correct" interpretation.

Strategy Lesson Experience

Initiating: Invite students to read the following story silently. After reading, talk about the story, concentrating on the characters.

An Adventure With Sally and Andrea

Yesterday, I heard a story about what happened when Sally and Andrea went shopping Saturday. Sally bought a suit at a department store and had it wrapped in a very nice-looking box. They were on their way to a nearby restaurant to have lunch.

As they were driving down a beautiful street, their car accidentally hit a cat that was running across the street. Sally stopped the car and they got out to see if they had killed the cat. Yes, the cat was dead. They were very upset because they both loved animals. They decided to try to return the cat to its owners. They removed the suit from the box in which it was packed, and put the dead cat carefully into it.

Sally and Andrea knocked on doors all over the neighborhood, but they couldn't find the owners of the cat. At last, they decided to take the dead cat to the animal shelter. But since they were very hungry they decided to have lunch first. They stopped for lunch at a restaurant and parked their car in the parking lot. They left the cat in the department-store box on the rear seat of the car.

Their table in the restaurant was near a window, so they could see their car while they were eating. As they ate, they saw a well-dressed, middle-aged woman walk past their car. She stopped, walked back to the car, and looked in the rear window. She looked around to make sure she wasn't being watched. Then she opened the car door, reached in, and took the box from the rear seat.

Sally and Andrea couldn't believe what they saw. This woman had just robbed them. Should they call the police? They were trying to decide what to do when the thief walked right into the restaurant and sat down at the counter. She put the box on the seat next to her, looked at the menu, and gave her order to the waitress. Sally and Andrea decided to do nothing for a few minutes. They would watch the thief and see what she did next.

As the woman was waiting for her order, she turned to the box and slowly began to lift the cover. All at once she screamed as loud as she could and fell to the floor in a faint. As she fell, she let go of the cover of the box, and the box closed. No one saw what was in it.

Naturally, everyone in the restaurant gathered around the woman who had screamed and fainted. After a few moments, the woman's eyes opened. But as soon as she saw the box, she began to shriek. Then she fainted again. Someone called an ambulance. When the ambulance arrived, the woman's eyes opened, but she was only partly aware of what was going on around her. She was placed on a stretcher and carried into the ambulance.

Just as the ambulance started to drive away, one of the waitresses ran out of the restaurant, carrying the box and shouting, "Stop! Wait! You forgot her package!" The ambulance stopped, and the waitress gave the box to one of the ambulance attendants. He put it carefully next to the woman on the stretcher so that she would know the box was safe beside her. Just then the woman sat up, looked around her, and saw the box next to her. She started to scream again, almost as loud as the ambulance siren as it started on its way to the hospital.

For a few minutes, Sally and Andrea couldn't say anything. When they came into the restaurant, they were feeling sorry for the cat. Now they were feeling sorry for the woman who had stolen the box with the dead cat inside. One thing was sure to be true, they agreed: that woman would think twice before she ever tried to steal anything again.

(ADAPTED BY BARRY SHERMAN)

Transacting: Ask students to talk about the story by telling about the characters. If, after discussing for a while, the readers have not commented on the characters in depth, consider the following:

- Who are the important characters in the story and how do you know?
- How do the characters feel about each other? Give evidence.
- How do you feel about the characters in the story? Do you like them? Would you like to have them for friends?
  Encourage students to ask each other: How do you know that? or Why do you believe that?
- Is the time or place in the story important to the characters? Would it make any difference if the time and place were different? In what ways would it make a difference? How would the characters act differently if the time or place were changed?
- What are the problems faced by each character, and how do they solve their problems?
- Would you solve the characters' problems in the same ways? What other solutions are there to the problems? Would they work any better? Why do you think so?

Encourage exploratory talk (Barnes 1992) in which students question each other and thereby expand each other's thinking. Such discussion helps students apply what they have read to other situations and settings as well as to their own lives.

Applying: Select three or four stories that have a great deal of information about characters and their relationships to their settings; the students may be involved in the selection process.

Divide students into groups and ask each group to select and read one of the stories, thinking of themselves as witnesses to the events. Ask the students to pretend that the main characters in each story have been reported to the police as missing persons. Each group will act as witnesses for the story they read, but they will become detectives using information they receive from another group of witnesses. The procedure is as follows:

1. After the students finish reading independently, they work with others in their group to make a list of characteristics of each main character and the most likely place where each could be found. Encourage students to focus on significant aspects of each selected character rather than with trivial details. They are not to share their story with any other group.
2. Decide which group will be the detectives for which story. Provide the detectives with the list of characteristics made up by the witnesses. The detectives then interview the witnesses about the characters. Ask students to concentrate on significant aspects of the characters' personality and relationships with time and place. Discuss the kinds of questions that would be good to ask in this situation.
3. Ask the detectives to write a report for the Bureau of Missing Persons that describes the characters and settings. They are then to read the original story and compare it with their report.

Expanding: Encourage students to add a section possibly called "Words or Phrases I Like" to their personal or class language book (See *Applying* in "Strategy Lesson: Language in Written Texts," page 121). In this section they list language they especially like that refers to people, places, or times.

Ask students to think about the books they have read. What characters do they remember? How did the author help the readers remember? Have students place a bookmark or self-adhesive note on any section of the book they are currently reading that has strong characterizations. Share these excerpts in class and discuss why they were selected.

Use students' favorite comic strips to explore the relationships between time, place, and characterization. Think of Snoopy and his doghouse, Doonesbury and current world events, or B.C. and prehistoric times. Some students may want to rewrite an episode, changing the time, place, or personality traits. Discuss the impact of these changes and how in changing one element in a story other elements also change.

Ask students to think of the person in their lives who has had the most important influence on them and then write a brief character sketch about that person. Invite students to share their stories. They can discuss the similarities and differences between what the reader or listener and the author believe about the person in the story. In a similar assignment students may want to write about a person who has had a negative effect on them.

Invite interested students to read about a famous person and to share information about that individual:

1. Did personality help make him or her famous?
2. Did the place in which the person was born or live affect his or her fame?
3. How did other people influence the person's life?

Invite students to represent a favorite character from a story through sketching, collage, or other media.

Readings for Expanding This Strategy Lesson

Books for Primary Grades

Adler, David A. *Benjamin Franklin*. New York, NY: Holiday House, 1992.
    The life of the accomplished American who achieved greatness as a writer, scientist, inventor, and statesman.

Baylor, Byrd. *Guess Who My Favorite Person Is?* New York, NY: Charles Scribner's Sons, 1977.
    Two people share their favorite things with each other: colors, dreams, places to live, sounds, and other favorites.

Say, Allen. *El Chino.* Boston, MA: Houghton Mifflin, 1990.
    A biography of Bill Wong, a Chinese American who became a famous bullfighter in Spain.

Wild, Margaret. *Our Granny.* New York, NY: Houghton Mifflin, 1993.
    A spirited celebration of the variety of grannies and the characteristics of one special one.

Yashima, Taro. *Crow Boy.* New York, NY: Viking, 1955.
    The special qualities of a culturally different child in a classroom are sensitively portrayed.

Books for Older Readers

Freedman, Russell. *Franklin Delano Roosevelt.* New York, NY: Clarion, 1990.
    Photographs and text trace the life of Franklin Delano Roosevelt from his birth in 1882 through his youth, early political career, and presidency, to his death in Warm Springs, Georgia, in 1945.

Freedman, Russell. *Eleanor Roosevelt: A Life of Discovery*. New York, NY: Clarion, 1993.
  A photobiography of the wife of a president who had a public life and career of her own.

Giblin, James Cross. *Edith Wilson: The Woman Who Ran the United States*. New York, NY: Viking, 1992.
  A biography of the first lady who gave vital support to her husband, President Woodrow Wilson, and to the nation during and after World War I.

Giblin, James Cross. *Thomas Jefferson: A Picture Book Biography*. New York, NY: Scholastic, 1994.
  A picture book biography of the life of Thomas Jefferson.

Kheen, Sally M. *I Am Regina*. New York, NY: Dell, 1991.
  The story of a ten-year-old girl whose life changes forever after her father and brother are killed and she is captured by Allegheny Indians. Befriended by kindly Nonschetto, Regina begins her new life.

Kinsey-Warnock, Natalie. *The Canada Geese Quilt*. New York, NY: Dell, 1989.
  Spring brings many changes to ten-year-old Ariel's life. The prospect of a new baby in the house leaves her feeling strange and left out. Grandma helps Ariel feel a part of things by working with her secretly on a quilt for the baby.

Lowry, Lois. *Anastasia Krupnik*. New York, NY: Dell, 1979.
  To Anastasia Krupnik, being ten is very confusing. If she didn't have her secret green notebook to write in, she would never make it to her eleventh birthday.

Spinelli, Jerry. *Maniac Magee*. New York, NY: HarperCollins, 1990.
  They say Maniac Magee was born in a dump. They say his stomach was a cereal box and his heart a sofa spring. They say. What's truth, what's myth? It's hard to know. But when Jeffrey Lionel Magee wanders into Two Mills, Pennsylvania, a legend is in the making.

Stanley, Fay. *The Last Princess*. New York, NY: Aladdin Books, 1994.
  Recounts the story of Hawaii's last heir to the throne, who was denied her right to rule when the monarchy was abolished.

Thompson, Wendy. *Ludwig van Beethoven: Composer's World*. New York, NY: Viking, 1990.
  With words, music, and full-color artwork, Beethoven's life and work as a composer is placed in the context of his world.

Turner, Robyn Montana. *Frida Kahlo*. Boston, MA: Little, Brown, 1993.
  Celebrates the life and work of Frida Kahlo, a famous Mexican artist.

Zhensun, Zheng and Alice Low. *A Young Painter—Wang Yani*. New York, NY: Scholastic, 1991.
  Examines the life and works of the young Chinese girl who started painting animals at the age of three and in her teens became the youngest artist to have a one-person show at the Smithsonian Institute.

STRATEGY LESSON: AUTHOR'S STANCE FOR FICTIONAL TEXTS

Evaluation: Who Will Benefit

This strategy lesson will benefit students who do not recognize the role of a "first-person character" or the role of the author.

Specific Rationale

Authors sometimes become characters in their own stories by writing in first person or by using the first person pronoun to identify the authors' point of view. In many languages there are different classifications of pronouns with corresponding verb forms. In English the use of any pronoun class is determined by the identity of the character; thus the *first person* (I or we) is used when the character is the speaker; the *second person* (you) when the character is spoken to; the *third person* (he, she, it, or they) when the character is spoken of. Even proficient readers sometimes confuse the storyteller with one of the other significant characters.

Strategy Lesson Experience

Initiating: Before providing students with the following story or one in which the author is a character in the story, remind learners that authors can be in their own stories. It is not as important to know the characters' names as it is to be able to tell how they act, why they act as they do, and how they influence events. If "Who Told This Story?" is read, tell students that the characters and the setting of the story are described first, followed by each character telling the story from his or her perspective. Ask the students which character is telling each version and what evidence supports their decisions.

Who Told This Story?

Characters:

Jimmy, small for his age, is riding his bike fast, calling and waving to his friends.

Bob, the same age as Jimmy, is tall and skinny. He is walking to school by himself. He looks at everyone and everything he passes very carefully.

Ms. Cool is a teacher at Bob and Jimmy's school. She rides a motorcycle to school so that she can find a place to park. She has never had a motorcycle accident.

Scene: A rainy Monday morning.

Jimmy is just about to bike across the driveway leading to the teachers' parking lot as Ms. Cool turns into the driveway on her motorcycle.

Bob runs into the driveway shouting. Jimmy swerves and runs off the curb, hits a tree, and falls off his bike. When Jimmy gets up, his pants are torn and the wheel on his bike is bent.

VERSION 1

My new bike is busted. It's really totaled. That kid. I'll kill him if I get my hands on him. He yelled to scare me and then got in my way. If I hadn't gone off the sidewalk, I would have hit him. He's going to pay for my bike. It's new and my mom just bought it for me. The light on my bike is broken and my wheel is bent. He's going to have to pay. He got in my way. Ask her, I bet she saw it.

VERSION 2

I just—I just—I just prevented a terrible accident. I saved his life. I was walking into the school yard when I saw him riding his new bike. He was so proud of it and was showing off and everything. Then I saw her turning left into the driveway. She didn't see him because he was behind the tree. But he was coming so fast I knew I had to stop him or he was going to get hit. I jumped out and yelled "Look out." I hope he didn't get hurt when he fell. I bet he will thank me for saving his life. Ask her, she'll tell you all about it.

VERSION 3

I'm still shaking. If he hadn't run out and tried to save that kid, I would have hit him. He did a brave thing. I was just turning into the driveway. It looked clear to me. I saw him running and then saw that kid on his bike swerve away from my motorcycle. I guess we are really lucky. I can't help thinking about what might have happened if he hadn't done some fast thinking. It looks as if that kid just has a bent fender and I don't think there is a scratch on my motorcycle. I'm going to recommend to the safety patrol that he get an award for bravery. I'm sure that kid will be grateful to him, too.

(DOROTHY WATSON AND YETTA GOODMAN)

Transacting: After their reading, invite students to talk about the three interpretations. Consider the following:

1. Who had the correct version of the story? Explore the idea that each person told the story correctly from his or her own perspective. Discuss how people get different slants on a story because of their own vantage point.
2. Should Bob pay for Jimmy's bike? Help students anchor their opinions to the story details and inferences. The students may want to have a mock trial in which the three characters are witnesses.

3. Why did each character act the way he or she did? Use evidence from the story to provide motives.

4. Is the "I" character in a story always the author? Emphasize the importance of knowing who is telling the story.

5. Why would an author write a story in first person? Explore how this device makes a story more personal. Explore the differences between oral and written stories. Relate first person stories to oral storytelling.

Applying: Ask students to think about the discussion questions above as they read "The Four Doors."

The Four Doors

My name is Antonio and I live in this big house with four doors. There are four families living in my house, but we Romeros are proud, because we have the nicest door of all. When you come see me you will know which door is mine. My door has a window so we can look out when the doorbell rings and see who is coming to visit. Every year we paint our door with beautiful paints. And we paint the mail slot shiny black, so the postman will say, "Ah, what fine people the Romeros are, they have the nicest mail slot I've ever seen."

My name is Felisha and I live in this big house with four doors. Four families live in this house, but we Johnsons are proud because we have the nicest door of all. When you come see me you'll know which door is mine right away. We have a beautiful silver screen door in front of our hard brown door. In the winter my big sister Denise and I take out the screens and put in the storm windows. But now it is summer and we can open our hard brown door and let the air come in without all the mosquitoes and flies. Our screen door has our initial "J" for Johnson, and there is a mail slot right in the door so the postman will say, "Ah, what fine people the Johnsons are. I don't even have to open this shiny screen door to deliver the mail."

My name is Ramona and I live in this big house with four doors. Four families live in this house, but we Billingsleas are proud because we have a good door. If you come to see me you will know my door right away. We haven't painted it since we moved in. The doorbell doesn't work. My little sister broke the window with a baseball last fall. And when the mailman comes by he always says, "When are you going to fix that mail slot?" But what I like most about my door is when my mother and father come home at night, and they look at that broken window and say, "We'll have to fix this door someday, but we're not home very often—so we'll just talk and play with our children tonight."

(Debra Goodman)

Invite students to read "The Four Doors" silently, for the purpose of selecting one of the vignettes to act out. After the group has created one or two incidents that occur in front of their door they need to choose a narrator (storyteller) and act out the scene.

Using information from their earlier discussion, invite students to talk about point of view and the role of the author. They can write an episode for the fourth door from their own first person perspective.

Books such as *Now Everybody Hates Me* (Martin & Marx 1992) for elementary age readers illustrate point of view: The "sweet tempered" little girl that Patty Jane sees in her mirror is not the one that brother Theodore sees. (Patty is sent to bed for whacking her brother and calling him a dumbbell. According to Patty she just touched Theodore hard. She didn't call him a dumbbell. She called him a . . . dumbhead.)

The Giver (Lowry 1993) for middle and secondary school readers is rich with conflicting viewpoints. Talk about values, tradition, justice, and injustice is bound to come about as readers explore the characters' diverse roles and perspectives.

Expanding: Involve the students in first-person storytelling. You might begin by telling a story about yourself, providing tapes of a storyteller for the students to listen to, or asking a storyteller to visit. Discuss differences in points of view and in the storyteller's role. Encourage students to tell their own stories. They might begin by telling a favorite joke as if it actually happened to them. Some students may want to interview parents or grandparents for folktales, stories, or superstitions from their background. Invite them to retell these stories as if the events had happened to them. As they become more confident as storytellers, students may want to read stories for oral telling or continue to make up their own adventures.

Select an exciting happening at the school, community, national, or international level. Ask students to describe the people involved. They might list the characteristics of the people and the setting, using no emotional words or phrases. Then ask the students to discuss the story from the point of view of two different people, using the first person pronoun in each story.

Students may make a wanted poster or a vote-for-me poster for themselves, another classmate, or their favorite character in a story. The text for their poster should focus on the character's major personality traits and be told in the first person.

Study the techniques of conflict resolution. How can what we learn about resolving our own differences help us understand someone else's viewpoint?

Readings for Expanding This Strategy Lesson

First Person Narratives

Cleary, Beverly. *A Girl from Yamhill*. New York, NY: Dell/Yearling, 1988.
> One of the most popular children's authors tells the history of her childhood growing up in Portland, Oregon. Vignettes that show up in her Henry and Ramona books are part of her life, presented with humor and sometimes sadness.

Fanelli, Sara. *My Map Book*. New York, NY: HarperCollins, 1995.
> The author draws maps of treasures, her home, her family, her community, her tummy, and other important aspects of her life.

Hoyt-Goldsmith, Diane. *Totem Pole*. New York, NY: Holiday House, 1990.
> David, a young Tsimshian boy, introduces himself and his father, a woodcarver of many objects including totem poles, and tells the legends and history of his people. Photographs by Lawrence Migdale provide a realistic portrayal of this Alaskan tribe.

Hoyt-Goldsmith, Diane. *Cherokee Summer*. New York, NY: Holiday House, 1993.
> A nonfictional account of the historical and present lives of Cherokee Indians living in Tahelquah, Oklahoma is told by young Bridget. Photographs by Lawrence Migdale expand the reader's views of the community.

Matthaei, Gay and Jewel Grutman. *The Ledgerbook of Thomas Blue Eagle*. Charlottesville, VA: Thomasson-Grant, 1994.
> Blue Eagle narrates this fictional account of his childhood on the Plains and his experiences at Carlisle Indian School. The illustrations by Adam Cvijanovic are based on narrative pictographs of important events in the lives of Plains Indians.

MacLachlan, Patricia. *All the Places to Love*. New York, NY: HarperCollins, 1994.
> Eli tells the story of his interactions with his grandparents, his parents, his little sister, and the favorite places in his rural community.

Meltzer, Milton. *Starting from Home: A Writer's Beginnings*. New York, NY: Puffin, 1988.
> Milton Meltzer, a major author of adolescent literature, relates his memoirs from his early beginnings in New York City through his adolescent years. His insights into American history are evident throughout his narrative.

STRATEGY LESSON: SETTING (TIME AND PLACE)

Evaluation: Who Will Benefit

This strategy lesson will help students who are reluctant to explore the significance of setting in a story and do not easily infer meaning from text as they read.

Specific Rationale

Many human characteristics are universal; stories reflect this universality regardless of the time and place in which the characters live. It is not difficult, consequently, for readers to relate to how and why people in stories act as they do. On the other hand, there are many respects in which a character's life experiences and those of the reader differ. Such differences may be related to the time and place in which the character lives. For example, understanding how rural life affects the experiences, dreams, and hopes of a character depends to a great degree on the reader's concepts of rural life. The problems motivating characters in the past or the future may not easily be related to by the modern experiences of the reader. Setting is sometimes, therefore, more subtle and more difficult for students to deal with than is characterization. Often in stories and articles that are not well constructed, setting is not developed in relation to the character and makes little impact on the story; therefore, readers are not consciously aware that time and place can be significant to plot, theme, and action.

Strategy Lesson Experience

Initiating: Invite students to read silently the following story or another story with strong evidence of setting. After reading, discuss the story, concentrating on where and when it took place.

Summer Visit to Grandmother Rosa

Spending my summer vacation with Grandmother Rosa was the most exciting thing that happened to me every year. I could hardly control my excitement when we all started getting ready for the long trip to Grandmother Rosa's big house in the country. Every June, together with my mother and father, I packed a few clothes in a small suitcase. Then, after a few more days of preparation, we took a taxi to the rail-road station.

The old train was always waiting for us, its noisy steam engine ready to start the long trip from the big city to the small, quiet village where Grandmother lived. That village was hundreds of miles away from the city and dozens of years back in time. It took twelve hours for the old train to make the trip to Grandmother's village.

It was a very small village that had not grown or changed for many, many years. Grandmother's house was built on the highest spot on a hill. From the house, we could see all the other houses, the few stores, and the river down below. The Iguape River was an important part of life in the village. Men and children fished there, women washed clothes in it, and it served as a highway to get from town to town. The only way to get across the river was to ride the old-fashioned ferryboat. The river overflowed every year in the rainy season, its water spreading over its banks to form a large lake. When it stopped raining, the river became narrower and narrower, until, many days later, it was back to normal.

We had to cross the river to get to Grandmother Rosa's house. And every year, by the time the train arrived at the station, it was night and very dark because there was no electricity in the village. If the moon was out and full, we could see where we were going. If not, we couldn't even see the ground we were stepping on. It was like being blind, trying to guess what lay ahead of us. But we always got to the river safely. After crossing it on the old, creaking ferry, we walked up the slope of the hill that led to Grandmother's house. Finally, we arrived at the old house on top of the hill. We saw the flickering light of the oil lamp shining through the front windows, telling us that we were welcome.

No matter how late the train arrived at the village, Grandmother Rosa was awake and waiting for us, burning her small oil lamp. She sat on a chair near the oil lamp, among the shadows dancing on the wall, waiting for her visitors.

The large table in the kitchen was filled with all kinds of food she had been preparing for days. She had prepared each dish herself. Grandmother Rosa was a small woman, and she lived alone. She raised chickens, pigs, vegetables, and fruits. She took care of all the chores by herself. She was her own butcher and cook; she baked all her own breads and cakes, and canned her own fruits and vegetables. She chopped wood for the ovens and stoves, and even took care of her own flower garden.

In the kitchen, Grandmother Rosa had a large woodburning stove. When it was lit, it made a lot of smoke. Over the years, there had been so much smoke that the kitchen walls were black. Outside, in the yard, my grandmother had a big oven for baking. Is there anything like the smell of fresh-baked bread?

Every year, when we arrived, after the long walk and crossing the river in darkness, Grandmother Rosa opened her door and hugged us and kissed us again and again. As we walked into the warmly lit kitchen, the delicious smells of different foods reached us.

It was at that moment that we were flooded with happiness at having reached Grandmother's kingdom, with all the gifts that she so lovingly offered us. It was then that we suddenly knew why we had traveled for so many hours, and why we walked so far in the darkness of the night to get to the flickering light in the house at the top of the hill. Here was Grandmother waiting in the middle of the kitchen, with her heart bursting with love for us.

(IRLENE S. SHERMAN)

Transacting: Encourage students to talk about the characters in relation to the setting. Consider the following points, if they are not addressed:

- When does the story take place? Does it happen in modern times, in the future, in the near past, or in ancient times? How do you know? Students don't necessarily need exact dates but need some general information about time. Explore cues that provide information for readers. Students may decide the story could have taken place in more than one time period. How is that possible?
- What language does the author use to help readers know when and where the story takes place? Focus on dialogue and any special language the author uses that suggest time. If there is none, talk about how such clues would help them understand settings.
- In what ways is this story similar to today's times? How is it different? Is it important to the story whether it takes place now or at another time? Why? Explore how the time of the story is or is not significant to understanding it.
- Where does the story take place? Does it take place near here? Does it take place in another country? How do you know?
- In what ways is the place similar to where you live? In what ways is it different?

Applying: Invite students to choose a story they are reading or to consider "A Summer Visit to Grandmother Rosa," investigating the setting in ways such as the following:

- Draw a map following the action of the story. Label each place on the map, relating it to action in the story.
- Draw a time line of events in the story. Focus on important parts of the story rather than insignificant detail.
- List aspects of the story related to time and setting that differ from their equivalents in the students' own lives and the aspects that are most similar to the students' lives. List only the most important. Making a chart might facilitate thinking:

Time and Place	Same	Different
12-hour train ride		fast trains
oil lamp		electricity
Iguape River	We live near a river	

Expanding: Encourage students to collect terms that describe setting and record them in their personal or class language books. Ask students to collect examples or make notes of language in stories that depict a different time or setting. Provide opportunity for learners to share their findings.

Invite students to relate historical fiction to periods of history by making interrelated time lines. The westward movement in the United States, for example, can be related to Laura Ingalls Wilder's books. *My Place* by Nadia Wheatley and Donna Rawlins (1987) is a powerful book for students to explore characterization, setting, and time. *My Place* depicts a neighborhood in Sydney, Australia, showing how over a two-hundred-year period many different indigenous and immigrant populations moved in and out of the area. Students can discover the organization and the features the authors use to write the book (a child about ten years old, a pet, a family activity, a description of the community, a recreational activity, a map, a tree, and so on). Each class member can write a similar vignette to represent his or her own family and neighborhood. A text set of books on islands that can be used for this activity is at the end of the next strategy lesson comparing fiction and nonfiction.

Interested students might make maps based on stories they believe lend themselves to map making, labeling the places where the significant action takes place.

Students may want to interview members of their family who have traveled a great deal. These interviews may develop into stories with time lines or maps related to their relatives' lives. Whenever relevant, such activities may be related to geography or history.

Readings for Expanding This Strategy Lesson

Books for Primary Grades

Anno, Mitsumasa. *Anno's U.S.A.* New York, NY: Philomel, 1983.
In wordless panoramas a lone traveler approaches the New World from the West in the present day and journeys the width of the country backward through time, departing the east coast as the Santa Maria appears over the horizon.

Anno, Mitsumasa. *Anno's Britain.* New York, NY: Philomel, 1982.
The illustrations lead the reader on a journey through Great Britain, moving freely through time and space.

Bouchard, David. *If You're Not From the Prairie . . .* New York, NY: Atheneum, 1995.
Those born and raised on the prairies are passionate about their bittersweet experiences with this diverse land. This book is a visual and poetic journey back to those times and the feelings they elicit.

Brown, Margaret Wise. *The Quiet Noisy Book.* New York, NY: HarperCollins, 1993.

Brown, Margaret Wise. *The Noisy Book.* New York, NY: HarperCollins, 1993.
In each of the "noisy" books, (originally written in the 1970s) Muffin, a little dog, is incapacitated so that he is unable to see, but he can hear. The title of the book indicates the setting in which Muffin hears many sounds.

Dewey, Jennifer Owings. *A Night and Day in the Desert.* Boston, MA: Little, Brown, 1991.
Depicts the unique environment of the desert, with its plant and animal life and special climatic conditions.

Field, Rachel. *If Once You Have Slept on an Island.* Honesdale, PA: Caroline House, 1993.
Poem describes the change one will experience after sleeping on an island.

Hartman, Gail. *As the Roadrunner Runs.* New York, NY: Bradbury, 1994.
Simple maps show how different animals, including a lizard, a jackrabbit, a roadrunner, mules, and deer, travel through an area of the Southwest.

Jakobsen, Kathy. *My New York.* Boston, MA: Little, Brown, 1993.
A letter from a girl living in New York describes in words and in pictures the sights to see in the city.

Knowlton, Jack. *Geography From A to Z*. New York, NY: HarperCollins, 1988.
 A glossary of geographic terms, from "archipelago" to "zone," with definitions and descriptions of the Earth's features.

Parnell, Peter. *Winter Barn*. New York, NY: Macmillan, 1986.
 A dilapidated old barn shelters a wide variety of animals, including snakes, porcupines, cats, and a skunk, during the sub-zero winter temperatures of Maine, while they wait for the first signs of spring.

Priceman, Marjorie. *How to Make an Apple Pie and See the World*. New York, NY: Knopf, 1994.
 A girl gathers the ingredients for apple pie from settings around the world.

Siebert, Diane. *Heartland*. New York, NY: Thomas Y. Crowell, 1989.
 Evokes the land, animals, and people of the Middle West in poetic text and illustrations.

Books for Older Readers

Juster, Norton. *The Phantom Toll Booth*. New York, NY: Random House, 1961.
 A marvelous fantasy through the doldrums and other interesting places. It involves the language play of the author.

FOCUS III: GENRE (LANGUAGE OF DISCOURSE)

STRATEGY LESSON: DISTINGUISHING BETWEEN FICTION AND NONFICTION

Evaluation: Who Will Benefit

This strategy lesson for distinguishing between fiction and nonfiction will benefit students:

- who make it clear through their retellings or discussions of events that they are not clear about the distinction between fact and fiction or between fantasy and reality;
- whose retellings focus on surface events and on characters but who do not suggest inferences about the nature and intent of the materials;
- who read only one kind of material, such as horse stories or motorcycle stories, and make little or no effort to expand their reading; or
- whose miscue analysis profile shows that sixty percent or more of their sentences have no syntactic and semantic acceptability.

Specific Rationale

The distinction between fiction and nonfiction is not always intrinsically clear. Even sophisticated adults may be uncertain whether or not a piece is or is not fiction. For example, in her autobiography written late in life, Eleanor Roosevelt (1961) reported a supposedly word-for-word dialogue that took place when she was seven years old. Is it possible that fictionalizing takes place in the dialogue reported in an autobiography? Readers may believe that a particular newspaper or journal column is factual if they are unaware that the columnist regularly writes satire. A spoof on research appearing in a professional journal might be taken seriously by readers who do not recognize the author's intent and do not expect to find satire or parody in a professional journal.

For elementary school students the distinction between fiction and nonfiction may be understood best by contrasting fantasy and reality. In helping learners explore this question, it is important to examine the cues that readers use to predict fiction and fact: 1) the title of the work and the table of contents; 2) previous experience with the author's work; and 3) the language of the material.

Title of the work and the table of contents.   Cover designs, including the title, provide information that help a reader predict the content of the material. Knowing what will *not* be in a particular piece of writing narrows the scope of what readers predict.

Consider the titles *The Secret of Childhood, The Disenchanted,* and *A Journey to the Center of the Earth* or select titles that are in the school or class library. What cues in the titles help readers determine that each work is either fiction or nonfiction? Once a reader has made initial predictions based on the title, the preface and table of contents can be used to confirm the predictions and to provide additional information from which the reader can make new predictions. Explore with students instances in which it is helpful to use information such as a table of contents and how it helps them know what to expect as they continue to read.

Previous experience with the author's work.   Familiarity with the author also focuses the scope of predictions that can be made about the reality of subject matter, that is, whether it is fiction or nonfiction. Consider these examples: *The Secret of*

Childhood by Maria Montessori (1966); *The Disenchanted* by Budd Schulberg (1968); and *A Journey to the Center of the Earth* by Jules Verne (1965). If you know anything about Jules Verne as a French novelist, you are more likely to predict a science fiction genre than if you have never heard of him. If you are aware of Maria Montessori as an educator, you know what to expect in terms of her philosophy and of the age of the children about which she writes. Shulberg writes fiction about a certain time and place with colorful characters. Knowing authors usually means having read their work, being aware of whether they typically write fiction or nonfiction, and having some familiarity with their writing style.

Language of the material.   The first paragraph from each of the books listed above provides language cues that help confirm or disconfirm a reader's earlier predictions and help the reader make new predictions.

> For some years childhood has been the object of intense social interest. Like other great movements this interest has not been aroused by any single individual but it has burst forth like a volcano shooting forth fires in all directions. Science provides the incentive for this new movement by drastically reducing the rate of infant mortality. Then it came to be realized that children were frequently worn out from the drudgery of their school work.

> (FROM *THE SECRETS OF CHILDHOOD*, MONTESSORI 1966, 1)

> It's waiting, Shep was thinking. You wait to get inside the gate, you wait outside the great man's office, you wait for your agent to make a deal, you wait for instructions on how to write and then when you finish your treatment and turn it in, you wait for that unique contribution to art, the story conference.

> (FROM *THE DISENCHANTED*, SCHULBERG 1968, 1)

> Looking back at all that has occurred to me since that eventful day, I am scarcely able to believe in the reality of my adventures. They were truly so wonderful that even now I am bewildered when I think of them.

> (FROM *A JOURNEY TO THE CENTER OF THE EARTH*, VERNE 1965, 1)

What language cues help confirm predictions that the material is fiction or nonfiction? Some cues might include:

- the degree of formality and the use of figurative language;
- how the language refers to people, places, and events;
- how the language indicates whether the characters are real or fictitious; and
- the kind of mood the language choices convey.

In the following lesson, learners will explore aspects of written language that provide cues for predictions about the subject matter and about whether or not the text is fiction or nonfiction. Such an exploration helps readers make use of their initial contact with a text. Good predicting strategies facilitate gaining meaning.

Strategy Lesson Experience

Initiating: Begin the discussion by considering the two titles: "Whale" and "How the Whale Got His Throat." These might be placed on the board or on a transparency to control the language features on which the readers need to focus. (Or you might adapt your own selections that are more appropriate to the age and interests of your students.)

After discussing the cues provided by revealing only the titles of the passages (or the covers of the books if available), reveal the authors' names. Discuss any additional cues students get from the authors' names. If the books are available, explore the ways illustrations provide additional cues.

Give each student a copy of the first paragraph of both pieces. After they have a chance to read the paragraphs silently, read both selections aloud. The students may feel the need to reread portions silently as they discuss the cues provided by the language in the first paragraphs.

"How the Whale Got His Throat"

In the sea, once upon a time, O my Best Beloved, there was a whale, and he ate fishes. He ate the starfish and the garfish, and the crab and the dab, and the plaice and the dace, and the skate and his mate, and the macereel and the pickereel, and the really truly twirly-whirly eel. All the fishes he could find in all the sea he ate with his mouth so!

(FROM *JUST SO STORIES,* RUDYARD KIPLING 1952, 9)

Whale

Whale is a huge sea animal that looks much like a fish. But whales are not fish. They belong instead to a group of animals called *mammals.* Other mammals include chimpanzees, dogs, and human beings. Like these mammals, whales have a highly developed brain and so are among the most intelligent of all animals.

(FROM *THE WORLD BOOK ENCYCLOPEDIA* 1995, 256)

Transacting: Consider the following questions if they have not been explored in the initiating discussion.

1. How does the title help in predicting whether the text is fact or fiction?
2. How do readers know the selections are different? Explore similarity and differences of the subject matter presented in the two passages and in how it is presented.
3. How does knowing the source give information about the subject matter?
4. What effect does knowing or not knowing the authors have on predictions of what the writing might be about? Help students understand that when they know authors or have heard about them, they also know more about the material.
5. Does *not* having an author's name tell anything? Explore the notion that an author always exists even if no name is given.
6. In what other ways are the two pieces similar?
7. In what other ways are the two pieces different?
8. Do the authors have different purposes for writing? What are they?
9. For what purposes would readers select these pieces to read?

10. Is there something in the way the author uses language that makes a reader believe that one of the selections is more factual or true to life than the other? Explore the students' ideas, encouraging them to support their hypotheses with examples from other material. You might discuss the following:
   a. How the author talks to the reader
   b. The use of real as opposed to unreal creatures (Are there garfish? How would you find out? References to different people, places, and animals help readers decide that one selection may be fact and the other fiction.)
   c. Unfamiliar spellings
   d. Style ("ate with his mouth so!" vs. "Like these mammals, whales have a highly developed brain . . .")
   e. Use of the terms *article* and *story* to differentiate between fact and fiction (In what materials would you find articles, and in what materials, stories?)
11. How do illustrations and diagrams help readers determine fact or fiction?

Applying: Select a nonfiction article and a fictionalized narrative on the same subject. An article on baseball from an encyclopedia or newspaper and a short story or poem about a baseball hero such as "Casey at the Bat" provide good contrast.

Invite students to work in small groups or in pairs. Explore the materials by using the questions suggested above. Encourage similar discussions about other material students read.

Invite students who are interested to read Katherine Paterson's *Lyddie* (1991) and the stories in *The Lowell Mill Girls: Life in the Factory* (1991) edited by JoAnne Weisman. *Lyddie* is the fictional story of Lyddie Worthen, who worked six days a week from dawn to dusk in the mills in Lowell, Massachusetts. *The Lowell Mill Girls: Life in the Factory* is a collection of essays and historical fiction that presents different perspectives on the history of Lowell's female workers in the 1840s. Without detracting from the beauty of these works, encourage students to be alert to the variety of ways in which the mills, Lowell, and the general conditions of the workers are described. The students may want to keep lists of differences and similarities between the books, adding to them or changing them as they gain additional evidence from their reading.

Suggestions for other paired readings of books or text sets are listed at the end of this lesson. Use newspaper and magazine articles, travel brochures, and maps related to a similar topic to explore genre differences.

Expanding: Encourage students to find an encyclopedia article, a newspaper article, and a poem about a favorite animal or any subject currently of interest to them or within the curriculum. Learners can share with the class the different genres, organizations, and styles authors use to handle similar content.

Students might look for feature articles about favorite sports figures or television or movie stars and a review of a game, television show, or movie in which the person they chose appears. They might compare the language in these two pieces of material, following a procedure similar to the one above.

Interested students might enjoy taking a feature or news article from the newspaper and rewriting it as a narrative or poem. Students might select a comic strip or a television show and rewrite it as if they were newspaper reporters and the incident had happened on the street where they live. They can then discuss why they chose the language they did and how their language choices were necessary for certain genre use specifications.

Readings for Expanding This Strategy Lesson

Ancona, George. *Cutters, Carvers & The Cathedral.* New York, NY: Lothrop, 1995.
   A fascinating photo essay that shows the workers who refurbished The Cathedral of Saint John the Divine.

Ancona, George. *The Golden Lion Tamarin Comes Home.* New York, NY: Macmillan, 1994.
The story of the reintroduction into the wild of golden lion tamarins born in captivity.

Bunting, Eve. *Night of the Gargoyles.* New York, NY: Clarion, 1994.
When night comes the gargoyles swoop down from the ledges where they spend their days.

Franklin, Kristine. *When the Monkeys Come Back.* New York, NY: Atheneum, 1994.
When the Costa Rican jungle is cut down the monkeys disappear. Doña Marta finds a way to bring the jungle and the monkeys back.

Hindey, Judy. *A Piece of String Is a Wonderful Thing.* Cambridge, MA: Candlewick Press, 1993.
Relates in verse the origin and uses of string.

Wallace, Karen. *Think of a Beaver.* Cambridge, MA: Candlewick Press, 1993.
Pictures and rhythmic text provide a close-up look at the habits and homes of North American beavers.

Zoehfield, Kathleen Weidner. *How Mountains Are Made.* New York, NY: Harper-Collins, 1995.
This book in the "Let's Read and Find Out Science" series describes how mountains are made. Other books in the series include *Look at Your Eyes* (Showers, Paul. 1992. New York, NY: HarperCollins.), *Tornado Alert* (Showers, Paul. 1988. New York, NY: HarperCollins.), and *Rockets and Satellites* (Branley, Franklin. 1987. New York, NY: Crowell.).

Paired Reading of Fiction/Nonfiction

Carle, Eric. *The Very Hungry Caterpillar.* New York, NY: Putnam, 1972.
The title provides a vivid description of this exciting picture storybook.

French, Vivian. *Caterpillar, Caterpillar.* Cambridge, MA: Candlewick Press, 1993.
A girl learns about caterpillars and butterflies as she watches her grandfather grow them on the nettles in his garden.

Paired Readings or a Text Set on Islands

Dean, Julia. *A Year on Monehegan Island.* New York, NY: Ticknor and Fields, 1995.
The author chronicles one year in the life of Monehegan Island and its residents, creating a portrait of a way of life that has almost vanished.

Field, Rachel. *If Once You Have Slept on an Island.* Honesdale, PA: Caroline House, 1993.
Poem describes the change one will experience after sleeping on an island.

Foster, Sally. *The Private World of Smith Island.* New York, NY: Cobblehill Books, 1993.
Describes in text and photographs the geography and history of Chesapeake Bay's Smith Island and the day-to-day life of its inhabitants.

Thaxter, Celia. *Celia's Island Journal.* Boston, MA: Little, Brown, 1992.
Relates the experiences of a young girl growing up in the mid-nineteenth century on an isolated island off the coast of New England where her father keeps the lighthouse.

Wallis, Lisa. *Island Child.* New York, NY: Lodestar Books, 1991.
A child on an island goes for bike rides, crunches icicles, and searches for sea glass on the shore.

STRATEGY LESSON: LANGUAGE IN WRITTEN TEXTS

Evaluation: Who Will Benefit

In addition to helping the readers mentioned in the evaluation section for "Integrating Informational Material," the next strategy lesson, this strategy lesson will help those learners who are unaware that:

- everything they read has the potential of informing them not only about the topic of the piece, but about related topics, consequently adding to their storehouse of background information;
- the language authors select to express meaning should be considered within the context of the entire narrative; or
- words and phrases can take on different meanings in different contexts.

Specific Rationale

Much of the rationale for this lesson is found in "Meaning Through Context" (Focus I, pages 69–71) and "Integrating Informational Material" (Focus III, pages 122–123). An additional purpose for this lesson is to help all learners become consciously aware that when they are reading, they are learning more than the information contained in the story itself. As learners construct meaning they are learning the language of discourse and the importance of context as well as gaining proficiency in the process of reading.

When students are reading for their own enjoyment, the process should not be interrupted for instruction. Therefore, in these lessons students will read an entire story and then consciously think about and discuss the concepts developed and integrated into their schema.

Strategy Lesson Experience

Initiating: Ask students to read the same folktale silently. Whenever they come to words or phrases they do not understand, they are to provide a synonym substitution or a nonword as they continue reading. The main purpose of this lesson is to help readers understand the story. When students finish reading, ask them to look through the story again and place a light pencil mark over any *significant* words or phrases that are new or used in an unusual way. Discuss the synonyms or nonwords they used and why they selected the ones they did.

Transacting: Encourage an exploratory discussion of the story that leads students to understand that the main purpose for reading is to construct meaning. Address each text item checked: Have you heard of or seen this word or phrase before? If you have, relate that experience to the way the item is used in this story.

Discuss how language takes on different meaning in different stories. Learners should know that this is how their ideas or concepts grow. Explore different meanings they have for specific words or phrases. Point out that there is language we know predominantly from reading, such as *Once upon a time* or dialogue carriers; we may never or seldom hear these spoken, just as there is oral language that may seldom be seen in print, such as tags like *you know*.

Continue exploration: Can we say this sentence another way without changing the meaning? How do we find out what the words or phrases mean in this story? What language cues help us know what the words or phrases mean? How much does the entire narrative help us understand smaller units of language? Help students understand that meaning changes depending on context; when they relate new words, concepts, or ideas to what they already know, they can often figure out meanings for themselves.

Applying: Invite students to develop a notebook that is entitled "My Language Book." In one section of this book they record sentences that contain words or phrases that are used in interesting or unusual ways. On the next line they might rewrite the sentence in their own words without changing the meaning. They may want to share these lists with each other periodically to see which kinds of books have words or phrases in common or to add to a "Class Language Book." These lists might be discussed in individual conferences with the teacher to monitor concept development. Many students will enjoy this activity as long as it is used when they show interest and used to stimulate discussion about language.

Expanding: Invite students to write on the board a mystery word or phrase from "My Language Book" that they think others won't know. These words may also come from their reading in science, math, social studies, and so on. For a couple of days classmates try to find the term in some context or to guess its meaning. When a number of students have some ideas, let the originator lead a group discussion about various meanings that this particular word or phrase can have depending on context.

Remind students to use words or phrases from their personal or from the class language books in their writings and discussions. Interested students might make a collage or illustrate language that they have added to their books.

Students may want to collect language that helps readers develop concepts by using their "literary senses" to hear, see, smell, and feel.

Readings for Expanding This Strategy Lesson

Maestro, Giulio. *What's a Frank Frank?* New York, NY: Clarion, 1984.
   A collection of original riddles making use of homographs—words that are spelled the same but have different meanings.

Mahy, Margaret. *Keeping House.* New York, NY: McElderry Books, 1991.
   A humorous story tells how a woman keeps house.

Terban, Marvin. *Mad as a Wet Hen!* New York, NY: Clarion, 1987.
   Illustrates and explains over 100 common English idioms, in categories including animals, body parts, and colors.

Terban, Marvin. *Eight Ate: A Feast of Homonym Riddles.* New York, NY: Clarion, 1982.
   A collection of original riddles, each using a homonym as the answer: i.e., bizarre-bazaar, foul-fowl.

Terban, Marvin. *Guppies in Tuxedos.* New York, NY: Clarion, 1988.
   Traces the origins of more than 100 eponymous words—words derived from the names of people or places.

STRATEGY LESSON: INTEGRATING INFORMATIONAL MATERIAL

Evaluation: Who Will Benefit

This strategy lesson will benefit students:

- who parrot facts and focus on trivial details but are unable to discuss significant information or generalizations;
- who do not understand or enjoy informational material;
- who do not realize that information can be gained by reading fiction; or
- whose miscue analysis profile shows that more than sixty percent of the sentences produced are syntactically acceptable, but of those, more than sixty percent of sentences show extensive change of meaning.

Specific Rationale

Informational material can be difficult to read for a number of reasons: a heavy or unknown concept load, hard-to-predict grammatical structures, or lack of concrete experiences, in addition to lack of interest.

Concept load.   Many times texts, especially but not exclusively information materials, present concepts or ideas that are new or contrary to the present beliefs of the learner; consequently, they have difficulty integrating such ideas into their already developed schema. For example, a text might present in a few short paragraphs a wide range of ideas that evolved over a long historical period. Authors who write such material are often unaware that in an attempt to generalize and simplify they conceptually overload the material. Such material should be avoided until readers are confidently using strategies for constructing meaning.

Consider this excerpt, a paragraph from a biography that a secondary student might be asked to read. As you read it, consider what background knowledge a reader must have in order to understand the concepts included. Put a check over words or phrases that represent a concept requiring background knowledge.

> In June 1884, along with thirty other students from an entering class of 103, Fitzgerald passed the Latin School's demanding final examinations. A copy of one of the exams given in this period remains in the files of the Boston School Committee. It opens with Latin, calling upon the students to translate Cicero and Virgil on sight and to explain the syntax of *honore, salutis,* and a dozen other words. In the section on history, the students are asked first to describe the forms of government and the classes into which people were divided in Greece during the Heroic Age, and then to explain the causes of the Pelo-ponnesian Wars and the terms of surrender and finally to evaluate Caesar's campaigns in Gaul (Goodwin 1987, 66).

This passage illustrates the complexity of such concepts as: Latin Schools in Boston; translation at sight; syntax; forms of government; classes into which people are divided; causes of wars; terms of surrender; and names and places such as Fitzgerald, Cicero, Virgil, Caesar, Greece, Gaul, and many others.

Those who have an extensive background in history, whether enriched through reading fiction or nonfiction, may be unaware of why this paragraph is difficult to read. As informed adults, teachers are often unaware of the degree to which informational materials, even when written for younger readers, contain new and unfamiliar concepts.

Grammatical structures.   The structure of written material may be unfamiliar to the readers and therefore hard to predict. (See the strategy lesson "Hard-to-Predict

Structures (Reader-Selected Miscues)" in Chapter 5.) In the paragraph above, did the last sentence, with two long independent clauses and many adverbial phrases, cause problems? Could the relationships developed through the independent and dependent clauses in the last sentence cause a reader to reread and wonder about meaning?

When both the structure or syntactic complexity and concept load are complex and impenetrable, students should be encouraged to replace the text with easier material. Students need a variety of ways such as concrete experiences, concept-related materials, and strategy lessons to build adequate schema for new information they want to learn.

Concrete experiences.   Reading to learn is limited by depth of background knowledge. If schema does not already exist to integrate new information, real-life experiences on which to build knowledge are crucial. It is virtually impossible to learn to knit or to assemble a toy from how-to written directions unless some prior experience precedes reading the knitting or assembly instructions. When students become interested in aspects of science, social studies, or math, first-hand experiences will not only make the subsequent reading easier but will provide motivation to read because students will have questions they want to answer. If field trips, experiments, and demonstrations are not possible, photos, posters, videos, CDs, and so on are important and accessible resources. Teachers find it useful to carefully examine texts their students will read in order to consider the concepts that may cause their students problems. They may discuss with their students what the students find difficult to understand. Teachers then plan nonreading experiences to provide the background their students need to support developing schema.

A variety of topically-related materials written and presented in various degrees of difficulty and formats provide students with both accessibility and choice. A criterion for selection is that the grammatical structure is highly predictable so that students are not overwhelmed by complex sentence structures as they are learning new concepts. Many teachers compile bibliographies of related materials that grow with time. Students can be involved in developing such bibliographies as they find new materials about a particular concept. Text sets of concept-related materials include books and magazine and newspaper articles as well as nonprint materials such as photographs, maps, and musical selections, among many others. Readers need to become aware of their own responsibility in developing and integrating concepts as they read. The lessons in this chapter and throughout this book will help build this awareness.

Strategy Lesson Experience

Initiating: Talk with students about the need to construct meaning as they read content-related materials. Examine the materials selected and discuss how informational material is organized to support developing concepts.

Introduce the "Read-for-Information Guide" on an overhead or give each student a copy. Reading the guide with the group will give them a chance to ask questions about the procedure. You may choose to generate a similar list with your students based on the class discussion.

Read-for-Information Guide
1. Think about why you want to know this information.
2. Make a list of some of the things that you already know about the subject. Call it *What I Know.* Add to this list as you gather information.
3. Make a list of questions you have about the subject. Call it *What I Want to Know.* Add to this list whenever another question emerges.
4. Think about resources you can use to find the answers to your questions.

5. Look for answers to the questions that are most interesting or most important to you.
6. Organize the important information by placing together ideas and concepts that relate to each other.
7. Share your information with others. You may want to present it as a play, a television show, or a group discussion through illustrations, on a poster, as a mobile, or in other creative ways.

Invite students to use the guide with an informational piece such as "Spiders," presented below. They can use a similar process when they inquire into their own topics.

1. Discuss possible reasons or purposes for learning more about spiders.
2. List on the board under *What I Know* things students know about spiders. If anyone raises questions or challenges, ask the challengers to write their questions under *What I Want to Know*. Label each question and statement with the name of the student who provides it. The student may then assume responsibility for the concepts in his or her particular statement or question. Whenever the student learns important new information, it should be added to the *What I Know* list.
3. Ask if anyone has additional questions about spiders. Add these to *What I Want to Know*, or if no questions were raised earlier, start such a list. Continue to add to this list all questions or challenges students raise throughout the lesson. You may want to put the lists on a computer so they are easy to add to and change. The two lists might look like the following:

What I Know	What I Want to Know
Eight legs (Carlos)	Is the silk made from spider spit? (Teresa)
Spiders bite (Daniel)	Will webs cause infections? (Nanci)
Spin silk webs (Carol)	Insects have six legs, how can spiders be insects? (Margaret)
Webs can stop bleeding (Althea)	Are they poisonous? (Antony)
Spiders are insects (Pat)	Can they grow into big monsters? (Bob)
Good for gardens (Virginia)	Is it bad luck to kill a spider? (Ann)

4. List under *Resources* names of books and other print information learners may be aware of. They may suggest encyclopedias and dictionaries. Encourage them to think of people they know who they might interview or use as consultants or experts. Accept these suggestions and encourage students to consider a wide variety of people, books, magazines, and newspapers. Encourage interested students to find out where books about spiders are located in the school and local libraries. Provide a few suggestions to get started, but leave the research to them. Enlist the help of librarians. Help students think about questions that might be posed to resource people from the school or community, such as pet-store owners, science teachers, exterminators, biologists, workers in nature centers, and knowledgeable family members or friends.
5. Ask students to select questions from the list that are most important or most interesting to them. Ask them to keep their questions in mind and a pencil in their hand as they read "Spiders." As they read, they can highlight answers to questions or make notes about anything they think might be important, but that they don't understand. (See "Strategy Lesson: Hard-to-Predict Structures (Reader-Selected Miscues)" in Chapter 5.)

Spiders

How many spiders have you seen in the last week? If you are observant—that is, if you watch the world around you carefully—you have probably seen more than one. Spiders live in most places in the world. They live both indoors and outdoors. They come in many sizes, shapes, and colors.

Although many people are afraid of spiders, spiders do not usually bite unless they are disturbed, and very few spider bites are poisonous. Spiders are helpful. Each year they eat thousands of harmful insects, which they trap in webs.

The body of the spider has two parts joined by a slender waist. It has eight legs. The top or front part of the body contains the spider's head. The bottom or back part of the body is called the abdomen. On the bottom of the spider near the back edge are its spinnerets. Spiders use their spinnerets to make the silk used for spider webs and for their egg sacs. These spinnerets look like tiny tubes.

When a spider starts to spin a web, it presses the spinnerets against something hard and out comes some of the liquid silk. This silk hardens in the air. Different kinds of spiders make different kinds of webs.

Many people are interested in spiders. Scientists study the behavior of spiders under different conditions. There are many superstitions about spiders. Some people can tell exciting or scary tales about them. What do you know about spiders?

(Yetta Goodman)

Transacting: If the following does not emerge in the talk about "Spiders," explore:

1. What information helped you answer your questions? Was the information important? Why do you think so?
   Ask students to add significant information under their *What I Know* list. Encourage them to use short phrases and their own words by modeling how you take notes. Help them explain what they think the ideas or concepts mean. Encourage exploratory discussion, challenges, and questions.

2. Do you think the new information is true or not? Why do you think so?
   Help students question what they read. If they are not sure if something is correct, have them leave it as a question under *What I Want to Know*. When they believe they have accurate information, they can then put it under *What I Know*. Help them understand that even printed resources contain inaccuracies.

3. Was any information recorded under *What I Know* inaccurate and did it need to be changed? What evidence do you have? The students cross out any statements they believe to be inaccurate and change any that need to be corrected.

4. Discuss any new concepts formed. As students discuss spinnerets, web-making, and egg sacs, explore the depth to which they understand each concept. If their concepts are not sufficiently developed for this task, ask questions that help them reconsider any narrow or inaccurate interpretations. Avoid giving answers. List all new questions under *What I Want to Know*. List all new information that is acceptable to the students under *What I Know*.
   The list now may look like this:

What I Know	What I Want to Know
Eight legs (Carlos)	*Insects have six legs, how can spiders be insects? (Margaret)*
Spin silk webs and egg sacs (Carol and Daniel)	*Can they grow into big monsters? (Bob)*
Webs can stop bleeding (Althea)	*What do spinnerets look like? (Teresa)*
~~*Spiders are insects (Pat)*~~	*Do all spiders have spinnerets? (Emilio)*
Good for gardens (Virginia)	*Is it bad luck to kill a spider? (Ann)*
Few spider bites are poisonous (Susan)	*What different sizes, shapes, and colors do spiders come in? (Peter and Antony)*
Spiders can help people (Oscar and Nanci)	*Do all spiders make webs? (Pat)*
Silk comes from spinnerets (Carol)	*What kinds of webs do spiders make? (Linda) (Teresa)*
	What superstitions do people have about spiders? (Carlos)

5. Encourage interested students to select questions they want to read more about as they continue to follow the "Read-for-Information Guide." Help them think of questions that are related. Provide options for those who wish at this point to read topics of more interest to them.

Applying: Encourage students to organize information for presentation purposes. Organizing information involves at least two separate activities: categorizing the material and selecting significant information.

As the list of *What I Know* increases, help students classify their concepts or ideas. They can collect information on note cards or cut their list apart and paste each statement on index cards so they can rearrange the categories when they need to add to them. Or they may wish to number or color code all statements related to a particular concept. Help students discover different ways to organize their information.

If students find a great deal of information about a single concept, they may want to limit their presentation, for example: How Spinnerets Work, How Spiders Weave Webs, Superstitions about Spiders. These topics are sufficient for an individual presentation even though each topic deals with only one of the questions asked.

Evaluate the "Read-for-Information Guide" with students. Add or make changes to identify the clues that helped the learners find and understand their information most easily. Replace or omit anything they did not find useful. Through this evaluation students may want to develop a new "Read-for-Information Guide." If such evaluation is done periodically, students consciously think through the strategies they find most useful in helping them to read selectively and to organize their thinking, their report writing, and any oral presentations.

Encourage students to present or share what they have learned. Explore a variety of sharing possibilities such as keeping an observation log of spiders making webs. Individual student researchers might compare their work with other experts. Learners might show slides or pictures of the webs and provide a time line indicating changes in the web. Students might apply thread to paper to replicate the different stages and kinds of webs. Facilitate sharing by encouraging creative presentational forms: scrapbooks, demonstrations, debates, panels, interviews, travelogues, and so on.

Expanding: Encourage students to use their new concepts in a variety of ways, including class discussions and written material. Students might add their new concepts with related words and phrases to a "Class Language Book" (see p. 126).

Encourage students to present their study in an interesting and exciting way to younger children. Written reports can be developed into a class encyclopedia. Ask student editors to verify the information. Students may choose to write to encyclopedia companies and other resource centers to find out how they ensure accuracy of material and how they update their material. Students may then revise their class encyclopedia.

Students may present their research findings in an exhibit, with the researchers available to answer questions or explain procedures. Invite students to use similar methods whenever they read informational material in social studies, math, science, and other content areas.

STRATEGY LESSON: GENERALIZATIONS

Evaluation: Who Will Benefit

This strategy lesson will help readers who can't see the forest for the trees; that is, they may be able to identify facts and information given in text, but are unable to generalize larger concepts from them.

Specific Rationale

Authors of nonfiction material often have an idea, law, or precept they want readers to generalize. These generalizations are built from an accumulation of particulars. Readers will be helped to understand such generalizations if they ask themselves: "What is the most important information I can learn from this text?" and "What do I infer from the material that leads me to this generalization?"

Strategy Lesson Experience

Initiating: Ask students to read from material selected for current theme studies in social studies, science, or other content areas. The student may select sections that are causing them problems or are of importance. Editorials on significant current events are also good resources.

Transacting: Explore the concept of forming generalizations. Discuss the notion of going from particular knowledge to seeing relationships between the particulars to forming rules, laws, and assumptions—generalizations. After reading a content area selection, discuss the following:

1. What was the most important idea(s) presented in this passage? List all ideas that learners share.
2. What particulars from the piece help readers infer what the author thought was most important?
3. Why did the author want readers to know this generalization?
4. What in the selection did you find most interesting and why? What was least interesting and why? Readers need to understand that the author and the reader are not always interested in the same things, and therefore, the reader may construct a different generalization from the one intended by the author.
5. For what reasons would you reread this article? When would you write down some of the ideas? Explore the notion that reading at varying speeds, taking notes, or going over written information must be related to the reader's purpose. Encourage students to reread the article after this discussion. Did our discussion help in your rereading of the article? Stress the importance of knowing the purpose of one's reading in selecting what will be most important to focus on during reading.

Applying: Gather a collection of content area selections into a text set of books, newspapers, and magazines that focus on a single concept or subject. Relating to theme studies makes lessons such as this one more relevant.

Invite students to read about a topic they select. Before reading ask the learners to write down two reasons why they want to read the article or to write two questions about the topic. After reading, ask the students who selected the same articles to meet together to discuss the following:

1. Are their reasons for reading similar or different?
2. Are their questions similar or different?
3. In one or two sentences, what is this article about?
4. What specific ideas from the text leads to this generalization?

Expanding: Invite interested students to express the author's main idea as a diagram, model, or political cartoon. Also explore with students the benefit of jotting down the author's details in a right-hand column and the author's generalizations in the left-hand column. They can also make notes about whether or not they agree with the author's generalizations.

Discuss the idea of highlighting particulars in one color and generalizations in another. Use terms such as *concept* and *generalization* in discussions with students. Duplicate material for students to try their hand at this kind of highlighting. Such experiences may help students find out what study aids help them.

STRATEGY LESSON: HUMOR

Evaluation: Who Will Benefit

This strategy lesson will help readers who do not respond to humor in their reading. The lesson is not meant to tell readers what is funny, but rather to encourage them to explore the semantic/pragmatic cues that they consider to be humorous.

Specific Rationale

As they grow and develop, people find a variety of things to be funny. What is funny to a six-year-old may not be to a twelve-year-old, and a twelve-year-old may not understand why her parents are laughing. An adult and a twelve-year-old may both laugh at the same incident but find different aspects of it funny. What is funny and why it is funny are very much related to how a situation is characterized, how it is understood, and how it relates to the reader's culture.

There are many kinds of humor and many reasons for people to laugh. It is helpful to discuss humor with readers, although it is important not to decide what is funny for them.

In exploring humor with students, you may have to deal with jokes or stories that make fun of specific groups of people for reasons of national origins, racial differences, religious differences, family relationships, and physical characteristics. Take this opportunity to discuss how humor can be used to put people down or keep people "in their place." Jokes made at the expense of a whole group of people may hurt the whole group in the same way that jokes made against an individual hurt the individual. (Relate this discussion to the strategy lesson on the use of eye dialect in Chapter 6 and to issues of prejudice.) Through discussions readers can see how others view humor and expand their own definition of humor.

Strategy Lesson Experience

Initiating: Reproduce three cartoons for use on the overhead. Ask the students to read all three cartoons.

Transacting: When students have finished reading invite them to respond to the three cartoons. If the following questions have not been answered, explore:

- Do you think the cartoons are funny? Why?
- Which cartoon is funniest? Why?
- What makes anything funny? Why? Explore all possibilities. Encourage students to explore with each other by questioning all answers.

Applying: To talk about the concept of humor, encourage students to bring to class examples of cartoons, bumper stickers, posters, joke books, and so on. Older students may enjoy combining entertainment and opinion through political cartooning. Discuss cartoonists' reasons for creating such cartoons.

Expanding: Invite interested students to select their favorite cartoons and read them first to a child of six or seven and then to someone older. Then the students ask them why they do or do not think the cartoons are funny. Discuss how different age groups react and why. As students present findings, ask class members to share their reactions to the cartoons. Students will observe different points of view among peers as well as among different age groups.

In a period of time during the school year, invite students to keep a separate collection of books or a list called "These Made Me Laugh." When a substantial number have been collected, students can share their favorite funny books, exploring what characteristics make a story or article funny. If students respond well to this lesson, expand to satire and sarcasm using similar formats.

Explore issues of pathos, satire and other aspects of literature in similar ways.

Readings for Expanding This Strategy

Cutler, Jane. *No Dogs Allowed.* Canada: Sunburst Books, 1992.
> Five-year-old Edward Fraser thinks he's a dog, and his older brother, Jason, is none too pleased. Younger brothers are bother enough, but a pet brother is intolerable.

Gwynne, Fred. *The King Who Rained.* New York, NY: Windmill Books/Dutton, 1970.
> Humorous use of puns. (There are similar Fred Gwynne books.)

Lindbergh, Reeve. *The Day the Goose Got Loose.* New York, NY: Penguin, 1990.
> When the goose gets loose chaos results.

Pikey, Dav. *Dogzilla.* San Diego, CA: Harcourt, 1993.
> Puns and clever plays on words highlight this take-off as a monstrous mutt terrorizes the residents of Mousopolis.

FOCUS IV: WORD AND PHRASE SEMANTIC CUES

There are relationships between the semantic and syntactic cueing systems. The lessons concerned with word and phrase semantic cues include knowledge of syntax. In using these lessons, the teacher may find it helpful to relate to Chapter 5, especially "Strategy Lesson: Varieties of Grammatical Function."

STRATEGY LESSON: PREDICTING PRONOUNS

Evaluation: Who Will Benefit

This strategy lesson will benefit readers who:

- overuse graphic information and make pronoun substitutions that disrupt comprehension; or
- indicate through their retelling or discussion that they have confused characters because they misunderstood pronoun references.

Specific Rationale

It is not uncommon for readers to miscue on pronouns, making such substitutions as *he* for *we* or *her* for *him.* Careful examination of these miscues reveals whether readers are inferring text information and predicting appropriate pronoun substitutions, revealing their knowledge of the English pronoun system, or whether they are confused about characterizations and are not inferring and predicting from the syntactic and semantic cues. Substitutions, omissions, or insertions of pronouns may be produced for a variety of reasons:

1. *Using appropriate context for appropriate predictions.*

   George was lying face down on the grass with his bicycle bent out of

   shape beside him. The doctor and I stood over him. "Let's lift him

   carefully," he said to me. He placed the board under George's body . . .

Miscues of this type indicate that the reader is concerned with meaning. The sentence starting "Let's lift him" cues the reader to expect both characters to be involved in the subsequent action. The substitution of *we* for *he* in the first instance indicates the reader's appropriate prediction about what might occur. The reader confirms by self-correcting, indicating an awareness of the subject of the dialogue carrier. The second *we* for *he* substitution changes the meaning of the sentence only slightly, is acceptable in the story, and requires no self-correction. Both miscues indicate the reader's meaning construction and awareness of the author's intent.

2. *Using conceptual understanding to produce pronoun substitutions.*

   The dog was a big, brown police dog and was ready to protect the

   chickens from any harm. When the coyotes attacked the chickens, the

   dog stood her ground. She was ready for a fight.

In this case, the substitution of *it* for *her* and *she* reveals the reader's concept about animals. (Even a substitution of *he* for *she* would have provided conceptual insight.) Animals of all kinds can be considered neuter if no name or personification is provided to help identify gender. Many people think of *dogs* generally as *he* and *cats* as *she* unless the context provides additional cues about the animal that establish a concept of maleness or femaleness for that animal. It is only necessary to deal with the concepts of gender if they interfere with a reader's understanding.

3. *Having insufficient or confusing contextual cues for the support of prediction.*

Readers' experiences may cause them to expect an alternate gender and therefore an alternate pronoun, especially if the text is ambiguous.

Mr. Rudy paid the baby-sitter. "Does that seem right?" *She*
He smiled and

nodded. "That's fine, I usually charge only $2.00 an hour."

If readers think of baby-sitters as girls, and if the text provides insufficient cues, a miscue such as the above may result. The writer did not immediately provide redundant information about the gender of the baby-sitter. This might cause a problem in developing appropriate characterization if the confusion is not resolved through further reading. In the above reading the meaning of the story is not disrupted by the miscue.

4. *Overusing the graphic cueing system.*

Persia has just had a family of five little kittens. All the children in

the neighborhood gather to watch the mother cat take care of *he*
her

kittens. She cleans them with *he* her rough tongue. *He* She really knew how

to take care of *he* her babies.

Although the miscues coded in the above example rarely occur as a consistent problem, there are some readers who produce substitutions that are neither semantically nor syntactically acceptable. Such readers pay attention to graphic information and substitute look-alike words rather than attending to the semantic cues. They appear unconcerned that meaning is disrupted or that their reading doesn't sound like language.

Strategy Lesson Experience

This lesson encourages students to make use of context clues as a means of predicting appropriate pronouns. The materials below focus on *he* and *she* pronoun slots. If students have problems with other pronoun substitutions that interfere with meaning, use these materials as models for selecting materials or for writing your own. Provide content that contains enough semantic cues so that the reader predicts largely on the basis of meaning.

Initiating: Invite the students to read "A Family Picture" and to talk about the members of the family.

A Family Picture

Judy
Eleven years old
Long brown hair in a pony tail
Taller than Matt
As tall as Mama and Papa
Blue jeans, a white shirt, and barefoot

Matt
Twelve years old
Long dark hair
The shortest in the family
Blue jeans, a striped tee shirt, and brown
shoes

Mama
Thirty years old
Short curly hair
Taller than Matt and as tall as Papa
A green jogging suit

Papa
Thirty years old
Short brown hair and mustache
Taller than Matt and as tall as Mama
A yellow sport shirt and blue pants

Ginger
Five years old
Long yellow, orange, and white hair
A big Collie
A collar

(Yetta Goodman)

As a group, compose a brief story about one of the family members described in "A Family Picture." The sketch might describe the family member engaging in a special activity and should include at least one other member.

Individually or with a partner choose another family member, write another sketch, and then compare stories. Ask volunteers to write their stories on a transparency or on the board. Illustrations may accompany the sketches.

Transacting: The following questions will help readers focus on the function of pronouns. Use terms such as *pronoun, noun,* and *proper noun* as appropriate.

1. Why did you use this particular word or pronoun?
   Students will realize that if they know the people or animals being described they also know how to refer to them. Explore the notion that information comes from what they know about the characters; the pronouns only confirm

their predictions. Students might discuss when proper nouns are used and when and how pronouns are used to refer to characters.

2. Why did you decide to call the dog *he* instead of *she* or *it?*
Why do we sometimes call animals *it* and other times *she* or *he?* Explore the idea that *it* is often used if the author doesn't know the sex of the animal. In some dialects of English, such as British, infants are referred to as *it.* Students might want to consider why this is so. There are usually more cues in a story indicating the gender of people than of animals.

Invite students who may need more work on pronoun references to write their own stories focusing on a character and incident of their own choosing. After writing, duplicate or place on an overhead transparency each sketch, including the one written as a group. Omit pronouns, replacing them with a five-space blank. Ask students to read one sketch to themselves, mentally placing an appropriate word in the blank as they read. If they cannot decide what to put in the blank, they are to continue reading, later returning to the blanks. Then read the story together, stopping at each blank for the pronoun insertion.

If the following questions have not been discussed, consider:

1. Why is this pronoun appropriate?
Encourage students to talk about the semantic cues that support their answers. Focus on the idea that cues to any word are embedded in the context of the story. The amount of context can range from a phrase to the entire discourse.
2. Who are the references to? How do you know?
Help students understand that the blanks are place holders for people in the story. Help them generalize that they can find semantic cues to characters that will help them predict appropriate pronouns.

Applying: Invite students to read the following two selections that may be similar to the sketches they just wrote. Talk about what they might do if they are not sure of what to put in each blank. Help students understand that they can continue to read and search for cues that indicate the person or animal referred to. The point to emphasize is that if readers understand who is being discussed they will know what pronouns are appropriate. A focus on meaning of the whole text selection rather than on a linguistic unit (the pronoun, in this case) leads to greater comprehension.

My Little Brother and My Big Sister

Sometimes I get so mad at _____ little brother and _____ older sister! They bug _____ to death! Last night _____ brother took _____ crayons and scribbled all over _____ homework paper. Because _____ messed it up _____ had to do the whole thing over again. _____ is always getting into my things. _____ big sister is just as bad. _____ thinks the whole house belongs to _____. _____ washes out _____ clothes and hangs them all over the bathroom. Between the two of _____ I think I'm going nuts. Sometimes _____ wish I had never heard of brothers and sisters. Look! Someone has been in my room again. I can tell because my sweater isn't on the floor where I left it. What nerve! What's this? _____ left me a note.

Hi,

Billy and I have gone for a walk. _____ cried all afternoon because _____ thought you were mad at him about the homework paper. _____ is really sorry.

We made some cookies and left them for you in the kitchen. _____ love you.

Helen

Gosh, I've got a nice brother and a neat sister.

(Dorothy Watson)

In the following selection, students may choose to insert a proper name rather than a pronoun. After the reading, discuss how they made decisions and why they chose proper names instead of pronouns and vice versa. In English pronouns are used unless names are needed to disambiguate the persons being referenced.

A Pet for Franklin

The morning was bright and sunny as Franklin and _____ mother walked to the pet store. Franklin was excited. _____ was soon going to have a pet of _____ own. In a few minutes _____ would pick out just the pet _____ wanted.

They entered the store and began to look around. Franklin had no idea what to choose. _____ saw so many wonderful animals to pick from. How would he ever choose just one? _____ mother smiled as _____ watched _____ face. _____ understood _____ problem and waited patiently.

Suddenly they heard a whistling noise. _____ looked up over _____ heads into a cage filled with feathers flying in every direction.

"Mother, what are those great birds?"

"Parakeets," _____ answered.

"Just what I want!" _____ said. "I can teach _____ to talk."

Franklin's mother smiled. "Are you sure you want a parakeet?"

"Absolutely," _____ answered.

Franklin and _____ mother walked to the counter where a man was putting away pet food.

The man smiled when Franklin said, "_____ want to buy a parakeet."

The man asked, "What color bird do _____ want?"

Franklin answered, "I don't care just so long as it can learn to talk."

"Then you want a male parakeet. They seem to learn to talk better than the females do."

Franklin's mother smiled at that comment but paid for _____ bird anyway. _____ also bought a cage and some food.

_____ was very happy as _____ walked home with new pet.

"Great day," said Franklin.

"I'm glad," said _____ mother. And if the new pet had already learned to talk, _____ might have said, "Good choice!"

(Dorothy Watson)

Expanding: Encourage students to talk about the pronouns they use when referring to animals. When they think of a dog, cat, horse, or cow, do they usually think of *he, she,* or *it?*

Invite students to keep track of how different authors refer to various animals. Interested students might interview family members to find out if they have a gender preference for certain animals.

Explore pronoun references to inanimate objects such as ships, cars, and hurricanes. Consider how such conventions develop. Students who know another language can contribute information about gender marking in other languages.

With the class write a short story without pronouns. Discuss with the students that some languages don't have pronouns. What other cues are available in the text to provide information about gender?

Students may want to keep a record of pronoun referents they find ambiguous in their reading. They should record the page number, book, author, and where the pronoun occurred. These can be used for additional class discussions on pronoun references after the students have collected three or four examples each.

Readings for Expanding This Strategy Lesson

Adamson, Joy. *Born Free*. New York, NY: Bantam Books, 1960.
   The life histories of Elsa, a lion, and her cubs interacting with humans
   and their own natural habitat. Pronoun references to animals provide
   challenges.

Cowen-Fletcher, Jane. *Mama Zooms*. New York, NY: Scholastic, 1993.
   A boy's wonderful mama takes him zooming everywhere with her because
   her wheelchair is a zooming machine.

Kopper, Lisa. *Daisy Thinks She's a Baby*. New York, NY: Alfred A. Knopf, 1994.
   Baby doesn't like it when Daisy the dog copies everything she does; but
   when Daisy becomes a mother, Baby likes that a lot.

STRATEGY LESSON: RELATIONAL WORDS AND PHRASES

Evaluation: Who Will Benefit

This strategy lesson will benefit students:

- whose reading and retellings indicate that they have trouble predicting relational structures involving words and phrases such as *though, even though, although*, and *as though*; therefore they lose text continuity;
- who frequently miscue on relational units or frequently regress to reread them; or
- who do not take the entire discourse into consideration to construct meaning from all relational information.

Specific Rationale

Structurally, stories and articles include paragraphs, sentences, clauses, and words that show complex relationships between and among people, events, places, things, and ideas. These relationships are often indicated by a clause marker, an adverb, or a conjunction. Examples of these relationships include:

Cause
Since my mom spilled coffee on my paper, I didn't bring it.
He tripped on the step and hit his head; *consequently*, he took an unexpected visit to the hospital.

Contrast
I like my brother; *however*, I sometimes have to get away from him.
I have a bad tooth and the dentist frightens me. *Nevertheless* I go for a checkup every six months.

Time
The pot boiled over; *subsequently*, the odor of burned stew filled the room.
When the boys got home from school the wind began to blow; *then* the rain poured.

Purpose
Stop playing the piano *so* I can go to sleep.
He edged closer *in order* to get a better look.

Students who never miscue on relational words or phrases may nevertheless not understand their meaning. This lack of awareness may become evident through the reader's retelling. There are several possible reasons for students' problems with grasping meaning relationships.

In some cases there is a difference between the oral and written terms used for the clause relationships. Sometimes the relational word is seldom used in oral English. In other cases the relational word is not common in the speaker's dialect. Compare these oral and written forms:

Oral:	He walked *like* he was hurt.
Written:	He walked *as though* he were hurt.
Oral:	He finally paid his book fine *so* it's possible to take books out of the library again.
Written:	He finally paid his fine, *thus* making it possible to take books out of the library again.
Oral:	I asked *did* she want to help me.
Written:	I asked *if* she wanted to help me.

In the following examples it is possible to predict more than one relational word. It is not until later in the sentence that it becomes obvious which prediction is appropriate. The reader's sentence is syntactically and semantically acceptable beyond the miscue (see slash mark in each example), therefore making it difficult for some readers to self-correct.

> *then*
> He went to the store when he was not hungry / in order to purchase his food
>
> with greater objectivity.

> *what*
> It all happened so fast that I could not for the life of me remember that I was
>
> supposed to be / at the doctor's office at three o'clock.

Sometimes a syntactically acceptable sentence can be produced with an alternate relational word. However, when the acceptable sentence produces a change of meaning, problems in understanding may occur:

> *what*
> He didn't know that the boy wanted to be brave or dead.

Often the relationship exceeds clause and sentence boundaries. In the following examples the reader needs to predict on the basis of the semantic cues of an entire paragraph or even of the entire text. The less knowledge readers have of the content of the material, the more difficulty they have understanding such relationships.

> Preventive dental care is important for all children. An important aspect in dental care is regular visits to the dentist. *Unfortunately,* this practice can be accompanied by pain.

> All you have to do to get a loan is flash a credit card or write a check. For more substantial amounts of money *though, or* if you haven't yet established credit, you still have to take out an installment loan.

Students should consider the role of relational words by focusing on how events, characters, and setting interrelate with each other to construct the plot, theme, and concepts or generalizations of the text. A focus on constructing meaning within the context of the entire discourse is the greatest help possible in predicting appropriate relational wording. Such a goal provides semantic cues to confirm or to self-correct if the prediction does not fit the syntactic pattern of the text.

Children use *and, but, so,* and *because* appropriately in oral language from a very early age. They also understand that events, characters, and settings have relationships to each other. Learners need to expand on this knowledge to help them comprehend written language as easily as they do oral language.

Some relational words and phrases may need to become the object of a strategy lesson. For example, *though* causes problems for a number of reasons. Although relationships expressed through phrases that include *though* are found in written materials for readers as young as seven or eight, many speakers do not use such complex relational terms in their oral language until they are older.

Even though, as though, although, and *though* have different meaning relationships in different contexts, although they often seem to express contrasting relationships:

It seemed *as though* I would never get there.

The odds were against him. He went, *though.*

Although (*though*) older than his brother, he was much shorter.

Since *though,* as an adverb, can appear in different places in a sentence it is often difficult to predict:

She walked *even though* her knee hurt.

Even though her knee hurt, she walked.

Since *though* is movable within the sentence, readers often predict *thought* or *through* in certain syntactic slots. Additionally, *thought* and *through* are similar graphophonically to *though,* and since they occur more often than *though,* they are likely to be predicted in some *though* slots:

thought
I left though John was happy.

through
He left without a peep, though the door had smashed his foot.

If readers are inferring meaning rather than focusing on the graphophonic system, they will become aware when their predictions are not acceptable and will make efforts to correct. Some readers, however, are so tied to graphophonic information that they consistently make substitutions such as *thought* or *through* for *though.* These students may also be helped by "Strategy Lesson: Repeated Substitutions" in Chapter 5.

The following lesson will focus on helping readers infer the relationships expressed by *as though, even though, although,* and *though.*

Strategy Lesson Experience

Initiating: Discuss the points made in the "Specific Rationale" above. Ask students how they might translate some of the examples into conversational speech or use similar examples that are more relevant to the students' experiences. Talk about the similarities and differences between the written and oral expressions of relational wording.

Either write a passage that contains relational wording or use one of the following selections. Read the paragraph aloud if the learners do not tend to use the forms in their oral language. Discuss what is learned about the character(s) in the passage. What opinions of them are formed? Help learners concentrate on inferring information from all the semantic cues in the paragraph, not just in a few surrounding words.

Selection 1

The Blue Stars hockey team is the best team in the league. The captain of the team is Leonard Thomas. He is tall, very strong, and a great hockey player. He does, however, have a big problem that drives people crazy. Leonard acts as though he is the only good player on the team. In fact, he acts as though he is the best hockey player in the world.

Selection 2

Rudy and May are my best friends. We're in the same class in school. We live on the same street. The three of us get along well most of the time. Every afternoon we go to one of our houses. Sometimes we do homework. Most of the time we talk about our teacher or other kids in class. I really like Rudy and May a lot but sometimes they make fun of me, and that hurts my feelings. Sometimes they act as though they are my enemies instead of my friends. They act as though they aren't hurting my feelings.

Selection 3

Eli and Grace walked down the narrow street. Eli tried to look as though he wasn't scared. He smiled at Grace and said, "We will be home soon." They walked quickly, looking back every once in a while.

In order to act as though everything was the same as always Eli asked, "How was school today?" But all he was really thinking about was the weird noise and a blue light that seemed to be coming out of nowhere.

If students don't mention that *like* can be substituted for *as though*, talk about that possibility. What else can be substituted for *as though* without changing meaning?

Explore the notion that authors often choose to use more formal language in their writing than is common in oral language. An important point is that just as authors have options, readers have the option of restating sentences to construct meaning.

Transacting: Prepare a few sentence pairs such as the following. Use content area material if possible. Invite students to read each pair.

1. The kids in our class do not like to go on trips together most of the time.
2. The day they went to the zoo they enjoyed themselves.

1. The pool was small and crowded with swimmers.
2. Ken put his inflated air mattress in the pool.

1. Wendy jumped into the pool and swam across.
2. The water in the pool was ice cold.

Ask students to combine the first pair of sentences into one sentence without changing the meaning. After they decide on a new sentence, write their dictation on the board. After working on the next sentences individually or in pairs, ask students to share their sentences. If none of the sentences include *although, even though,* or *though* as possible relational words, add some samples to the list.

After a discussion that gives them an opportunity to transform the sentences, ask the students to read the passages below. They may want to fill in the blank or think the word *blank*. Remind them that they might consider a phrase as well as a word to fit the blank. These techniques provide students with ways to transform and re-arrange sentences without changing the meaning. Teachers may prefer writing their own sentences, using names of students and events in which they are interested.

Pat did not like to drink milk. Her mother said that milk was good for her and that she should drink it.

Restatement: Pat's mother said that milk was good for her and she should drink it _____ Pat did not like milk.

Most of the time Linda doesn't play baseball well. She tries to be a good player, but usually strikes out or flies out to an outfielder. Today Linda hit some good ones. She got a single and was hit home. She almost made it to third the second time she came up to bat, but she was tagged out.

Restatement: Today Linda played ball very well _____ she isn't usually a good ball player.

Karen always asked questions. She wanted answers to everything she didn't understand. She knew she might get into trouble, but she kept asking questions anyway.

Restatement: Karen kept asking questions _____ she might get into trouble for asking them all the time.

Margaret worked hard to get enough money to buy expensive skis. Both her parents had jobs, but they were not rich. Margaret's parents told her they didn't think she should spend a lot of money on skis, but she bought expensive ones anyway.

Restatement: Margaret bought expensive skis _____ her parents told her not to spend too much money on them.

Invite students to share their restatements and to talk about how the restatements kept the original meaning. If the learners do not use some form of *though* in the sentences, provide *even though, though,* or *although* where appropriate as alternatives.

Applying: Before students read the selections below, review the purposes of the lessons they used during the *Initiating* and *Transacting* phases. Remind them that the strategies they have been using include:

- concentrating on what the sentence means in relationship to other sentences and to the entire discourse;
- mentally rearranging or transforming the sentences to make them easier to understand;
- substituting a known word or phrase that retains meaning when encountering an unfamiliar word or phrase; and
- thinking "blank" or skipping a word when unable to make an appropriate substitution.

After they read the following selections, ask students to mark in the margin of the text where they used one of the options or strategies suggested in this lesson.

Bikes

Tom and Danny were good friends. The two boys went everywhere together. When Tom went to the movies, Danny went too. When Danny went bike riding, Tom went too. One day Tom said to Danny, "I want to get some books to read. Let's go to the library."

Danny didn't like books but he wanted to be with his friend, so off he went, even though he didn't like libraries very much either.

When the boys got to the library, Tom took books from the shelves and began to read parts of them. Danny looked around for something to do. He saw a sign on a table that said "Books on Bikes." Danny loved anything about bikes so for the first time books looked interesting to him.

There were so many different books and magazines about bikes! Danny couldn't believe that there could be so many. Some told how to fix bikes. Other books showed how bikes looked a long time ago. Some of the magazines showed how different parts of the bike had changed over the years.

Danny was still looking at the books and magazines when Tom said, "Come on, Danny, it's getting late." Danny looked at his watch. He and Tom had been in the library for an hour. Even though he still didn't like libraries, he had found something interesting and had enjoyed himself.

"Maybe we'll come back again sometime," Danny said.

"You act as though you like libraries," Tom said.

Danny acted as though he didn't hear his friend, but he was smiling.

(YETTA GOODMAN)

The Stormy Night

Linda walked to the window, where her brother Jud was standing. He was looking at the rain hitting the windowpane.

"What a terrible storm," he said as lightning flashed and a loud clap of thunder sounded.

"I hope Mom and Dad are all right," said Linda, joining her brother at the window. "I hope they stay at the restaurant. I don't want them to drive home in this thunderstorm, even though I wish they were here."

"Me, too," her brother whispered, but he was feeling a little uneasy alone in the house with his sister on a dark, stormy night. Linda went back to her reading. Jud still watched the storm.

It began to rain harder, the lightning became brighter, and the thunder much louder. It seemed as though the storm was right on top of them. Suddenly, after a very loud thunderclap, the lights went out. Now, Linda and Jud were in total darkness.

"Where are you?" asked Jud. "I can't see you."

"I'm over here, in the next room," answered Linda. "I can't see you either."

"Keep talking," Jud said. "Even though I can't see you, I can hear you."

"Okay. I'll keep talking, and you do the same thing. We'll both try to get closer to each other. But be careful not to hit your head or stub your toe."

So Linda and Jud began to walk slowly toward each other, even though they couldn't see anything in the darkness. They slid their feet along the floor so they wouldn't stub their toes. And they kept talking. Outside, the storm was still raging. The rain was falling as hard as ever, even though there was less thunder. It seemed as though the main part of the storm was moving away.

"We're getting closer," said Jud. "I can even hear your breathing."

"Just keep on moving," said his sister.

"Ouch!" Jud screeched. "I just hit my toe against the table."

"You must be moving too fast. Slow down."

"Where are you now?" asked Jud.

Linda thought a moment, then laughed and said, "I think I passed you, although if I did, we should have bumped."

Just then the lights went on. Both Jud and Linda laughed when they saw that they had passed each other. In fact, Jud had almost walked into the next room.

A while later, their parents arrived.

"I thought you would be upset when the lights went out," said Dad. "What did you do?"

"Oh, nothing much," said Linda, winking at her brother. "It was nothing to get excited about."

(BARRY SHERMAN)

Discuss the strategies the students used for constructing meaning. This lesson should be short and to the point.

Expanding: Read *What Good Luck, What Bad Luck* (Charlip 1972) to the students. Talk briefly about the pattern of the text. Then invite learners to write their own picture books using relational terms as themes. For example, if a book were called *Even Though*, one page might say, "*Even though* an elephant weighs a ton . . . " (accompanied by an illustration) followed by a page that says, "It can dance on the head of this pin" (another illustration). A book called *Except* might start with, "I flew around the world in my own super jet last night . . ." followed by, ". . . *except* I was dreaming at the time." Writers might share their books, while listeners make predictions based on the terms used.

Suggest that students be on the alert for the use of relational words in their reading, especially in the content areas. Interested students might categorize the words according to whether they suggest cause, contrast, time, or purpose.

If students keep their own personal dictionaries, they may want to add relational terms they are exploring. Any one relational word or phrase seldom occurs more than a few times in a story. It is, therefore, important for students to read widely if they are to encounter a variety of such words or phrases.

Readings for Expanding This Strategy Lesson

Charlip, Remy. *Fortunately.* New York, NY: Four Winds Press, 1964.
   Good and bad luck accompany Ned from New York to Florida on his way to a surprise party.

McNaughton, Colin. *Suddenly.* San Diego, CA: Harcourt, 1994.
   A story about the adventures of Preston, the little pig, who always seems to avoid the wolf.

STRATEGY LESSON: NEGATIVES AND MEANING

Evaluation: Who Will Benefit

This strategy lesson will benefit readers who:

- omit or insert negatives resulting in loss of meaning; or
- omit or insert negatives in materials because of misconceptions or limited experience.

Specific Rationale

It is not only the presence of negative words, such as *not, no, never,* and *none,* that indicates negation in English; the meaning that readers infer from a story also provides cues.

Often, relational words such as *although, yet, but,* and *nevertheless* support the semantic cues being developed across the text and help the reader predict negatives. Words such as *do* and *any* tend to be used differently in sentences that contain a negative than in those that do not.

Substitutions of a negative for a positive or vice versa can happen especially when:

- *There is little or no change of meaning.* When the statement is insignificant to the major plot of the story, the substitution is probably inconsequential.

   He wasn't a little bit sleepy so he continued to sing.
   <small>was</small>

In dialogue, questions can be asked that cause no difference in meaning regardless of whether a negative or positive statement is used.

   Hold the hammer right! Don't you know you have to hold it at the end?
   <small>Do</small>

In these cases the use of negatives makes little difference to the story and, therefore, is not considered a problem.

- *There is a misconception or misunderstanding.* For students who focus on meaning, the strategy of predicting negatives will only cause problems when they do not fully understand the events of the story because of their own misconceptions about or lack of familiarity with the events.

   The children always set the table before dinner. They placed the napkins carefully and set the large bowls in place. During the roundup, when the men were out on the range, the tables were not set carefully.

Readers may not understand the social behavior at the ranch; and if that behavior is not developed throughout the story, they may easily omit the *not* in a passage such as the one above.

   Each evening they made a wide circuit of the bedding grounds and built fires on high points, where they could be seen for miles around.

If students are unaware that fires scare away animals and assume that the fires are to be hidden, it would be reasonable to insert a negative in the verb phrase *could be seen.* In this case, the negative results in a logical and possible, although changed, meaning.

- *A two-word negative appears in text.* Occasionally readers predict a negative contraction for a two word negative (for example *don't* for *do not*). The reader may then realize that the negative is in its full form (*do not*) and will self-correct or produce what sounds like "I don't not want to go." Such readers are overemphasizing graphic information and may be unaware that a contracted form (don't) for a full form (do not) or vice versa is appropriate for proficient reading and does not need to be corrected.

The best way to help readers predict negation is to help them focus on meaning construction. In addition to the context which provides clues to negation, certain words and phrases provide information indicating that a negative may occur or has occurred.

Many modern languages have an obligatory double-negative form. However, most forms of written English use the negative only once in a sentence, except for dialogue representing dialects that retain the double negative. Double negatives such as in *He don't do nothing nohow* have the advantage of providing redundant information for the reader or listener. Since the redundancy of the multiple negative is not available in most written English, readers must rely on other cues to predict negation appropriately.

The lesson that follows helps the reader think of the developing meaning of the story as well as to explore language cues that signal negation.

Strategy Lesson Experience

Initiating: Provide students with a copy of "Scenes for Negatives and Positives" (or write similar ones that reflect your students' interests). The questions accompanying each scene give students various ideas for dialogues. Some of the stories will elicit language that includes negatives and others will not. Put students into small groups to write out or act out the scenes.

When the groups have selected the scenes they want to write or act out, ask each group to describe the setting. This is done so that the group will have images of the people and places in the scene. The students may want to tape-record the scene or write the narrative as a shared story on the board or transparency. Together the class might compare the conversations to determine how the language of each differs depending on whether it describes a negative or positive incident. Help students consider the language, mood, and plot development that suggest the negative and the positive.

Scenes for Negatives and Positives

Scene: Penny, Jill, Liz, and Carol are going fishing. Each brings along different bait but enough for all the others. One brings artificial bait (you decide what kind); another live worms; a third, cheese; and a fourth, (your favorite bait).

- What would their dialogue be if they all decide to use the same bait and not to use any of the other three?
- What would their dialogue be if each likes her own bait best and rejects the other three?
- What would their dialogue be if they decide all the baits are equally good and each will use some of the bait brought by the others?

Scene : Kate and Jeff have a large dog. Dad asks them to wash it.

- What would the dialogue be if the children refuse to wash the dog?
- What would the dialogue be if the children agree to wash the dog?
- What would the dialogue be if one child agrees to wash the dog and the other child refuses?
- What would the dialogue be if one child agrees to wash the front end of the dog and the other child agrees to wash the back end?

Transacting: Invite the students to talk about the three or four conversations possible for each scene. If the following questions have not been answered, consider:

1. In what ways do the dialogues suggest that there might be a negative or a positive statement or incident? On the chalkboard make two columns, labeling one *Negative Characteristics* and the other *Positive Characteristics*. List the characteristics suggested by the students in the appropriate column. In a third column, indicate how the language differs. List a sentence from the story as an example when appropriate. Ask the students to check the characteristics as they proceed through each dialogue to see if additional semantic cues are given for their decisions.
2. In what ways does the mood of the characters suggest whether incidents will be stated in a negative or positive way? Follow the same procedure of listing the characteristics in the appropriate columns. Use the other dialogues to make comparisons and to support the categories developed.
3. What words or phrases are used with negatives that are either not used, or used in different ways, in positive statements? Encourage the students to consider phrases or whole sentences within the total text, as well as words.

Applying: Continue adding to the list of negative and positive characteristics if there is interest. Then, reproduce these columns and encourage students to keep adding to the list from all their other reading. If the lesson becomes too analytical or takes too long, students may lose interest. Follow their lead by using their suggestions, and stop the discussion when interest wanes. It is sometimes useful to place the most interesting examples on a classroom chart. The students can add to this any examples they find. Additions can be discussed every few weeks or so, depending on class interest.

Ask students to be on the alert for instances when authors inform their readers that a negative or positive will be used. Any material is suitable, including their current reading, environmental print, and their own writings.

Expanding: Invite students to select a short passage from any material, including content area resources. Ask a volunteer to read the passage as the author wrote it and again make changes either to positive or negative forms that retain the meaning. Encourage listeners to talk about the two texts. Which seems genuine? Why? Discuss what happens to the language surrounding negative and positive words or phrases when such changes are made.

STRATEGY LESSON: NEGATIVE CONTRACTIONS

Evaluation: Who Will Benefit

This strategy lesson will benefit students who:

- substitute inappropriate look-alike words for negative contractions, for example *want* for *won't,* and who do not correct such miscues.
- read an acceptable contraction for a full form, or vice versa, and then correct such high-quality miscues:

© *shouldn't*
I ∖ should not be in this room.

© *have not*
They ∖ haven't had breakfast yet.

- predict a negative contraction, but when they encounter the full form insert "not" following the contraction:

don't not
I do not go to his house.

can't not
He cannot be in six places at one time.

- because of limited reading experiences, are just beginning to encounter contractions in print.

Specific Rationale

Readers with limited reading experiences may have seldom encountered contracted word forms. Such readers may predict the negative, for example, reading *cannot* for *can't.* As they become aware of the miscue, they self-correct. Although rereading does not usually interfere with constructing meaning, it is inefficient since the reader is concentrating on surface information which slows the reading. The focus of this strategy lesson is to make students aware that:

- written language and oral language have many things in common; and
- it is acceptable to read a contraction for a full form, or vice versa, and that such miscues need not be corrected.

Strategy Lesson Experience

Initiating: This lesson helps students become aware that contractions are alternate options in oral and written language and that reading a negative contraction (won't, can't, don't, wouldn't) for the full form, (will not, cannot, do not, would not) does not produce a change in meaning.

After children finish sharing a big book, they could return to the written text to search for examples of contractions or for full form phrases that could be contracted. For example, in the big book *Little Blue Ben* by Phoebe Gilman (1989) the following appears:

He can't be in there.
It's too cold. It's too wet.
"Oh, yuck!" says Blue Ben.
"These eggs are not yummy!"

Discuss the possibility of reading *cannot* for *can't* and *aren't* for *are not.* Talk with students about what the apostrophe represents in negative contractions.

If students point out other contracted forms such as *it's* (*It's too cold. It's too wet.*), discuss the appropriateness of substituting *it is* for *it's*. If big books are not available, use other appropriate reading materials.

Transacting: Ask students to think of something they do on a regular basis: go to the mall, play games, take a bus to school, read, write, and so on. On the chalkboard categorize negative and positive reactions to the activity:

> I like to go to the mall. I do not like to go to the mall.

Ask the students who have a positive response to explain why. Do the same for those who have negative responses. List the comments, being careful to record negative contractions or full forms exactly as the student says them. When there are at least five or six examples in each list underline and discuss all the contractions and full forms. What difference does it make if we use *do not* or *don't*? Help students realize that these different forms do not make a difference in meaning. Rather, they represent an option a speaker or an author uses sometimes because of the rhythm of the sentence.

Applying: Pursue this lesson only if students continue to need help with contracted forms. Write on the board or on a transparency:

Tomorrow I will _____ .
Tomorrow I will not _____ .
Tomorrow I won't_____ .

When I am in the kitchen I can _____ .
When I am in the kitchen I can't _____ .
When I am in the kitchen I cannot _____ .

I like to _____ .
I don't like to _____ .
I do not like to _____ .

Invite students to complete the sentences. Ask if there is any difference in meaning when they use the full or contracted forms. Discuss any preference they have for one over the other and why.

Expanding: Encourage students to ask questions about all forms of language. An inquiry concerning negative contractions might introduce the student researchers to "language hunts" in which they engage in the following experiences: tape-record a conversation, analyze the recorded data, and report their findings to the class. List, giving as much context as possible, all the negative contractions or full-form equivalents heard in one recorded event:

- fifteen minutes of a television comedy show
- fifteen minutes of a mystery show
- fifteen minutes of a news broadcast
- fifteen minutes of a social studies discussion in class
- fifteen minutes of an address by the President
- other

Record all the negative contractions or full-form equivalents in the following:

- four pages of their favorite book
- comics in the newspaper

- a front page newspaper story
- a news magazine story
- a page of a science book
- other

Using the results of the investigations, discuss whether contractions or full forms are used more in oral language or in written language and which forms are used in different genres. As students are researching this area, ask them to be alert to other language forms that might be interesting topics for study.

5

Focus on the Syntactic Cueing System

GENERAL RATIONALE

Through the years, there has been a great deal of change in the way linguists look at language. Linguists do not view grammar prescriptively, thinking that there are iron-clad rules governing how people speak, read, and write. Rather, linguists consider language to be a medium for human communication. Like all other aspects of culture, language constantly changes and has variations from group to group and from place to place.

By studying the ways people speak and read, linguists have discovered that every language has rules. These rules cannot be imposed on students through grammar books, curriculum mandates, or even by teachers. Rather, they are intuitively learned by growing up in a society that uses the language.

The term *grammar* or *syntax* refers to the structure or organization of language that facilitates making meaning. When very young children intuitively pick up language cues, including the relationship of sentences to each other, they use their knowledge of syntax to construct meaning. Children also intuitively become aware of the relationships between units of language. They come to understand that morphemes such as *-s* and *-ed* on the ends of words change tense and plurality. They understand the relationships of words within phrases, phrases within clauses, sentences, and paragraphs, and the relationships of all these units that result in a cohesive whole text.

To construct meaning in English we depend a great deal on the order of linguistic units. For example, the position of the words within sentences influences the relationship of concepts. The words *tickled, Betty*, and *Mary* tell nothing about who has done the tickling or who got tickled. A structure or frame must support the semantic intent, as in *Mary tickled Betty.*

Because of the structure or syntax of language, readers, writers, listeners, and speakers can understand complex meanings. For example, readers can predict a question through the use of markers such as *why, when,* or *who* positioned at the beginning of a sentence. Inverted sentence order, as in *Is she? Can you? Did he?*, also helps readers predict questions. Word order also signals declarative and imperative sentences, as in *I'm going to take the leap* and *Run for your life, Sally.*

English words can be categorized into five grammatical functions: nouns, verbs, adjectives, adverbs, and function words. We use grammatical terms according to the function they serve in a sentence. For example, *the* is a noun in the sentence *The is a word that occurs frequently in English* because it is the subject of the sentence; it refers to an abstract idea and is followed by a verb phrase. *The* can also be inflected like a noun, as in *There are five the's in the previous sentence.* In *To measure the temperature, very few people fry eggs on the sidewalk,* both *the's* are indefinite articles that refer in general to temperature and sidewalks. In *The story about the Mississippi River ended,* both *the's* are definite articles; that is, they refer to specific nouns.

English has a limited number of word orders, or syntactic patterns, and each has distinguishing characteristics. This syntactic or grammatical patterning makes it possible for readers to predict and then confirm their reading. Certain grammatical functions fit into structures while others do not. For example, the first blank below can only be filled with a verb and the second only with an adjective:

We happily _____ our old school song.

She played a _____ tune on the flute.

Dialect groups within a language use overlapping but not identical rule systems while speakers of different languages use sets of rules that are different from other languages. Humans could not communicate as easily as they do if the members speaking the same language did not know and use their language's cueing systems. Teachers promote proficiency with the rules of language by facilitating authentic communication and normal interaction with and among learners. And through strategy lessons we engage students in talking about language as an object of wonderment and inquiry.

It is important that educators become knowledgeable about language in general and the language of their students specifically. Through such awareness we are less likely to impose inappropriate and inhibiting rules and instructional procedures on learners. Such restrictions are particularly discouraging and defeating for students whose languages or dialects are different from that of the teacher.

Some important points concerning syntactic function and grammatical relations that apply to reading include:

- Within the context of all language cues, syntax is the frame that supports meaning.
- Children are proficient language users by the time they enter school; they intuitively know how to use the syntax of their language.
- Reading demands the application of a language user's knowledge of syntax. In other words, to construct meaning from a text, the reader must use its structure.
- A reader's language or dialect may be reflected in syntactic changes in the text without loss of meaning.
- Readers substitute, omit, and insert words and phrases within the syntactic structure of a sentence.

STUDENTS WHO NEED TO FOCUS ON THE SYNTACTIC CUEING SYSTEM

Students with little or no confidence in their reading ability need to become consciously aware of their knowledge of the structure of language. Insecure readers need to take risks as they use the structure of language to infer and predict a writer's intentions.

By listening to students read during teacher-student conferences, teachers can determine if the reading *sounds like language,* that is, if miscues result in syntactically acceptable structures. Teachers might ask: As you are making sense of your reading, does the language in the story help you keep reading? Where does the language bother you? Students need to know that the aim of reading is to make meaning and that grammatical patterns help them do that. The intention of the following strategy lessons is to help students develop insights into their uses of the syntactic cueing system that will in turn help them construct meaning.

The *syntactic acceptability* score from Procedure III of the Reading Miscue Inventory (RMI) profile helps identify students who need support to make appropriate use of their knowledge of syntax to predict and confirm as they read. Before choosing predicting and confirming strategy lessons that focus on syntactic cues, it is important to examine the different qualities of students' miscues. Gloria, a second-grader, made the following RMI Procedure III scores on a story she read.

Syntactic Acceptability	Y 60%	N 40%	
Semantic Acceptability	Y 55%	N 45%	
Meaning Change	Y 84%	P 10%	N 6%
Graphic Similarity	H 62%	S 28%	N 10%
Retelling	48%		

Following are typical miscues from Gloria's reading:

Who
"You are too little," said Father.

Her   s-s-some
"Here is something you can do."

Gloria's miscues are not corrected even though they are syntactically and semantically unacceptable. Gloria's scores and the pattern of her miscues indicate that she will benefit from strategy lessons that focus on the syntactic cueing system.

In contrast, in the examples below Carol uses grammatical information to correct her miscues.

ⓒ
and they kill a fair ⎰number‚of people.

Carol inserts a period after *number*, predicting the end of the sentence. But she then sees *of people*, and makes the decision to disconfirm her prediction by orally rereading the end of the sentence appropriately.

ⓒ
hope
His sister, Suzanne, ⎰was hopping around and calling to him.

Carol reads *His sister, Suzanne, was hope around* and realizes that what she has read does not sound like language and is not making sense. She disconfirms her prediction, returns to the beginning of the verb phrase, and corrects. Carol's profile of miscues (syntactic acceptability Y 93 percent, N 7 percent) and her very complete retelling do not indicate a need for syntactically focused strategy lessons.

The following *pattern* of reading behaviors may indicate a possible need for strategy lessons that focus on sampling, inferring, predicting, and confirming syntactic cues:

- Readers who are so insecure with the language of a written text that they will not predict, even when syntax is supportive.
- Readers who predict a syntactic structure that is not acceptable with the rest of the sentence and fail to disconfirm and self-correct their prediction based

on text that follows the miscue. These readers' scores are seldom higher than 60 percent for syntactically acceptable structures.

- Readers who are not confident reading a new genre.
- Readers who overcorrect; that is, they make syntactically and semantically acceptable miscues, but decide that it is necessary to correct anyway.

STRATEGY LESSON: COOPERATIVE CONTROLLED CLOZE

This strategy lesson is an outgrowth of the collaborative work of Brian Cambourne and Yetta Goodman.

Evaluation: Who Will Benefit

Students who are hesitant to predict words or phrases in order to continue reading will benefit from this lesson. When these reluctant readers meet an unfamiliar word or phrase they often do one of the following:

- pause for a long time before attempting other strategies;
- deliberately omit words and phrases;
- produce nonword substitutions that have high graphic similarity, but do not fit syntactically; or
- resist making use of their own knowledge and experiences as they read.

This strategy lesson provides a chance to talk about the structure and function of language in a supportive setting. It helps readers know they have intuitive knowledge about language that they can use in their reading.

The lesson lends itself to any age group, across genre, and in all discipline areas. By careful design of the rate and type of deletion, Cooperative Controlled Cloze can be adjusted to challenge, assure success, and accommodate the reader.

Specific Rationale

Cooperative Controlled Cloze (CCC) helps readers simultaneously focus on language and on their own comprehension. That is, students examine and talk about both the language of the text and about their own construction of meaning. Working with each other, students decide what words or phrases go into specific slots. This experience shows that learners are capable of thinking and talking about language as an object of study as they construct meaning.

As readers collaborate in making decisions using a wide range of cues in order to predict and construct meaning, they become consciously aware of their language knowledge and their abilities as readers. Such awareness helps readers become more confident and autonomous and encourages them to take charge of their own learning.

Throughout the decision-making discussion, teachers keep notes about students' comments that provide insights into learners' understanding of the reading process and of language, and also indicate which areas need more support through additional strategy lessons. Teachers' records are evidence for continuous evaluation of reading and language learning growth.

Although CCC are texts that students have not read, the texts contain a large portion of familiar language and relevant content. The material is presented in its entirety: a short story, a complete incident, or a fully developed concept. CCC can be made from materials found in content textbooks, magazine articles, encyclopedias written for students, and literature for children and adolescents. Students may volunteer to use some of their own writings.

In constructing material, the complexity of the placement of slots must be considered. Complexity is a function of the number of deletions, the predictability of the inserted words and phrases, and the concept load of the material. The greater the number of deletions the more difficult the task for the reader. Teachers must consider the confidence of the reader when determining how challenging the experience should be and therefore how many deletions to make. The point is to build strength through success, not to undermine the reader's confidence.

Predictability is relatively easy within a context that is highly constrained grammatically. That means there is a small set of options that leaves little doubt in the reader's mind.

The hill was hard to climb and _____ path was muddy.

On the other hand, when there are many options, predictability is diminished, and readers may have trouble deciding on an appropriate language structure. The following sentence is somewhat troublesome because it can be read without inserting any word in the blank:

He is the kind of person _____ everybody likes.

If students are unaware that they bring their own experiences and language knowledge to reading and are also unaware that a range of clues helps them understand a single-word concept, then words that embody concepts may be chosen for deletion.

His love of truth and _____ was well known.

The grammatical function of the slots constrain the reader's focus. For example, pronouns cause readers to focus on monitoring the story line for characters. It may become necessary to reread or even read ahead to discover the linguistic cues that point to the character's gender or whether there is more than one character. Function words, such as *the, a, in,* and *to* focus students' attention on the relationship between setting and characterization. (See "Strategy Lesson: Repeated Substitutions," Chapter 5, page 208.)

The first few sentences of a paragraph used for CCC usually remain intact to provide a context and greater predictability, especially for those inexperienced with the strategy.

Usually, the shorter the sentence in which the slot occurs or the shorter the story used for selected slotting, the more difficult the task. Compare "The Peddler and the Tiger" below with these sentences:

The boy rowed across the river in a small _____ painted black with a yellow strip on the stern.
The yellow-striped black _____ was easy to see.

The Peddler and the Tiger

One night an old tiger was out in the rain. It was very dark and the rain was falling hard. The _____ was wet and cold. He tried to find a _____ place so that he could get out of the rain. But he could find _____. There was nothing but rain. How it did _____. At last the tiger came to an _____ wall and he lay down against it. It was not quite so _____ and miserable, so he fell _____. While he slept a peddler came _____. The peddler had lost his donkey and was trying to find him. It was so dark the peddler could hardly _____. The rain fell _____ and faster. He was freezing _____ and soaking _____. The peddler looked for a _____ place but could find _____. At last he came to the old _____ against which the tiger lay asleep. The peddler saw the dim _____ of an _____ close to the wall. "This must be my _____ ," he said. So he took the tiger by the ear and began to kick and _____ him. "You old rascal," he said. "At _____ I have found you. What did you run _____ for?" To say the least the tiger was surprised. As he began to stir himself the peddler jumped on his _____ and shouted, "Get up now, I want to go _____." The sleepy tiger got up and _____.

Strategy Lesson Experience

The words or phrases to be replaced are carefully chosen to maximize the purpose of the lesson. It is preferable that the teacher guide students through a CCC experience at least once before they work on their own. If the teacher leads the lesson, the material can be placed on an overhead transparency, and after talking with each other, students might fill in the blanks. When small groups are working together, the material may be duplicated. Sometimes the group works with one copy in order to encourage collaboration, discussion, and consensus. Other times each student has a copy and different responses and justification for the choices are encouraged.

Initiating and Transacting: As teachers initiate the CCC strategy lesson, they make suggestions that lead to thinking about language and content and demonstrate the use of questions such as: What would make sense? How do you know? Can you find anything in the text that supports your decision? Are there any alternative suggestions? If we read on will your suggestion make sense? Will it help to reread? How does this help? The teacher uses accepted linguistic terminology such as *noun*, *prepositional phrase*, and so on, demonstrating the use of linguistic terms in context.

All responses, regardless of the degree to which they fit the slots, should be accepted but questioned with *Why do you think so?* In this way, students see that the teacher challenges all responses, not just those thought to be wrong or inappropriate. Students are encouraged to ask questions and to challenge each other in a supportive way.

The use of any cloze procedure must be carefully considered; therefore, the rationale for CCC should be discussed with students, including how and why the passage is constructed as it is. The usual procedure for CCC can be altered for the group, but in general is as follows:

1. Read the passage aloud together.
2. Discuss each blank until everyone agrees, or the members write their own choices in the blank. There need not be consensus, but all answers should be justified.
3. Share agreements and disagreements to see if anyone can be convinced to change responses.

4. Read the passage silently. When each student finishes reading make any appropriate changes.
5. Discuss whether they prefer their choices over the author's choices and why. Students come to understand that both authors and readers create their own meanings.

Applying: Middle grade or secondary students may find it informative to categorize their responses according to which insertions they and their peers easily agree on and which stimulate thought and discussion. It may help learners to consider what it is in their backgrounds and the language structures that permits agreement or disagreement.

If each member of the group fills in the blanks independently, they can then compare their responses and either change their answers to agree with others or justify them. Encourage justification on the basis of linguistic information, content, or personal experience.

Expanding: An interested student may volunteer to become a linguistic researcher who takes notes during the group discussion. The purpose of the research is to study the various strategies students use in filling the slots. The researcher may want to focus on the language used by students as they talk about the experience. How people work in groups may be another topic of study. When the researchers report to their peers, the students evaluate their own ability to think and talk about language.

Students may want to predict a larger structure, such as the ending of a story. Invite them to cooperatively write the ending of a story such as "The Peddler and the Tiger."

Readings for Expanding this Strategy Lesson

Rebus Books

Marzollo, Jean. *The Rebus Treasury*. New York, NY: Dial, 1986.

> Rebus books use pictures, usually in noun and verb positions, to represent words, syllables, or phrases. These books are fun and involve readers in interesting ways to expand their opportunities to use blanks to infer meaning. Students can also be involved in writing their own rebus books to share with their classmates.

STRATEGY LESSON: NOUNS AS NAMES OF PEOPLE

Evaluation: Who Will Benefit

This strategy lesson will help students who cannot identify the characters or fail to ascribe certain traits to characters when retelling a story. Such readers may miscue on names, as Ruth did when she repeatedly encountered the name of the main character, Sven, throughout a six-page story. (*UC* indicates an unsuccessful attempt to correct a miscue. Omissions are indicated by circles around the omitted word. Substitutions are written directly over the word for which they were substituted.)

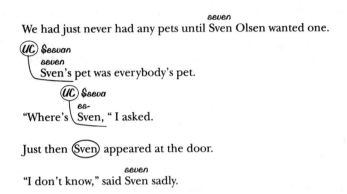

Many readers who read the story from which Ruth's miscues were selected predict *seven* for the first occurrence of *Sven* in the story, but by the second instance, they substitute a proper noun such as *Steve* or *Seever* and usually retain the name throughout the story. Ruth never indicated through her intonation that she was aware that Sven was a name. She tried nonwords ($esvan and $seva), omitted *Sven* in the fourth occurrence, and finally returned to *seven*. Ruth's retelling confirmed that she was unaware of the Sven character in the story. Readers such as Ruth often make miscues that have high graphic similarity between the text and the observed response (*Sven* looks very similar to *seven*) but result in unacceptable linguistic structures.

Some readers are so concerned about pronouncing a name correctly that they either substitute a different name each time it appears, or omit the name throughout the entire story. If, during the retelling, such students show an understanding of the characters, they need to know that what they did in their reading was acceptable because it did not disrupt comprehension. However, they also need to know that their reading can become more efficient if they consistently substitute the same name.

This lesson will help students whose miscue profiles show a graphic similarity score of 75 percent or higher along with syntactic and semantic acceptability scores of 60 percent or lower.

Specific Rationale

Nouns refer to concrete or abstract things or ideas and they function as the subjects and objects of clauses and phrases. Nouns are usually predictable and readers generally have little problem predicting their occurrence in text. Nevertheless, some nouns cause problems in reading.

Proper nouns frequently have spellings that are not common in English, such as *Scavuzzo*, *Papazian*, *Wyche*, *Pakaranadom*, and *Gutierrez*. Readers' background knowledge and the context of the story helps them determine if the proper noun refers to a male or female person, an animal, a geographic location, or even to a commercial brand name. Unless they are familiar with the names based on their culture and background knowledge, students are apt to become inefficient readers if they concentrate on trying to pronounce or sound out proper names, such as the ones in the examples below:

Stanislaw Zychiewicz's family has lived in Chicago for three generations.

Yaityopya Niguisa Nagast Manguist is a country in Africa. It is known to Americans by the name Ethiopia.

The family name of the common squid is Loliginidae, the genus is *Loligo,* and the species is *pealil.*

Readers must rely on their sophisticated use of syntax and focus on searching for meaning rather than concentrating on sounding out proper names. Proficient readers use the following strategies to understand how names fit noun slots. (You might verify these strategies by recalling how you handled the names in the examples above.)

1. Predict a name slot. (Pronouns can often be predicted for the noun.)
2. Omit the name or substitute another name, nickname, pronoun, or initials for the proper name.
3. Determine some physical, occupational, or personal characteristic.
4. Determine the significance of the name to the entire text, and concentrate only on names that the reader believes to be important.

Strategy Lesson Experience

Initiating: Invite students to select one or two troublesome parts as they read the following story silently. Then, discuss with them the four points listed above as they relate to concerns the students raise.

My Friend Larry

When Larry was as old as you are, something always gave him trouble in school. His full name was very long. Everybody thought it was hard to say Larry's name when they saw it written. That was because Larry's full name was Lawrence Annicchiarico. You can imagine the problems that such a long name caused.

Every September, at the beginning of school, Larry's new teacher tried to say his full name: "Lawrence Anni—, Lawrence Annic—, Lawrence, how do you say your name?" And Larry would tell his teacher how to say his name. Of course, by that time, everyone in the class was laughing. Even his friends would laugh. Luckily for Larry, the fun only lasted a day or two. And as he grew up, the laughing over his name bothered him less and less. But then, when he was eighteen, a new problem began.

A few months after his eighteenth birthday, Larry went into the U.S. Army. In the army, soldiers are called by their last names. But "Annicchiarico" was a hard name to say. It was also very long, so the officers shortened the name to "Anni." And this is how Larry became known as Anni to his fellow soldiers.

You can imagine that Larry was not too happy about the name. It sounded like the girl's name "Annie." Sometimes, when Larry and a few friends visited a new town or city, people would laugh when they heard his friends call him Anni. In one way, Larry was lucky. Nobody would laugh too long because he was tall and strong, and people did not want to make him angry.

After Larry left the army, he decided to become a teacher. His long name helped him teach his students an important lesson. That lesson may help you, too.

The first day of school, Larry began by saying, "Hello. My name is Mr. Annicchiarico." He looked at the class and saw that the children were going to have problems with his name. He had to shorten it to make it easy for the class and for the other students in the school. So he wrote his name on the board and said, "This is how my name looks when it is written. It is a very long name and hard to say. Okay. From now on, whenever you want to speak to me, instead of 'Mr. Annicchiarico,' say 'Mr. A.' And when you read my name, instead of trying to sound out all of the letters, read 'Mr. A.'"

And so, Larry became known as Mr. A. in his school. And he taught all his students that they could do the same thing whenever they came to a hard name in a story. If they came to a Russian name such as "Svidrigailov," they could read "Sam" or "Sid" instead. The French name "Jean-Pierre" could be read as "John" or "Jim" or "J.P." The name Mr. Zychiewicwz could be changed to "Mr. Z." You try it the next time you come to a hard name in a story you are reading.

(BARRY SHERMAN)

Transacting: Students having trouble with unfamiliar proper names will report that they had a problem with the name *Annicchiarico*. These readers might discuss the strategies Larry Annicchiarico gave to those who had trouble with his name.

Consider the following questions for additional discussion about "My Friend Larry" and in preparation for discussion for the reading of "The Mad Russian" that follows.

1. What do you know about the characters in the story? How did you get that information?

2. When you read a story, what should you find out about the characters? Is it necessary to know a great deal about every character?

You might list on the board the things students think they should know about characters and consider whether they are the things they learned about Mr. A. or the Mad Russian.

Explore the notion that the significant characters can be set apart from the insignificant characters based on what and how much the author tells about them.

3. What is the author's relationship to the characters? Is the author a character in the story? Is he or she writing about a friend or an acquaintance?

4. Is the pronunciation of the characters' names crucial to understanding the story? Why do you think it is acceptable to call the character in this story Mr. A.? When is it acceptable to omit or substitute another name for an unfamiliar one?

Help students understand that the purpose of silent reading is to gain understanding, to be entertained, or both. Understanding the character is more important than pronouncing his or her name.

5. When might it be important to pronounce someone's name?

Even when reading about famous people, it is more important that students recognize the subjects' historical significance, know what they are famous for, understand their relationships to other people, and grasp aspects of their personalities than it is to sound out a name.

6. How do you find out how to pronounce someone's name?

Discuss the limitations of asking teachers or looking in dictionaries. Sometimes the only reliable source for pronunciation is the person whose name it is. You might want to discuss how the same name can be pronounced differently depending on what language or from what part of a country it originates. Explore the notion that many non-English names are Anglicized even by television and radio reporters.

The Mad Russian

Alexei Mikhail Feodorovich Lermontov was born in New York City in 1916. Two years earlier, his mother and father had come to America from Russia. That was why they gave him a Russian name. But most of his friends found his Russian name hard to say, so they called him "Al" or "Alex." Al's name wasn't really so unusual. "Alexei" in Russian is the same as the English name "Alex." The name "Mikhail" is the same as "Michael." The name "Feodorovich" means that Al was the son of a man named "Theodore." "Lermontov" was Al's last name, just like the American last names "Smith," "Jones," or "Evans." So his American friends might have thought of him as "Alex-Michael-Son-of-Theodore-Lermontov." But it was a lot easier for them to call him "Al" or "Alex."

When Al grew up, he got a new name. His friends started calling him "The Mad Russian" because he did crazy things from time to time, and "mad" is a word that can sometimes mean crazy.

The first crazy thing Al did was when he was in college. He was playing fullback in an important football game. The score was tied 12–12, and Al had the ball. As he started to run with the ball he lost his sense of direction. He was running the wrong way! All of a sudden, he realized that he was going the wrong way, so he turned around and started back. He ran so well that he scored the touchdown that broke the tie. His team went on to win 22–15. Al's run was amazing because he ran 32 yards the wrong way and 62 yards the right way. He had to run a total of 94 yards before he scored the touchdown! It was after this game that his friends started calling him "The Mad Russian."

Alexei did other "mad" things besides running the wrong way in a football game. He learned to fly an airplane, and he became a good pilot. But he also did a few crazy things in the air. Once he tried to fly under a bridge upside down. The plane crashed into the water, and Alexei nearly lost his life. The next crazy thing he did was when he decided to go into the jungles of South America to look for gold and diamonds. His friends didn't see him again for two years. Everyone thought he had died in the jungles. But the Mad Russian was not going to let a jungle stop him. Two years after he started out to look for gold and diamonds, he came back home a rich man.

Al did many crazy things, as if to prove to his friends that "The Mad Russian" really was a good name for him. He would tell his friends that he really should be called "The Mad American" because he was not a Russian at all—he had been born in New York City. But then his friends would say, "Listen, Al, anyone with a name like Alexei Mikhail Feodorovich Lermontov has got to be Russian. And everyone knows you're mad." At this point, Alex and his friends would laugh, and someone would remember one of the crazy things "The Mad Russian" had done. Al had been everywhere and had tried to do almost everything. But he loved to fly airplanes best. That is why he became a fighter pilot in the U.S. Army during World War II.

Al became part of a new fighter squadron on an island far out in the Pacific Ocean. From this island, Al and his friends flew their planes against the enemy. Al's plane was a twin-engine fighter called the P-38 or Lockheed "Lightning." He named his plane "The Mad Russian." The name was painted in big black letters on the plane's nose.

Al and his plane went through many adventures together. Some of them were very crazy. But the last adventure seemed to be the craziest of all. One of the planes in Al's fighter squadron had lost the use of one engine in an air battle. This damaged airplane was trying to return to the base. The plane was flying very slowly. "The Mad Russian" reduced speed and was flying alongside to protect the crippled airplane. The other planes in the squadron went on ahead. Al and his friend flew as fast as they could, but it wasn't fast enough. Suddenly, ten enemy fighters came at Al and his friend from out of the clouds. Al had been watching for signs of enemy planes and saw the ten planes immediately.

"Don't worry," said Al over the radio as he started to turn his plane around to face the enemy fighters. "With 'The Mad Russian' on your side, you don't have a thing to worry about. You just keep heading for home."

Al's friend wanted to help, but he couldn't get his one good engine to produce more power. He could only watch as Al's plane single-handedly took on the ten enemy planes. Because his own plane was too damaged to turn and fight, he had to keep heading for home. He knew that Al didn't have a chance, and he expected to be attacked from behind at any moment. But no plane attacked him, and he returned safely. But "The Mad Russian" did not come back, and no one ever saw Al again. Alexei was listed as Missing in Action, and he was awarded a medal for bravery above and beyond the call of duty.

Some people said that what Al did was the craziest thing he had ever done. They said that he should have kept heading for home and saved himself. How could he have expected to fight ten planes by himself? But "The Mad Russian's" friends knew better. They knew that Al never expected to beat the ten enemy fighters. He did what he felt he had to do, even though he would die.

World War II ended a long time ago. But today, on that lonely island far out in the Pacific Ocean, there are still signs showing that Al's air base had been there. Palm trees grow where P-38 fighters used to take off and land, but it still looks like an airfield. At one corner of the old runway, there is a stone with a picture of a P-38 carved into it. Below the picture are these words: In Memory of "The Mad Russian," Alexei Mikhail Feodorovich Lermontov, Craziest Guy of a Crazy Bunch.

(BARRY SHERMAN)

Applying: Invite students to keep a record of unfamiliar names they read over a two-week period. By recording the entire sentence or sentences in which each name is included with the reference to the name of the book and the page number, students have the context to discuss the syntactic cues that support their meaning construction. To provide even more information ask students to write down two or three things they learned about the person or place as they were reading the story.

At a group meeting or individual conference, ask students to share their examples. What did they learn about the characters? How did they find this out? Encourage learners to focus on understanding character description and development rather than name pronunciation. This is not to imply that we do not care about how names are pronounced; the point is that if pronunciation is the first thing readers attend to, it impedes meaning construction.

Expanding: Invite students to peruse a telephone book for unusual names and to list a few on the board. Since the telephone book provides little or no information about the people whose names are listed, is there anything that might be inferred from the spelling of the name itself? How many ways is the same name, such as Smith or Smythe, spelled? Can students discover whether the different spellings mean the names come from different parts of a country or represent different languages (Rodriquez–Spanish or Rodriques–Portuguese) from different countries? Discuss the national origins of class members' names. Students might interview parents, grandparents, or neighbors about how similar names can differ in spelling or pronunciation even in the same family. Has their family name ever been changed? Do they know why?

Study the listings of phone books from across the country to see if there is a preponderance of certain names in one area but few or none of the same names in other areas. Interested students might categorize some of the spelling patterns related to certain languages or national origins and develop some rules about the spellings.

Students may want to explore the names of famous people in social studies, math, science, and the arts. An interesting search is to check names in the phone book to see how many people are named after famous people and how the names have been altered. One random look through a city telephone directory produced Mildred Fillmore, likely named after President Millard Fillmore.

When names from other countries are heard on the radio or television, students might check with people from those countries to see if commentators are pronouncing the names as a native speaker would. Discuss with learners why people care about how their names are pronounced. Strategies for finding out how people pronounce their names is an expansion of this lesson.

Prior to any standardized test, remind students of this naming strategy and encourage its use in the reading of tests.

Relate the lessons to "Strategy Lesson: Characterization" in Chapter 4, page 99.

Readings for Expanding This Strategy Lesson

Books for Primary Grades

Lobel, Anita. *Alison's Zinnia*. New York, NY: Greenwillow, 1990.
> Allison acquired an amaryllis for Beryl who bought a begonia for Crystal— and so on through the alphabet, as full-page illustrations are presented of each flower.

Moser, Barry. *Tucker Pfeffercorn*. Boston, MA: Little, Brown, 1994.
> A retelling of the classic Rumpelstiltskin tale with a Southern setting.

Zelinsky, Paul O. *Rumpelstiltskin*. New York, NY: Dutton, 1986.
> A strange little man helps the miller's daughter spin straw into gold for the king on the condition that she will give him her firstborn child.

Books for Older Readers

Taylor, Sidney. *All of a Kind Family*. New York, NY: Dell, 1979.
Taylor, Sidney. *More All of a Kind Family*. Chicago, IL: Follett, 1954.
Taylor, Sidney. *All of a Kind Family Uptown*. Chicago: Follett, 1958.
> A Jewish family and their everyday lives—their enjoyment, trials, and tribulations—in New York City during the early 1900s. The names used in these stories are from American Jewish culture.

STRATEGY LESSON: NOUNS AS PLACE NAMES

Evaluation: Who Will Benefit

This strategy lesson will benefit students who:

- may read a place name without a miscue, but do not know that the reference is to a place;
- tediously sound out names rather than make an appropriate namelike substitution, such as in the reading of *Appalachian:*

"Robin climbed the A-A-A-Apple-a-chi-an Mountains."

- need assistance with the "Strategy Lesson: Nouns as Names of People" (see page 161).

Specific Rationale

Reading names of places is similar to reading names of people. When learners discuss places found in their reading, they need to understand that more important than pronunciation of the place name is the relevance of the place to the story or the article. The reader must be concerned with searching for cues to the type of place being named, such as a body of water, river, mountain, or town. The focus must be on the concepts related to the place. The place name is usually embedded in the total text that provides cues to understanding:

The water in the Oose flowed rapidly.

They reached the peak of Kosciusko after a hard climb.

They got on the bus headed for New York. The bus roared out of the rolling hills. They passed farmhouses and suburbs. They rolled along the highway, across the bridge, and into the big city. They came into the heavy traffic. As they found themselves among tall buildings the traffic got heavier and heavier.

In the first example, the text cues, *water, flowed,* and *rapidly,* suggest that the Oose is a body of water. However, the reader must have a conceptual understanding of how water flows and how its movement is described to be able to infer a body of water. In the second example, the concept that people climb mountains to reach a peak must be known by students if they are to use the language cues *reached the peak* and *hard climb* to determine that Kosciusko is a mountain. The text in the last example provides evidence to those with prior knowledge that the bus is headed for New York *City,* not the state of New York. The entire text provides cues for understanding the setting or the place; cues may or may not be found in the name itself.

Students must realize that to understand place names, they need a variety of available language cues as well as their own background knowledge. Such language cues include:

- the name itself: Culver City, Detroit River, Mount Rushmore, Niagara Falls, Saguaro Desert; and
- meaningful words or combining forms (burg, ville, port, and so on) embedded in the place name: Riverview, Woodland Hills, Bloomington, Petersburg, Morristown, Deerfield, Evansville, Middleborough, Williamsport, Bournemouth.

By exploring these and other place names as they appear in social studies, science, or other content area curricular materials, learners develop concepts about how place names originate and how they relate to specific places. It is important to stress that some names have only historical significance and may not provide appropriate cues for the place being named. Riverview may not have a view of the river but still carry the name. Highland Park may be an urban city that has no resemblance to a park and be located on flat land. Kansas City is a city in Missouri and also a city in Kansas, and Michigan City is located in the state of Indiana.

Students should be aware that even when the name itself contains meaningful words, it is necessary to rely on the cues in the total language context in order to build a complete picture of the place the author is describing.

Language cues can provide conceptual information that distinguishes a political division, such as a city or state, from a geographic location, such as a river or mountain. It is easier for learners to distinguish between broader and distinctly different categories of places than between narrower classifications; for example, rivers are more easily distinguished from hills and mountains than from lakes, streams, currents, and flows. The more similar the concepts, the greater amount of experience and knowledge is necessary to understand their differences.

Even informed adults have difficulty distinguishing similar kinds of places unless they have specific knowledge. For example, in Israel, Lake Tiberias and the Sea of Galilee are the same body of water. Although many people would consider a lake different from a sea, their definitions must overlap if different people at different times call the same body of water by either term. The possibilities for confusion of the lake and sea are reflected in dictionary definitions:

> **sea** (sē), n. 1. the salt waters that cover the greater part of the earth's surface. 2. a division of these waters, of considerable extent, more or less definitely marked off by land boundaries: *the North Sea* . . . 3. one of the seven seas; ocean. 4. a large lake or landlocked body of water.
>
> **lake** (lāk), n. 1. a body of fresh or salt water of considerable size, surrounded by land . . . *Lake Aral.* See *Aral Sea* (Flexner & Hauck 1987).

Although reading can enhance and broaden concepts, knowledge must be built through many non-reading experiences. Unless interest and motivation are extremely high, trying to learn something completely new by reading about it is a frustrating and often unsuccessful experience, even for the most proficient readers. Through field trips, students can gain first-hand information about geographical, historical, and national places. Even if the specific places under study are not close by, a visit to any geographical or historical location will help learners develop concepts of place. Videos, films, filmstrips, and pictures can prove helpful, especially if they supplement students' sharing of their real-life experiences.

Strategy Lesson Experience

Initiating and Transacting: Invite students who are having problems with understanding nouns as place names to read the following poems silently. Provide maps of the world, the United States, and of several states, including Colorado.

I'd Like to Live in Colorado

I'd like to live in Colorado.
I'd like to live out where it's green.
I'd like to be where mountains, trees,
And rivers are all waitin' to be seen.

I'd like to sit beneath an aspen,
Find a field in which to lie
And watch the Rocky Mountains
Climbing halfway to the sky.

I'd like to live in Colorado.
I'd like to see wildflowers grow,
And smell their perfume in the air
As I wander down dirt roads.

I'd even like the cities there,
Small mining towns that grew
Like Durango, Silverton, Ouray;
Big ones like Denver, too.

(Valerie Gelfat)

Goin' Down the Colorado

Get the raft, Sam,
And let's go!
Goin' down the river!
Find a spot
And throw it in!
Headin' down the river!

I got my paddle.
Have you got yours?
Paddle down the river!

See them rapids?
Hold on tight!
Rushing down the river!

Look out for rocks!
Yipes! There's one!
Dangers on the river!

Yes sir, we're goin' down the Colorado,
Going fast and hard.
Feelin' like we're on a tornado.
Feelin' mighty small!

It's a churning, whirling bathtub.
It's a race against the rocks.
It's a muscle-tearing contest
And a challenge to survive.

It's a mighty work of nature
That don't care if you live or die,
Yes sir, we're goin' down the Colorado
And we can't tell you why!!

(VALERIE GELFAT)

Invite students to talk about the poems. What images are formed? Some learners might want to sketch a scene or two that one of the poems brought to mind.

If the students haven't discussed the following, ask the first three questions about each poem; then move to a comparison of the poems by considering Questions 4 and 5.

1. What is being described in the poem, "I'd Like to Live in Colorado"?
   Accept generalized answers such as, "a place out west" or "back east," as well as more specific ones such as, "a state."
2. What language in the poem tells you the kind of place being described?
3. What cues help the reader determine what place is being described?
   Point out that personal experiences help learners select the language that reminds them of a particular place.
4. What are the obvious language cues that make the place in one poem different from the place in the other poem?
   If the students cannot easily distinguish between the state and the river in the two selections, encourage them to explore other language indicating this difference. Select terms that don't appear in the poem. If you are in or near Colorado or the Colorado River, invite students to share their personal experiences. Ask these informants if the author was accurate in her descriptions. Encourage students to compare a familiar river and state with those described in the poems.
5. What language would you use to make the places in the poems more real? What language would you use to write your own poems so that they describe the river or state you know best?
   Invite students, as they discuss various places, to locate them on a variety of maps and globes.

Applying: As students silently read a story such as "A Bus Ride Through Paris," encourage them to record, either on a chart or a log, information about place names that can be used in further discussions. Consider the following:

- new concepts about places, even if the names can't be pronounced;
- information that doesn't ring true based on personal experiences and knowledge;
- new places that are described well; and
- new places that are not adequately described.
  Indicate the significance of the place to the understanding of the story. Students might make guesses about the place based on additional reading and research, if they are interested.

Bus Ride through Paris

Hello, everybody. Today we will take a bus ride through the city of Paris, France. I will be your guide on this trip. I will tell you all about the interesting places that you will see.

Paris is often called *la belle Paris*—beautiful Paris—because this city is one of the most beautiful and interesting cities in the world. Paris has beautiful streets, beautiful old buildings, and a beautiful river, the Seine. The Seine River cuts the city of Paris into two parts. One is called *la rive gauche*—the Left Bank. The other part is called *la rive droite*—the Right Bank. Each part of the city is interesting in a special way.

We will start our trip through Paris on an island in the middle of the Seine River. Then we will drive over a bridge to the Right Bank. We will end our trip by driving across another bridge to the Left Bank where we will see the famous *Tour Eiffel*.

We are now on City Island in the middle of the Seine River. City Island, or *Île de la Cité*, as it is called in French, is the place where the city of Paris started out a long time ago. All of Paris was on this one little island for a few hundred years before the city began to grow. Today, there are interesting streets and buildings still standing on the island that remind us of what Paris probably looked like six hundred years ago. We will have time to look at only one building while we are on the island, the great church of Paris, the Cathedral of *Notre Dame de Paris*. This church is one of the most beautiful buildings in the world. It took a long time to build, and it is about seven hundred years old. Look at the wonderful windows made of small pieces of different-colored glass! Look at the carvings all over the outside of the church! *C'est magnifique.* It's wonderful! Wonderful!

Now we drive over the bridge to *la rive droite*—the Right Bank of the Seine River. Here we see the largest palace in the world, the Louvre. This palace is very famous because it is now an art museum.

As we leave the Louvre, we will come to one of the most beautiful streets in Paris—the *Avenue des Champs Elysées*. This wide, tree-lined street is loved by everyone who lives in Paris. When you look down the *Avenue des Champs Elysées,* you can see the famous monument called the *Arc de Triomphe*. This famous Arch of Triumph is the center of many streets called the *Place de l'Étoile*. The *Place de l'Étoile* looks like a star because twelve streets branch out in all directions from the *Arc de Triomphe*. Can you imagine the traffic jam when automobiles from twelve streets meet? *C'est terrible!*

Now we will drive across the Seine River to *la rive gauche*–the Left Bank. We will see the famous *Tour Eiffel*, or Eiffel Tower, as you say in English. When most people think of Paris, the first thing that comes to mind is the Eiffel Tower.

We will end our bus ride through Paris here at the *Tour Eiffel*. I hope you enjoyed your visit to *la belle Paris*. Maybe you will visit us again someday. Until then, *au revoir!*

(BARRY SHERMAN)

Students may want to draw maps of the Paris tour or of their own travel experiences. They may enjoy making maps based on a walk around their neighborhood or a field trip. Suggest that they use their maps along with photos or sketches to make a brief presentation to their classmates. Encourage the use of place names on their maps and in their writing or oral presentations.

Expanding: *Possum Magic* (1987) by Mem Fox is about Hush, a young invisible possum, and her grandma. Hush and Grandma Poss visit Australian cities looking for magic that will make Hush visible. Enjoy the book for its beautiful story and pictures. Discuss the names of places and of food that are an important part of the adventure. How does the language help readers understand and "feel" the story?

Have on hand atlases, maps, globes, and travel folders. Encourage students to refer to these sources for information about places mentioned in *Possum Magic* as well as other places they find interesting.

Invite students to think of places they have traveled or would like to visit. Encourage them to jot down all the information they know about this special place, check maps and resource books for additional information, and then write descriptions, perhaps using some of the names they find difficult to pronounce. Ask students to share their descriptions or stories with other learners. Can the readers visualize the places the authors have described?

Discuss why places in their own cities may have misleading names. For example, children from New York City may be familiar with residential areas that are urban, yet have rustic names such as Forest Hills, Fresh Meadows, Woodside, Bay Ridge, and Forest Park. Students may also be familiar with places in New York City whose names reflect their historical origins but not what they are today, such as Bowling Green, Wall Street, or Fort Tryon. Students might discuss what visitors expect these places to be and what they actually are.

If learners are interested, they may classify places and list the characteristics necessary to build concepts for the categories. This works especially well if the places fit with theme cycles that involve place names. The following organization may be helpful:

- Political entities: city, state, town, county, country, nation, republic, province, township, borough;
- Geographic entities (land): mountain, hill, slope, plains, flatland, plateau, desert, valley, mesa, forest, woods, jungle;
- Geographic entities (water): ocean, sea, river, lake, pond, stream, creek, rill, fall, pool, rapid, swamp;
- Buildings: house, school, library, store, office, government building, institute, station; and
- Monuments: statue, architectural structure, historical site.

Discuss how language cues in social studies materials are similar to and different from the cues to settings in fictional material. To establish contrast, you may want to use the poem "Goin' Down the Colorado" (page 170) and an encyclopedia article about the Colorado River. Discuss the different kinds of cues and syntactic patterns in each.

If the students show interest in travel, encourage them during any current events discussion to find the places on the globe or map. They might put pins or flags at the site. In addition, the students might simulate a travel agency, collecting brochures, making up information bulletins for class members, setting up an immigration bureau, discovering why people need visas, passports, immunizations, and so on.

Encourage students to examine newspapers to find out how the setting of a news article is determined. Students may note that the dateline tells where the story was written or transmitted and sometimes includes a place name; however, the story itself may indicate that the action took place elsewhere. Confusion in understanding datelines is not unusual and is worth clarifying.

Relate these lessons to "Strategy Lesson: Setting (Time and Place)," Chapter 4, page 110.

Readings for Expanding This Strategy Lesson

Lobel, Anita. *Away From Home.* New York, NY: Greenwillow, 1994.
Proceeds through the alphabet using boys' names and the names of exotic places in alliterative fashion.

STRATEGY LESSON: VARIETIES OF GRAMMATICAL FUNCTION

Evaluation: Who Will Benefit

This strategy lesson will help readers who:

- tediously sound out words, read haltingly, or consistently look to the teacher for help;
- are not confident enough to risk making predictions, and consequently will not omit words or make meaningful substitutions;
- know words in their more common syntactic positions but do not know them when they occur in less common ones; or
- do very little independent reading.

Specific Rationale

Except for nouns or noun phrases used for names of people and places, no other grammatical function within a sentence consistently causes problems for all readers. In fact, more than 70 percent of the time, most readers *retain the grammatical function of the text* when they make a word level substitution (K. Goodman & Burke 1973). The following miscues exemplify this phenomenon:

> *deer Whitefoot*
> He called his pet Lightfoot.

> *reached*
> Penny rushed up the front steps.

Even when miscues *do not retain the grammatical function of the text,* there is evidence that readers predict appropriate or acceptable grammatical structures:

> *to   climb*
> Pulling the kitchen stepladder out into the hall and climbing up on it, he reached the light.

> *the owner's*
> It was almost like his own voice speaking to him.

If the predicted structure is not confirmed by subsequent text, readers will often correct the unacceptable grammatical structure. Such miscues often are syntactically acceptable up through the point of the miscue because the reader has predicted a familiar language structure:

> ©   *the*
> And so he burst into the apartment.

At the beginning of this sentence, *And so the* is a syntactically acceptable structure. It is not, however, acceptable with the remainder of the sentence. The reader shows awareness of this phenomenon as he rereads and self-corrects.

Although most words do not have a universal grammatical function outside the context of a sentence, there are variations in the frequency with which words fill particular grammatical-function slots. *Circus* and *river* will most frequently occur as nouns; *trained* will most frequently occur as a verb:

The children went to the *circus.*
The boat went up and down the *river.*
They *trained* the parakeet to talk.

Students who do not read widely may predict the most commonly used grammatical function of a word and become confused when that word is placed in less frequently used positions:

He was selling *circus* balloons.
He wanted to be a *river* man.
He has a *trained* parakeet.

Although most readers naturally use syntax to predict text, some lack confidence in their ability to make use of grammatical knowledge. These insecure readers tend to focus on weak and less effective strategies, such as sounding out. It is important to help such readers build their confidence. They need to know that guessing or risk-taking is a good strategy.

Reading patterned literature to and with children allows them to complete predictable sentences and to make up new ones, thereby building confidence. (See "Strategy Lesson: Focus on Common Spelling Patterns Through Predictable Language" in Chapter 6, page 224.)

Many strategies that involve both predicting and confirming place responsibility on the reader to take risks and to guess; when predictions do not work, readers need to overcome the problem by using various confirming strategies.

The materials in this lesson encourage readers to explore options:

1. Substituting the word *blank* or omitting the word or phrase, and continuing to read when the reader has no immediate prediction.
   Additional context provides cues that enable readers to think of synonyms for unfamiliar words or phrases. Saying "blank" for the unfamiliar word provides a place holder to allow the reader to make syntactic or grammatical sense of the phrase or sentence and to permit the reader to retain the structure until meaning emerges. Readers making use of this technique sometimes say "blanks," "blanked," or "blanking" for inflected words, revealing their strength as users of language and their knowledge of grammar. However, most readers prefer skipping the word altogether. In either case, this strategy gives readers independence by allowing them to continue reading even when they are unwilling to try a substitution for the unknown word or phrase. Some students call this a "keep going" strategy.
2. Substituting a word or phrase that is appropriate grammatically and semantically for an unfamiliar word or phrase.
   As readers begin to justify their own synonym substitutions based on grammatical function and context, their attention focuses on overall meaning. This strategy not only helps readers concentrate on comprehension but also provides them with a way to rely on their own strengths. It legitimizes risk-taking in the process of learning. (For further development of this point see "Strategy Lesson: Cooperative Controlled Cloze," page 157 and "Strategy Lesson: Synonym Substitution," page 236.)

Strategy Lesson Experience

Initiating: The short selections that follow focus on words used in uncommon positions; the first focuses on words used in uncommon adjective positions, while the second deals with prepositional phrases.

If you find that a student has trouble with a grammatical function not included in these lessons, you may want to locate or write appropriate material. If so, you will find it helpful to refer to Chapter 3, "Criteria for Selecting and Writing Materials for Strategy Lessons."

Invite students to read "Tom's Birds" *(adjective position)* or "Little Red Riding Hood" *(prepositional phrases)* silently. As they read, ask them to think of a word or phrase that best fits the blanks so that the sentences make sense to them in the context of the entire story. If they are not sure what belongs in any blank, suggest that they think the word *blank* and continue reading. After the readers have gotten additional cues from the story, they can go back to the blank and try a word or phrase that best fits the slot. Explain that it is possible to think of more than one word or phrase for some blanks. Allow time for students to read the entire selection and then reread any section in order to build a complete meaningful story. At this point, either read the story aloud or ask a volunteer to read it. Ask all students to fill in each blank with their personal responses and to listen for the others' choices. With "Little Red Riding Hood," the teacher might read aloud while the students look at the map and respond with appropriate prepositional phrases.

Tom's Birds

Tom loved birds. He became interested in them when he started to feed the ones that came into his back yard each winter. Tom put crumbs on the ground behind his house. He then built two _____ feeders and hung them on tree branches so he could see them from his window.

At first Tom didn't know the names of any of the birds. He looked for information about them in _____ books. He discovered that there were cardinals, grackles, and sparrows visiting his feeders.

When his mom and dad saw how interested Tom was in birds, they decided to buy him some he could keep in the house.

A parakeet was the first to arrive. Tom worked hard every day to train his new pet to talk. He repeated the same words in the same way over and over again. After a long time and a lot of hard work Tom had a _____ bird. His parakeet could say things like "Hi, guys!" and "What's for dinner, doc?"

About a month later Tom's parents bought him a bright yellow bird. It was a canary. Tom loved to watch Tweety hop from perch to perch and turn its head from side to side as it chirped and peeped. After a while Tom was fed up with Tweety's chirping and peeping. He was ready for bird songs! He knew it would be as hard teaching his canary to sing as it was teaching his parakeet to talk. He also knew it would be worth the effort and that some day, if he worked very hard, he would have a _____ bird and a _____ bird.

(DOROTHY WATSON)

178

Little Red Riding Hood

One day Little Red Riding Hood's mother sent her to her grandmother's house with a basket of goodies. It was a long walk. She went __1__ to the path in the forest. As she walked along she saw a rabbit sitting __2__ . And she saw a bird's nest high __3__ . It was a nice day and Red Riding Hood was happy to be going to her grandmother's house, so she began to play. She ran __4__ and jumped __5__ . She climbed __6__ and then went skipping down the forest road. She saw a deer get a drink __7__ . She picked some flowers from the side __8__ . She was happy because she knew that her grandmother would like the flowers. But then she saw something that scared her. She saw a wolf hiding __9__ . She knew the wolf would want to eat her, so she began to run. She ran as fast as she could. She ran right __10__ of her grandmother's house.

(ADAPTED BY CAROLYN BURKE)

Transacting: Encourage students to discuss what they put in each slot as they read the story silently. Read each story together. Consider these questions if they have not already been addressed:

1. What words or phrases fit the slot and help the sentence and story make sense? Urge learners to consider the whole sentence or even larger chunks of the story to gain information.
2. What cues help you make a decision?
   Encourage students with different points of view to speak up as long as their choice is based on the context of the story. As students continue to provide responses, help them evaluate how appropriate their choices are. The ability

to fill in the slots, making meaningful sentences within the total story, indicates a reader's ability to use language proficiently. Point out that readers do not need every piece of information to make sense of the story. If they are thinking about what they are reading, learners supply a great deal of information themselves. Point out that all readers substitute words that make sense for words and phrases they are unsure of; most readers do this intuitively without knowing they are doing so. In this way, they continue to read and understand the selection without waiting for outside help. Explore the idea that the main purpose of reading is to construct meaning.

3. Are there any other words or phrases that would maintain the sense of the stories?

Elicit alternative words for "Tom's Birds" or phrases for "Little Red Riding Hood." If students don't suggest any, mention one or two to help them see that there is a wide range of possibilities. Learners' predictions will show increasing flexibility as they make several choices that fit and make sense.

Applying: To gain confidence, students having trouble predicting grammatical structures need as much contextual support as possible. Therefore, the text items chosen for deletion (selected slotting) should be highly predictable. However, once readers feel comfortable with their own knowledge, they may want to apply their newly found strengths to texts with deletions that are less predictable. Select interesting materials in which students have some background knowledge. Stories or articles used for this experience should provide a variety of encounters with different grammatical functions.

Point out to students that if they continue reading past a blank they often gain enough information to offer a suitable word or phrase. At other times they may get enough meaning from the text that precedes the blank.

Depending on how proficient the readers are, encourage them to: 1) omit the word and go on; 2) say "blank" and go on; or 3) substitute anything that makes sense in the story and sounds right in the sentence. By suggesting these strategies, students begin to understand that they must take control of their reading and that one way of doing so is to take a risk based on what makes sense and sounds right.

Students may want to work in pairs and then in larger groups to compare the versions each pair produces. They might discuss which of the versions they think are most appropriate and why they think so. (See the "Strategy Lesson: Cooperative Controlled Cloze," page 157.)

Expanding: If more work is needed and if students are interested, invite them to delete predictable adjectives, adverbs, and so on, from social studies, science, or math passages and then present the material to the class. Discuss the substitutions that class members make.

Find unusual or interesting newspaper headlines. Invite students to write stories to fit the headlines and then follow the selected-slotting procedure described above. Keep a collection of good stories on file to use with other learners.

Students may want to compile their own dictionaries, listing words or phrases that were unfamiliar to them when they started reading a selection but that they came to understand through their reading. Divide a small notebook into alphabetic sections and invite students to write the words they select in the appropriate section. Younger children often find it easier to use a file box, recording each entry in alphabetical order on a separate card. To provide context, it is helpful to record the entire sentence from the story as well as students' own definitions of the word as they understand it through their reading. After they have written their own definitions, they may want to check a published dictionary to confirm their own definitions and to note any differences.

STRATEGY LESSON: DIRECT SPEECH INDICATORS (WORD LEVEL DIALOGUE CARRIERS)

Evaluation: Who Will Benefit

This strategy lesson will benefit readers who:

- are unable to develop a picture of what various characters are like, what they say, and what they do, even though the story has a significant amount of dialogue;
- repeatedly substitute the words *said* and *and* for each other (also see "Strategy Lesson: Repeated Substitutions," page 202);
- produce a large number of syntactically and semantically unacceptable intonation miscues that relate to dialogue carriers; or
- focus so intently on graphophonic information that they miss the cues that indicate who is talking, for example:

      John was dragging a large tree branch. He saw his friends.
      "Bonnie and David," said John, "come and help me."

   A reader might miscue by reading the last sentence as:

      a. Bonnie and David and John. "Come and help me."
      b. Bonnie and David said, "John, come and help me."

In (a), the reader does not predict the dialogue-carrier verb *said*, sees another name, and connects it with the first two names by substituting *and* for *said*. The reader of (b) is not sure who is talking to whom.

This strategy lesson is *not* for readers who produce miscues in sentences that retain the story's meaning. An example would be a reading of the above as:

      John was dragging a large tree branch. He saw his friends⊙
      ⊙Bonnie and David,⊙(said⌿John⊙ "Come and help me."
      (Read as: He saw his friends Bonnie and David.
      John said, "Come and help me.")

Specific Rationale

Written language makes use of a set of print conventions to indicate direct speech. These conventions include dialogue carriers, paragraphing, and quotation marks.

Dialogue carriers are the short clauses that indicate who is talking:

      I said, "Stop that!"
      "Dinner's ready," *yelled Robin.*

Said is the most common verb used in dialogue-carrier clauses; however, other verbs are used to express feelings that accompany direct speech. Sometimes emotions are expressed in phrases that accompany the dialogue carrier:

      "She hit a home run!" *John yelled gleefully.*
      "You drew first blood," *Rambo mumbled menacingly.*

Authors generally begin a new paragraph each time the dialogue shifts from one speaker to another. *Quotation marks* are used to set the spoken message apart from the remainder of the text.

The conventions for indicating direct speech are relatively straightforward, yet factors exist that cause some readers to experience difficulty:

- Most of the conventions used to indicate direct speech in writing are seldom represented in oral language. When we report what a third party said, the intonation in our voice and the use of indirect quoting is the oral equivalent of punctuation and dialogue-carrier phrases in writing:

    Oral: He really meant it when he invited us all to his place.
    Written: Bob included everyone when he said sincerely, "I want you all to come to my house."

- Dialogue carriers with their accompanying punctuation can start a sentence, end a sentence, or occur in the middle of the speaker's utterance:

    a. Sarah yelled, "I'll be late. Don't wait up."
    b. "I'll be late. Don't wait up," Sarah yelled.
    c. "I'll be late," Sarah yelled. "Don't wait up."

- Dialogue is often in the present tense while the tense of the dialogue-carrier clause and the story is in the past:

    "Come and have pizza," Gale called.

- Authors often do not use dialogue carriers in extended exchanges between characters. Readers must rely on quotation marks and paragraphing as cues. These direct speech cues are supported by the reader's knowledge of the developing story.

Strategy Lesson Experience

Initiating: This lesson will help students understand *said* as an all-purpose verb within the dialogue-carrier clause. After the students have read "The Skating Rink" silently, ask them to look it over a second time in order to choose parts to read aloud.

The Skating Rink

Scene: Saturday afternoon at a crowded roller-skating rink. Two boys and a girl are standing at the edge of the rink with their skates on. They are talking to each other.

Johnny: It's crowded today!

Teresa: I don't think I've ever seen so many people here on Saturday afternoon.

Mike: I knew we shouldn't have come today. How can you have fun when there are so many people around? Let's get out of here and go to the show.

Teresa: No. Not me! I've got my skates on. And besides, we've already paid. Let's skate.

Johnny: Look over there! There's a bunch of guys from school trying to play whip.

Teresa: On this crowded floor? Where?

Johnny: [Pointing] Right over there. See them?

Mike: Yeah, I see them.

Teresa: I see them too. If they don't stop, they'll be thrown out of here. Better keep away from them or we'll be thrown out with them.

Johnny: Do you see those three girls skating with Ben? Aren't they in your class, Mike?

Mike: Yeah. One of them sits next to me. Let's skate over and break into their group.

Johnny: Good idea. We'll hit them from behind and surprise them.

Teresa: You go first, Mike.

Mike: Heck no. Why should I?

Teresa: It's your idea.

Johnny: Boy, are you brave! All right, I'll go first.

Teresa: I'll go with you.

Mike: Okay. Ready, get set, go!

[They skate off across the floor toward the other group of skaters.]

Bring attention to dialogue carriers by suggesting rewriting the play as a story:

1. If we wanted to rewrite "The Skating Rink" as a story, how would we show that the characters are talking to each other and also show what they are doing? How does language change from a play to a story to show that people are talking to each other?

The students might explore the following:

  a. In a story, descriptive language tells what is happening in the scene.
  b. The language indicates who is talking by including *Johnny asked* or *Teresa said*.
  c. The dialogue is placed on the page as part of the story.
  d. Quotation marks are used to show who is talking. (With younger children the terms *talking marks* or *speech marks* might be used until the concept is clear. When children understand that the marks identify someone's speech, talk about quotations and begin using the term *quotation marks*.)

2. If you were writing the story "The Skating Rink" how would you start? How would you describe the setting? How would you tell what the kids were talking about? How would you tell what a particular character said?

   As the students talk, act as their scribe, writing exactly what they dictate in story form on the board or overhead transparency. One or two students may want to edit the story for a class publication.

Transacting: Invite students to search for the differences in the play and the story. If it is appropriate for the age and of interest to the students, discuss the function and composition of *dialogue carriers.* Point out the special function of *said* in the story. *Said* can replace any verb an author may choose to use in the dialogue-carrier clause. If a dialogue includes people asking each other questions, *asked* and *answered* are commonly used instead of *said.*

When readers become aware that a certain character is speaking and understand the purpose of the dialogue, invite them to substitute *said, asked,* or *answered* for any unfamiliar verb used by the author. Ask readers if they can omit the dialogue carrier and still retain the meaning of the passage.

Applying: If learners need more help with this strategy, duplicate a student's, teacher's, or group's version of "The Skating Rink." Replace all the dialogue-carrier verbs (said, discussed, smiled, and so on) with a line. Invite the students to read the story silently and think of at least one word or phrase that can fit each blank.

Invite students to read "The Incubator" silently, thinking of at least one word or phrase that fits each blank. The readers might try *said* or *asked* first; then try other words.

The Incubator

Dave walked down three flights of stairs to the second floor. He went to the door that had the number 24 on it. The name Turner was written under it. He knocked on the door.

Richard's mother opened the door.

"Is Richard home?" Dave _____ Mrs. Turner.

"In his bedroom," _____ Mrs. Turner. She opened the door wide and let Dave in. He walked right to Richard's room. Richard and Dave were good friends. They had lived in the same apartment building since they were in first grade together. They used to be in the same class, but this year they were in separate classrooms.

Dave poked his head into Richard's room and looked around.

"Where are you?" Dave _____ .

"Here I am." Richard's voice came from the bedroom closet.

"What are you doing in there?" Dave _____ .

"Looking through my animal cards," _____ Richard.

Everyone knew that Richard loved animals. He told everyone that he was going to work in a zoo or be an animal doctor or something like that.

"What do you think I should do for my science project this year?" _____ Dave. "Mr. Grant just told us today that we have to have our project ready in six weeks."

"Why don't you hatch chicks?" _____ Richard. "I just saw on a TV program that you could hatch eggs in twenty-one days."

"Isn't that hard to do?" _____ Dave.

"Nope," _____ Richard.

"What do you have to do?" _____ Dave.

Richard _____ , "First, you've got to make an incubator. All you need is a fairly good size box with a cover. You line it with foil to insulate it. Then you put an egg carton in it. You fix up a light socket through a little hole on the side of the box and attach a light bulb of about seventy watts. You'll need to have a small bowl full of water in the box all the time. That keeps the humidity right. Then you'll have to get some fertilized eggs."

Dave _____ , "Where do I find the eggs?"

"Fertilized eggs are not easy to find," _____ Richard. "Sometimes you can get them at a health-food store, a feed store, or a live-poultry store. You should call those places to make sure they have them before you go."

"Okay. If I get the eggs, what will I have to do next?" _____ Dave.

Richard _____ , "You'll have to put a mark on one end of the egg."

"Why?" _____ Dave.

"You have to turn the eggs every day. If you mark them, and keep a written record of which day it is, and what side the mark is on, you won't get mixed up," _____ Richard.

"Is that all I need to know?" _____ Dave.

"Did I tell you about the temperature?" _____ Richard.

"No," _____ Dave.

"Oh, I must've forgotten," _____ Richard. "I guess we should look in a book to make sure we don't forget anything."

Dave _____ , "Do you have a book on hatching eggs? It seems like fun. I think I'd like to try it. Will you help me?"

"Sure!" _____ Richard. "I used to have a book on eggs around here. Let's see if we can find it."

(YETTA GOODMAN)

Encourage students to talk about the words or phrases they placed in each slot. Discuss the fact that *said* could be placed in most of the slots, but other words may make the story more interesting. Talk about other words or phrases that would make the story livelier.

Consider writing a short play. Invite students to talk about the content and then dictate the dialogue as you or a student transcribes it into the play genre. The students might first read the play as a radio script and then act it out. There are plays listed following the "Strategy Lesson: Direct Speech Indicators (Phrase Level Dialogue Carriers)" (page 187).

Discuss how a play is rewritten as a narrative passage. Encourage a student or small group to rewrite the play and share this with the class. Talk about the changes in text. If contrasts between genres arise, discuss the differences.

One small group might write plays and then present them to another group to turn into story format using dialogue carriers. Some students may want to write an appropriate ending to "The Skating Rink" in story form, making use of dialogue carriers.

Expanding: Ask students to watch for dialogue carriers that are new to them as they read or listen to stories or read dialogue in newspapers or nonfiction works. These can be listed on the board and recorded. Encourage students to consider using these new dialogue carriers in their own writing.

Invite students to write a simulated interview with a scientist, government official, sports figure, or entertainment personality who interests them. Articles in current magazines or newspapers will provide information they can use for such compositions. The learners may want to read interviews to see how journalists mark dialogue with words and with punctuation in newspapers and magazine articles. Interested students might conduct and write actual interviews with community leaders or speakers invited to class, or students can interview each other.

Tape-record a small group of students as they discuss an interesting object, are involved in a discovery activity, or talk in a literature study group. With the students, transcribe the discussion, using dialogue carriers and other dialogue conventions that help identify and describe each speaker's manner and tone.

Immerse students in listening to stories that contain a great deal of dialogue. Read aloud to the entire class regularly. Read stories to small groups or to individual students, encouraging them to attend to the print conventions for dialogue carriers. Parents, older students, or proficient readers may serve as readers as well. Read-along books with tape recordings or big book formats are especially helpful for this lesson. The experience demonstrates for students how proficient readers handle such print.

Readings for Expanding This Strategy Lesson

Waddell, Martin. *Farmer Duck.* Boston, MA: Candlewick, 1991.
   A hardworking duck nearly collapses when a farmer demands too much work from him. The story is carried through the question-and-answer dialogue.

STRATEGY LESSON: DIRECT SPEECH INDICATORS (PHRASE LEVEL DIALOGUE CARRIERS)

Evaluation: Who Will Benefit

This strategy lesson will benefit students who:

- need help with dialogue carriers in general;
- can retell events in the dialogue but often miss the tone of the story and the characters' feelings and personalities;
- do not like to read stories or articles that include a great deal of dialogue; or
- are becoming more facile with dialogue carriers but are still insecure.

(See "Evaluation: Who Will Benefit" in "Strategy Lesson: Direct Speech Indicators (Word Level Dialogue Carriers)" page 181.)

Specific Rationale

Authors make dialogues more interesting and complex by moving the dialogue carrier to different places within the sentence and by adding descriptive phrases or clauses to indicate body movement, facial expressions, and the condition of the speaker's voice. These phrases or clauses give added dimension to the characters and to their relationships with others:

> Robert *muttered as his face turned red*, "That isn't funny."
> "The new lightbulb will make all the difference," he *commented brightly*.
> "Don't ever do that again," Robin *screamed hysterically*, "ever again!"

Usually, readers who handle such phrases effectively read often or are read to a great deal. They understand that dialogue carriers not only identify the speaker, but may lead to descriptive information about the speaker. By focusing on meaning and using context to predict the mood or posture of the person talking, proficient readers can predict variable dialogue-carrier phrases. If their predictions are not acceptable with what follows, they know enough about the story to rethink or reread and self-correct when necessary.

Readers need experiences with variations in language in order to use appropriate strategies when unfamiliar language occurs. This strategy lesson provides such experiences.

Strategy Lesson Experience

Initiating: As an introduction to this lesson, read stories filled with dialogue and descriptive dialogue-carrier phrases to the class. During the reading, interpret the character through voice and gestures. Write several examples on the board or on a transparency. Distribute one or two books to each learner or to partners and invite them to look through the book until they find dialogue they might share with the group. Ask students if they remember any stories or if they are currently reading books in which there is a lot of talk between characters. One or two students may volunteer to make a small collection of books that contain a great deal of dialogue.

Transacting: To pursue the strategy, write sentences such as the following on the board one at a time:

- "Watch out for that bus," Paul _____ .
- "This is the greatest class in the school," Kassi _____ .

- "Thanks for standing up for me," Jerry _____ .
- "What flavor ice cream do you have?" Barbara _____ .

As each sentence is presented, encourage the students to talk about why they filled the blanks as they did. The following questions may be useful:

- If you were reading this sentence aloud how could you show what the speaker was feeling while he or she talked? Can you express the emotions through talking, dramatizing, or drawing?
  Ask a student to read the sentence with appropriate intonation.
- As a writer, how could you help a reader to understand the tone of the narrative? Encourage students to move the dialogue-carrier phrase to the beginning of the sentence or to interrupt the sentence in the middle, if it is suitable to do so, and then change punctuation:

  "Watch out!" Paul shouted, "for that bus!"

- How would a writer let the reader know the tone of voice the speaker was using?

  "Watch out for that bus," Paul said *in a commanding voice.*

- How could you let the reader know what the speaker was doing while talking?

  "Watch out for that bus," Paul said *as he pushed Gloria out of the way.*

- How might each sentence be written if the speakers were joking, crying, or fighting?

Applying: If students need additional support, invite them to read "Angie's Glasses."

Angie's Glasses

Angela ran into the house screaming angrily, "Carol! Carol!"

She found her sister in the kitchen talking on the phone.

"Carol," she said, "Johnny stole my glasses and won't give them back. Every time I chase him he gives them to Eddie and Eddie rides off with them on his bike—"

"Listen, will you stop running to tattle all the time." Carol's voice was filled with exasperation. "Why don't you just stay away from the boys and take care of your own business?"

"But Carol—" Angela began in protest.

"I'm trying to talk on the phone, Angie," Carol interrupted. "Will you please leave me alone?"

Angela stormed out of the house to find her brothers.

"Angie, Angie, can't catch me!" Johnny jeered.

Angela ran as fast as she could, but just as she was about to catch up with him he tossed the glasses to Matthew.

"Run, Matthew," Johnny and Eddie shouted at their younger brother.

Angela laughed because she knew she could catch Matthew.

"Boy, just wait 'til I catch you," she threatened.

But Eddie on his bicycle was faster than Angela, and he took the glasses from Matthew just before Angela caught up with him. Twelve-year-old Patty looked out the window just in time to see Angela angrily hitting her little brother.

"Angie," she demanded, "you leave Matt alone."

Completely discouraged, Angela sat down on the front porch steps and let the tears fall down her cheeks.

"Angie, Angie, can't catch me," her brothers teased her, holding the glasses nearby until she grabbed at them, then running out of her reach.

Then Beth came up the steps and sat down at Angela's side.

"What's wrong with you?" she questioned her sister.

"Everybody hates me," was Angela's tearful reply. "Patty and Carol keep yelling at me and Matthew gets to do anything he wants, 'cause he's youngest, and Johnny and Eddie stole my glasses—"

"Angie, Angie, can't catch me," Eddie screamed from across the street.

"Well," Beth announced, "we don't care about those silly boys. We're going to sit here and play cards and enjoy ourselves."

Angela ran to get the cards, and she and Beth started a game of War. Attracted by all the talking and laughing, soon their brothers came and sat nearby.

"Can I play?" Matthew asked in a pleading tone.

"Well," Beth thoughtfully replied, "I suppose so; we're not selfish, right?"

"Right," Angela agreed.

"Can I play? Can I play?" Johnny and Eddie begged at the same time.

Soon the five brothers and sisters were involved in an exciting game of War.

"Oh, I almost forgot," Johnny remarked offhandedly. "Here's your glasses."

"I don't need them right now," Angela replied. "Will you hold on to them for me, Johnny?"

(DEBRA GOODMAN)

189

Encourage students to discuss how the author informs the reader about the speaker's emotional state, movement, and voice quality by using cues in the dialogue-carrier clauses, as well as cues in the story as a whole.

Expanding: Ask students to look for dialogue in the last few stories they have written; invite them to share excerpts with the group. Is it possible that their stories might be improved by using some interesting dialogue, including dialogue carriers?

Readings for Expanding This Strategy Lesson

Books for Primary Grades

Alexander, Sue. *Small Plays for Special Days.* New York, NY: Clarion, 1977.
   Seven short plays for two actors about popular holidays with staging notes and costume suggestions.

Guy, Ginger. *Black Crow, Black Crow.* New York, NY: Morrow, 1991.
   A girl questions a crow outside her window. Her question inspires fanciful answers.

Books for Older Readers

Adorjan, Carol and Yuri Rasovsky. *WKID: Easy Radio Plays.* Niles, Il: Albert Whitman & Co., 1988.
   Includes four plays accompanied by advice on music and sound effects, a glossary of radio terms, and a section on director's hand signals.

STRATEGY LESSON: HARD-TO-PREDICT STRUCTURES (READER-SELECTED MISCUES)

Evaluation: Who Will Benefit

This strategy lesson will benefit students who:

- have trouble finishing or who avoid reading long stories, even though they are interested in the topic. These students prefer short books and may even count pages before they select a book.
- do a great deal of regressing or rereading, but still don't produce acceptable sentences. Such students tend to self-correct a word or two but tend not to self-correct unacceptable phrases or clauses.
- change sentence structure by omitting intonation or by using inappropriate intonation. The result of these transformations is often unacceptable sentences, yet no attempt to correct is made.
- are confused about the relationship of significant and insignificant information, or who treat information as discrete items, making no attempt to discern relationships.
- make word-substitution miscues that are not grammatically acceptable within the sentence. Miscue analysis indicates that even though readers usually substitute the same part of speech as the text word, the syntactic and semantic acceptability scores of students who would benefit from this lesson are less than 60 percent (K. Goodman & Burke 1973).

Specific Rationale

Readability is directly related to predictability. Readers predict familiar grammatical structures and concepts with greater ease and confidence than unfamiliar structures or concepts. Unfamiliar structures disrupt the reader's ability to predict the author's language, thus making the text more difficult. Readers handle such sentences as *Jerry loves Janice* or *Beverly gave a flower to her teacher* with greater proficiency than a sentence such as *See Sparky jump.* The subject-verb-object structure of the first two examples is more common in English than is the imperative form of the third sentence. The structure of a sentence is unpredictable, and therefore less readable, when a word such as *see* does not convey the expected meaning. The meaning in *See Sparky jump* is better expressed with *Watch* or *Look at Sparky jump.* The ability to predict familiar structures explains why so many beginning readers transform a sentence such as *Dad! See Sparky jump* into *Dad sees Sparky jump.*

Hard-to-predict structures can surprise even the most proficient reader for the following and other reasons:

- *Unfamiliar style.* Authors have distinctive styles because of their language background, their creative crafting of a text, and their conscious choice of grammatical structures. To convey mood, they may purposely choose short, tight sentences or long, rolling ones in the same way an artist chooses stroke, color, and texture, or a composer uses tempo, key, and volume. Grammatical structures may be hard to predict for readers who have had limited experiences with a particular style.
- *Differences between written and oral language.* Typical structures in either the written or oral language form may not be common in the other form. Distinctions are reflected in the purposes and circumstances of writers and speakers. For example:

a. Writers must provide their audiences with images of people, places, and events, since authors and their readers seldom share a common time and place:

At dawn Gabriel began to stir. They were in an isolated place; fields on either side of the road were dotted with thickets of trees here and there. He saw a stream, and made his way to it across a rutted, bumpy meadow; Gabriel, wide awake now, giggled as the bicycle jolted him up and down.

(FROM *THE GIVER*, LOWRY 1993, 167)

b. An author may choose to use formal language that many readers seldom experience:

The motionless, who struggle with no such unnecessary inherited encumbrances, find it labor enough to subdue and cultivate a few cubic feet of flesh.

(FROM *WALDEN*, THOREAU 1980, 3)

c. Language variations based on region, ethnicity, or age, as well as archaic language, can baffle a reader who may have limited experience. The following represents a special case of language variation in which the author creates language:

"Redunculus and um-possible," the BFG said. "They is going two times as fast as me and they is finishing their guzzle before we is halfway."

(FROM *THE BFG*, DAHL 1982, 115)

d. Written language can present new and abstract ideas. Philosophical, theological, or legal points of view can often be expressed in language that is very different from the reader's experiences with written or oral language. The reader often confronts new concepts but has no opportunity to ask questions or have a face-to-face discussion in order to clarify those concepts.

A swarm of conflict plagues their short-fused Hood.
Where Walking/death is forced to knock on Wood.

(FROM "BOYZ N SEARCH OF THEIR SOULAR SYSTEM,"
IN *SOUL LOOKS BACK IN WONDER*, E. REDMOND 1993, 4)

- *Limited reading experiences.* Students who read only basal readers or other controlled materials may have difficulty predicting certain grammatical structures. The constant use of reading materials that are controlled for vocabulary, patterns of spelling-sound relationships, or types of sentence structures can interfere with reading development. Reading such materials exclusively intensifies the reader's tendency to predict only those structures that are familiar. Readers must learn to anticipate and appreciate uniqueness in written language. The strategy lessons that follow help learners remain confident when they encounter complex grammatical structures and help them realize that all readers make some predictions that do not work and that it is acceptable to reread or rethink when a prediction has been disconfirmed.
- *Specific hard-to-predict syntax.* Stories and articles read by all readers often include hard-to-predict structures. Some phrases and clauses are difficult to

predict when *the main noun or verb phrase is combined with additional noun or prepositional phrases.* Consider this example:

> Years passed and more people came from
> towns and villages all over Venezuela to make
> their homes on the mountainside.

(FROM *THE STREETS ARE FREE*, KURUSA 1985)

Students who focus on word identification may lose the relationships of phrases within a sentence. When reading a passage such as the first example, they are usually more concerned with sounding out words like *Venezuela* and *villages* than with understanding that a group of people have moved over time for a particular reason.

Inexperienced readers do not make an easy adjustment from subject-verb-object sentences to more complex structures. They tend to predict that the sentence ends before it actually does, resulting in a dangling phrase or clause which they may not include as part of a complete sentence. The reader who has not developed proficient strategies for handling a series of phrases or clauses can easily confuse the meaning of the text by rearranging or transforming the text. For example:

> Years passed and more people came from
>   . *To*
> towns and villages all over Venezuela˄ to make
> their homes on the mountainside. . . .

(FROM *THE STREETS ARE FREE*, KURUSA 1985)

A second type of hard-to-predict sentence includes *a series of parallel phrases or clauses within a single sentence:*

> The children who used to play in the open
> fields could no longer play there, nor in the
> forest, nor in the streams.

(FROM *THE STREETS ARE FREE*, KURUSA 1985)

In oral language, intonation is used to cue the listener that a series of phrases or clauses is coming. In social studies or science materials, colons, numbers, or the listing of items in a column often serve as an organizational cue. In other writing, however, there are few cues signaling a series of ideas or items so a reader may predict other structures. Proficient readers adapt to such structures. If their initial prediction results in an inappropriate structure, proficient readers reread and rethink their predictions.

Another hard-to-predict structure is one that gives information that cannot be fully understood until the student has read further into the text. Such structures often consist of a *dependent clause preceding an independent clause.*

> As he opened the kitchen door, Mama and
> Nell were finishing the dishes.

(FROM *LITTLEJIM*, HOUSTON 1988, 44)

Sentences of this type require readers to predict what will occur and at the same time hold information in memory while they process the forthcoming text. Only as readers begin to understand how all the information fits together do they integrate the ideas into the developing story. Such sentences become difficult if readers are not concerned with predicting possible structures and holding on to ideas as they read, and if they do not continuously integrate what they are reading with what they already understand.

Strategy Lesson Experience

Initiating: Predictability is based on experiences with oral and written language. Even young children have varied backgrounds in terms of the language structures they encounter in their lives. What may be predictable for one reader who loves science fiction and the encyclopedia or for another reader who can handle a television guide with ease may not be very predictable for a third reader who believes that he or she can read only instructional materials.

Readers with limited experiences with a range of genre need to explore strategies that help them become aware that they are capable of reading grammatical structures they consider hard to predict. The Reader-Selected Miscue (RSM) procedure (Watson 1973, Watson & Hoge 1996) gives teachers and students an opportunity to pinpoint structures that individual students or small groups of students find difficult to predict. RSM is an evaluation that can be applied to any silent reading experience. Readers become informants concerning their own reading instruction.

The following procedures should be modified for the comfort and needs of learners:

1. Students read their choice of material silently without interruption for ten to thirty minutes. The only qualification is that students are reading materials they have not read before.
2. When readers encounter a problem, they mark it with a blank bookmark and continue reading. Students have access to as many 2-inch by 8-inch bookmarks as needed.
3. At the end of the specified reading period students return to each marked place and select three (adjust this number depending on the reader) miscues that are still puzzling. Because readers continued reading past the trouble spot, they may now have worked out the problem and, therefore, do not need to report all miscues.
4. On the bookmark, students write the structure (a whole sentence or more) in which the problem occurred, underlining the part they think caused the problem. For later discussion, the students might also note on the bookmark the title of the book and the page number of the troublesome text.
5. Collect the bookmarks.
6. Classify the miscues according to similarity of problems. As students develop an understanding of this process, involve them in the categorizing.
7. Select one classification of structures, provide a few examples, and invite those students having problems with that structure to come together for a discussion.
8. Write the miscue examples on the board, make transparencies, or duplicate copies for the students.
9. Students should bring their reading material to the group in case the entire text needs to be examined to figure out why a miscue was made. Use the students' examples as the basis for discussion.

Transacting: Start the discussion of each sentence with the student who selected it as a problem. Then invite the group members to suggest additional reasons why they think a particular structure might cause problems. Consider the following questions if they have not already been addressed in the discussion:

1. Why do you think this was a problem?
2. If you were not able to work it out while you were reading, do you think you know now what the sentence means?
3. How did (or could) you figure out the meaning? What strategies did (or could) you use to figure it out? Have you constructed even a partial meaning? Encourage students to refer to the original reading material whenever appropriate.
4. Can you restate or rewrite the sentence in your own words so that it makes more sense? What could the author have written to make this easier for you to read?

It may be useful to continue these questions with as many as six or seven examples if students remain interested. Help students understand that finding meaning is their major consideration. If they are able to restate or rethink the ideas in their own language, then they have constructed meaning, even if they had difficulty with the sentence structure.

The RSM procedure helps students understand how structure supports meaning making in text. Students now can try their hand at manipulating syntax to construct meaning with a variety of grammatical structures.

Applying: Make a transparency, write on the board, or make copies of "Sentences for Restructuring" (page 196) for students who need more help. With the students, transform one group of sentences into one, two, or three expanded sentences. Then ask individual students or pairs of students to transform another group of sentences.

Sentences for Restructuring

The weather was getting warm.
Pam invited friends to her house.
Pam had ice cream.
She had all flavors.
Pam had toppings of all kinds.
All the boys made their own ice-cream sundaes.
All the girls made their own ice-cream sundaes.

Lester looked in the window.
He saw his mother.
She sat at her computer.
She was thinking.
Lester saw the bookshelves.
He saw all the books.
The books belonged to his mother.
He saw the worn rug.
The rug was tan.
He saw the couch.
The couch was brown.
The couch was old.
There were books scattered on the couch.
The books belonged to his mother.
Lester smiled.
He had been away all summer.
He was home.
The good things never change.

As the students rewrite the sentences, encourage them to talk about the new structures and any changes of meaning. The following questions will help learners see the delicate relationship between structure and meaning:

1. Do the sentences sound acceptable to you?
2. Do different structures cause shifts in meaning?
3. Can different structures support the same meaning?
4. Do different structures make the sentences more interesting?

Use the students' examples to explore how variations in sentence organization affect meaning. Syntactic shifts are related to shifts in meaning, focus, and emphasis.

Social studies, math, and science materials may be the source of unique structures that some readers find difficult. Encourage students to select a variety of genre and formats for the RSM procedure. A small group of students may want to categorize common types of structures they discover within a particular genre.

Expanding: The ability to handle a variety of grammatical structures enables students to read a wide variety of materials. Engage students in sustained silent reading on a daily basis. With young children, or with those who have limited experience or success in reading, start with as little as ten minutes each day. Encourage the students to give themselves time to become familiar with a new author or genre. As students gain interest and stamina, increase the reading time.

Students of all ages, even adults, should be read to regularly and as frequently as possible. The importance of this experience lies not only in the appreciation and enjoyment of literature, but also in the exposure to a wide range of linguistic structures and styles uncommon in oral language. Tape-record a student's or teacher's reading for others to follow and read along with as they listen. Talk with students about the read-along experience, discussing the advantage of attending to the text as the story is being read. The point is to enjoy and understand the story while "absorbing" the sound and structure of language.

Learners may want to devise a record-keeping system related to their reading. Decide with students what aspects of their reading they want to record and the purposes and criteria for recording. The purposes might include: 1) showing progress; 2) remembering favorite books and articles so they can be shared; 3) listing disliked pieces in order to discuss why the material wasn't enjoyable; 4) recalling favorite authors in order to read more of their writings; and 5) recording interesting language structure, ideas, and knowledge to help with future reading and writing.

Record keeping should be based on the students' purposes and should change as students have experiences with recording and as their interests change. One first-grade class kept its individual records on bookmarks. Each student wrote his or her name on the card, as well as the name of the book and its author; students drew a happy or sad face to indicate their individual response to the book. A group of fourth graders kept a record of every book or article they read on a file card. They entered the title and why a friend might want to read it. The class members shared the books and articles with each other. They put copies of articles in a file for interested learners to read.

A group of sixth graders kept each individual's reading record in a folder:

Student's Name   _Jaime G._

Title	Author	Summary	Comments
La Calle Es Libre	Kurusa	Es un cuento acerca de la lucha de unos niños por agarrar un lugar de recreo.	Nos ayuda a conocer como lograr una meta.
Littlejim	Gloria Houston	It's about a boy who wants to read and write but his dad isn't happy with it.	You learn a lot about the past.

In some classes students record specific areas of concern like: *Sentences that caused me trouble and what they mean, Words I met for the first time and now understand, Hard-to-predict sentences,* or *Unfamiliar words and phrases.* The classifications should reflect the readers' concern for constructing meaning.

The more opportunities students have for extensive and intensive reading and writing experiences, the more familiarity they will have with hard-to-predict grammatical structures. It is essential to have a wide variety of readily accessible reading materials (See the "Materials/Functions Grid" in Chapter 2). Even though students have access to the school library throughout the day, it is important to have a well-stocked library with numerous references immediately available within the classroom. As a rule of thumb, teachers feel that the classroom library should contain a minimum of five top-quality books per child.

Encourage students to share their readings in a variety of ways. They might use drama, art, movement, music, or oral and written reporting. Newspaper articles may be presented as television or radio news broadcasts. Students reading the same title might discuss their shared reading in a literature study group and then plan a panel presentation for the class.

Help students take ownership of their learning by encouraging them to choose their own reading selections, decide what they want to share, and design their own presentations. When students are excited about what they read and are involved in deciding how sharing will be done, they will view reading as a joyful learning experience.

Readings for Expanding This Strategy Lesson

Books for Primary Grades

Calmenson, Stephanie. *Hotter Than a Hot Dog!* Boston, MA: Little, Brown, 1994.
    A little girl and her grandmother escape the city on a hot summer day by going to the beach.

Day, Alexander. *Frank and Ernest On the Road.* New York, NY: Scholastic, 1994.
    While making a delivery for a friend, an elephant and a bear become familiar with the experiences and language of truck drivers.

Jacquith, Priscilla. *Bo Rabbit Smart for True.* New York, NY: Philomel, 1981.
    These are African American folklore tales which tell animal stories.

Lester, Julius. *The Tales of Uncle Remus.* New York, NY: Dial, 1987.
    A collection of African American folktales which tell the stories of Brer Rabbit.

London, Jonathan. *Froggy Gets Dressed.* New York, NY: Viking, 1992.
    Rambunctious Froggy hops out into the snow for a frolic but his mother keeps calling him back to add other articles of winter clothing.

Books for Older Readers

Sutcliff, Rosemary. *Warrior Scarlett.* Oxford, England: Sunburst Press, 1958.
    Drem must kill a wolf single-handedly but how can he do this with his spear arm withered and useless? Sutcliff establishes the setting and time by representing the language of the period in this book and the next one.

Sutcliff, Rosemary. *Dragon Slayer.* Middlesex, England: Puffin, 1961.
    A retelling of the story of Beowulf.

Yep, Laurence. *Dragon's Gate.* New York, NY: HarperCollins, 1993.
    When he accidentally kills a Manchu, a Chinese boy is sent to America to join his father, an uncle, and other Chinese working to build a tunnel for the transcontinental railroad through the Sierra Nevada mountains in 1867. Rich, mature language patterns.

STRATEGY LESSON: PUNCTUATION

Evaluation: Who Will Benefit

This strategy lesson will benefit readers who:

- appear not to attend to punctuation, thus producing miscues that result in sentences that are unacceptable or only partially acceptable syntactically and semantically and that are not self-corrected; or
- consistently produce intonation-related miscues.

Specific Rationale

"You just ran through a stop sign!" "Read it with feeling." "Pay attention to the punctuation marks." These and similar instructional remarks reflect an assumption held by many teachers and researchers that readers are not attending to a key convention of print: punctuation. However, there is a problem with assuming that readers are paying attention to punctuation only when the voice takes on dramatic inflections or when there is a pause at commas and periods.

The purpose of punctuation in writing is to help the reader clarify linguistic segments of written texts. In English, where most punctuation occurs at the end of phrases, clauses, and sentences, punctuation marks help readers confirm their previous predictions. In Spanish, punctuation marks appear at the beginning of sentences and therefore can be used by readers as part of their predictions. Because readers are knowledgeable about sentence structure, they usually predict the tone of the sentence. This can be verified by listening to readers' intonations during their oral reading and through miscue analysis. Punctuation helps readers confirm their predictions by marking dialogue, exclamations, questions, and a series of related linguistic units including clauses, phrases, and sentences. Punctuation serves a similar and parallel function to the role of intonation in oral language, but it is a simplistic notion to consider punctuation and intonation as matches. Intonation does things that punctuation cannot do, such as show sarcasm or disbelief. On the other hand, punctuation shows linguistic units in a clearly demarked way.

The language user must constantly make syntactic and semantic decisions if punctuation marks are to provide usable information; that is, the reader must be committed to constructing meaning. To help understand this concept, read the following and complete the final sentence:

LeeAnn was only five years old and she had already been missing for more than three hours. When . . .

Whether you chose to predict a question such as *When will we find her?* or a statement such as *When Mom heard the police siren, she breathed a sigh of relief,* your basic decision concerning whether the sentence is a declarative or interrogative one was made based on your reading of the previous sentence as you sampled and predicted *When.* Only as you continue along a fourth line of text would you be able to confirm or disconfirm your prediction. The period or question mark at the end of the statement or question in addition to the language and length of the sentence become places where confirmation occurs.

Instances in which the reader's intonation suggests that punctuation marks are inserted, omitted, or moved are further documentation of the constructive role of the reader:

①   while

It was a great party⊙ While the adults congregated on the

②   The

patio⸴ the kids ran to the family room and booted up the new
computer game.

What can be simply described as the omission of the period (1) and a period
substituted for a comma (2) is a shift of the dependent clause of the second sentence to the first. For such grammatical transformations to take place, readers must
actively predict the structure; they do not wait for the punctuation to direct them.
Rearranging or disregarding punctuation reflects a decision readers make earlier in
the text. If readers understand the function of a punctuation mark, the mark itself
will not present a problem.

Strategy Lesson Experience

Initiating: Material for this lesson needs to be relatively brief, direct in its message,
and not overly complex in structure. Single-concept informational pieces such as a
description of the seasonal cycles work well, as do folktales and traditional tales having a simple plot, clearly delineated events, and repetitive phrasing.

Preparation of the material involves producing a version typed entirely in capital letters and without punctuation. All other written conventions, such as spelling
and paragraphing, are maintained.

Invite students who need help to read the piece into a tape recorder. Encourage them to make sense of the text and then be prepared to discuss the experience.
Once the reading begins, it should proceed without interruption.

There are some effects that punctuation-free text can have on readers:

- Reading will be slowed.
- Rethinking and rereading at points where predictions do not work out will be
  necessary.
- If the author is a consistent writer, predicting will become more effective as
  the reading progresses.
- If the reader knows a great deal about the topic, reading will be a meaning-
  constructing process.

Transacting: When students finish reading, encourage them to talk about the experience. They may want to listen to parts of the tape as a basis for discussion.

As students talk about and listen to their own readings, they need to:

- understand that they play an active role in the reading process;
- develop knowledge of points in a text that present the possibilities of alternate
  predictions;
- know punctuation as a way to confirm their decisions; and
- value self-correction as a reflective strategy that results from confirming meaning and acceptable syntax.

Applying: Invite student volunteers to share an example of their writing with the
discussion group. Ask group members to write a piece, omitting the punctuation. If
a student is willing, copy the piece onto a transparency. If an author reads a piece,
ask the listeners what punctuation is needed to understand the text. If the author
writes the passage on a transparency, ask one or two readers to read it aloud. This
provides authors and listeners with evidence of the support that punctuation can offer the reader. The value of prediction becomes evident.

Expanding: Students may want to collect punctuation conventions that seem un-familiar or unusual, keeping them in an individual or class notebook. The learners may want to place their examples on a chart:

Punctuation (Write complete phrase or sentence)	Source	Term	Meaning
"Harry repeated the magic words to himself—and disappeared	*Dragon Takes a Wife*	*dash*	*separates related parts*
h——	*Tip Magazine*	*long dashes*	*"questionable" word, letters are omitted*
called "barrio" *San José*	*The Streets Are Free*	*apostrophes or quotes accent mark*	*unusual word Spanish name*

Students might keep a record of places in their own writing where they used the same mark that an author used because they wanted to convey something to their readers. They may also find places in their writing that might benefit from revision with different punctuation. Exploring such invented punctuation tunes learners into the purposes of punctuation.

STRATEGY LESSON: REPEATED SUBSTITUTIONS

Evaluation: Who Will Benefit

This strategy lesson will benefit students who:

- repeatedly substitute one word or phrase for another across text that results in sentences that are not semantically and syntactically acceptable.

Specific Rationale

Since substituting words or phrases consistently is an issue in reading development, understanding the reasons for such substitutions becomes important in deciding when and how to use strategy lessons.

Repeated substitutions are evaluated by the same criteria used to evaluate all miscues: Does the structure in which the miscue occurs (including the miscue) sound like language? Does it make sense? When such questions are asked, it becomes clear that some repeated substitutions are of high quality. Such miscues should not become the focus of reading instruction since they represent an example of non-disruptive changes that result in repeated substitutions that are syntactically and semantically acceptable. However, when semantic and syntactic cues are largely ignored and the reader attends mainly to graphic cues, low-quality repeated substitutions often result. The strategy lessons for repeated substitutions are written to help readers who produce such low-quality substitutions. In deciding whether repeated substitutions are amenable to strategy lessons, it is important to consider the following discussions. For further discussion of repeated substitutions across text, see "repeated miscues" in *Reading Miscue Inventory* (Y. Goodman et al. 1987).

Some teachers believe that readers make repeated substitutions because they are not paying close attention to the graphic information or that they have formed an "habitual association" between two words and that until the habit is broken they will always be confused. They assume that if readers examined the print more carefully, the substitutions would not occur.

These theoretical assumptions lead teachers to design instruction that focuses the readers' attention on graphic differences between words. For example:

The words *doll* and *ball* are distinguished by attending to the *d* or the *b*, remembering that the stick comes after the circle in *d*, but before the circle in *b*.

The words *was* and *saw* are distinguished by attending to the initial letter of each word and making its sound.

Miss and *Mrs.* are distinguished from each other by focusing on their medial letters (*i* and *r*) and on the single versus the double *s*.

Teachers who give such advice tend to view repeated substitutions as visual problems best handled by intensifying the reader's attention to the shape and sequence of letters. Research on invented spelling (Wilde 1992) and miscue analysis (Allen & Watson 1976) contradict this interpretation. For example:

- Readers do not consistently substitute one word or phrase for another from one text to another. There are instances when such words or phrases are read as expected, and other times when there is a different substitution, not the associated one.
- No reader has a persistent problem with a specific letter. For example, the reader who seems unable to discriminate between *doll* and *ball* will not have the problem spill over to all other words beginning with *d* or *b*. Readers who

sometimes read *bog* for *dog* or *bad* for *dad* almost never reverse *d* in the final position, saying *dab* for *dad*.

- Repeated substitution pairs have a stronger tendency toward higher graphic similarity than other substitution miscues. However, there are many repeated substitutions that bear little or no graphic similarity to each other, such as the substitution of *wolf* for *coyote*, or *job* for *work*. Such high-quality substitutions reflect the reader's knowledge and attention to syntactic and semantic cues.

- Repeated substitution miscues are supportive of comprehension when they show use of all three cueing systems resulting in semantic and syntactic acceptability in the text. Such substitutions do not disrupt meaning. Repeated miscues that need instructional attention are those that rely on only one or two of the cueing systems, are not syntactically and semantically acceptable, are not corrected, and disrupt meaning construction.

If we view repeated substitutions in light of all the language cueing systems, we can generalize: The quality of any particular repeated substitution depends on linguistic and pragmatic contexts and on the use of self-correcting strategies.

Let's first examine high-quality repeated substitutions such as function words, including noun determiners, name, and pronoun substitutions, and then examine miscues that make little use of *syntactic and semantic information.*

Function word substitutions: Miscue research (K. Goodman & Gespass 1983) indicates that the largest percentage of repeated-substitution miscues are function words (determiners and clause and phrase markers, among others); the reader, in making the substitutions, almost always maintains grammatical function.

Although some function words carry semantic information, basically their role is to provide syntactic structure. For example, determiners announce that a noun phrase is coming up; clause and phrase markers establish the relationships between objects and actions.

To understand the syntactic role of function words, complete the following paragraph.

> While we are quite often oblivious _____ our environment, nature can periodically intrude upon our consciousness _____ a most startling manner. Yesterday I was working at my desk _____ I gradually became aware of thunder _____ rain. I continued to work, letting the weather serve only _____ background to my efforts. Gradually, almost imperceptibly, the noise increased. Just as gradually, and without conscious decision, I was drawn away from my work _____ the window, where I became _____ spellbound witness to a magnificently violent hailstorm.

The task of filling in the blanks was probably a relatively easy one. You might have found yourself predicting with the word already formed in your mind *before* arriving at the blank, or perhaps you handled the blank and the whole chunk of sentence *following* it, as a single unit. Even though the blank intruded on your attention more than a word might have, you still probably focused your attention on content-laden words such as *oblivious, environment, thunder, weather, witness,* and *hailstorm*. It is doubtful that anyone would bother to try out an alternative word once they constructed text that made sense and sounded syntactically acceptable. That is, a proficient reader would probably not switch to *of our environment* after predicting *to our environment*, or *and I gradually became aware* after predicting *when I gradually became aware*, or *the spellbound witness* after predicting *a spellbound witness*. Function words unobtrusively organize the text, thus allowing readers to focus on constructing meaning.

Since function words are highly predictable in certain linguistic contexts, it is natural for the reader's attention to be drawn away from the function word to meaning-bearing content language. The result is that a large percentage of repeated miscues will occur at these points.

High-quality noun determiner substitutions: Although there are slight shifts of meaning in the following examples, the miscues cause such minor changes that readers self-correct silently or ignore them in favor of moving on to more significant information.

Substitutions for determiners are made by all readers, because the grammatical slot for the determiner is based on the readers' comprehending of the text. There may be no way for readers to use their knowledge of whether the noun phrase should be definite or indefinite, because the material may be ambiguous. Substituting *a* for *the* and vice versa is the most common (K. Goodman and Gespass 1983):

> "Let's have a look at her," said Jock Duncan, our cook and doctor. We waited in
> *the*
> silence while he held Claribel against his ear, trying to hear a heartbeat.

> Think of it [baby sitting] as homework. Part of your education. You just happen to
> *a*
> do your studying in the room where your baby brother is sleeping, that's all.

> On the way to the station I kept telling my parents what had happened . . . At the
> *a*   *the*
> station Mr. Barnaby rushed us into the studio and pushed a crib for Andrew under
> one of the big cameras.

High-quality name and pronoun substitutions: The most significant function of a name is to signal the actions, words, and thoughts of a specific character. Sometimes the only additional semantic information comes from the presence of *she* or *he* to mark the character's gender. One of the most effective strategies that readers use is to substitute an alternative name. The substitution may be a real name or a name that shares graphic similarities, or an attempt at a phonetic reproduction. (See "Strategy Lesson: Nouns as Names of People," page 161.)

> *Judy*
> Juby is my oldest friend. He lives in Los Cordovas where the schoolhouse is.

> *Clarido*
> I first saw Claribel when I was working in my office.

> *Steven Awsom*
> We had just never had any pets until Sven Olsen decided he wanted one.

> *Andrea*
> Andre put one of his father's old axes on the sled.

Low-quality substitutions: Repeated substitutions such as *oh* for *no*, on first appearance, seem to support the graphic-perception argument. Such a substitution seems to ignore the syntactic role of each word that does not fill the same grammatical function slot.

However, readers may view these two words as similar syntactically because they have seen them in similar contexts in basal readers. For example:

No, no, no.	Oh, oh, oh.
No, Betty, no.	Oh, Betty, oh.
"No, Polly!" she said.	"Oh, Polly!" she said.
"No," said the man.	"Oh," said the man.

In these syntactic units the negative *no* and the interjection *oh* are interchangeable. The almost nonexistent story line, heavily dependent on pictures, does not provide the reader with supportive information on what language to predict.

The combination of weak semantic information and indeterminate syntax makes it possible for yet another word—*go*—to be substituted for *no* or *oh.*

Go, go, go.
Go, Betty, go.
"Go, Polly!" she said.
"Go," said the man.

These examples illustrate that when the text provides meager and inappropriate semantic and syntactic information it increases the chances of low-quality repeated-substitution miscues. Children often make such miscues when reading the artificial language found in commercial reading textbooks, but seldom make such miscues when reading the authentic language found in trade books (K. Goodman and Y. Goodman 1978). Additional examples are found at the end of this specific rationale.

Additional substitution miscues: There are additional types of substitution miscues that essentially can be classified into two groups:

- those miscues in which the syntactic slot is maintained without regard for semantic cues.
  The miscues result in oral reading that sounds like language but does not make sense even at the sentence level. For example, in a story about a baby brother, the word *typical* occurs thirteen times with story context represented by the following sentences, clearly building the meaning of *average* or *everyday:*

  . . . a pretty good brother . . . As little brothers go.

  He'd do just as good as anyone else his age.

  A baby like everyone else's baby.

  All babies cry . . . He wouldn't be typical if he didn't cry sometimes.

    A number of fifth- and sixth-grade readers encountering *typical* chose to read $*typeical* or *tropical.* Although these two responses show readers' attention to both graphophonic and syntactic cues, they do not reflect semantic considerations. However, in their retellings some students explained the meaning of their substitution miscue, indicating they were comprehending and constructing meaning across the text.
- those in which the syntax in the sentence is acceptable, but the miscue is not semantically acceptable within the entire text.
  These low-quality substitutions fit the syntactic pattern without regard for meaning. The available graphophonic, syntactic, and semantic cues prior to or closely surrounding the miscue are consistent with the prediction. However, when additional syntax and meaning indicate the need for disconfirming the earlier prediction and for self-correction, the reader does not choose to do so:

was
At last Pete saw a large policeman. He rushed up to him and said, "Please will you help me?"

and
"I see a monkey," said Shirley.

For less efficient readers, many repeated-substitution miscues fall in this low-quality syntactic category. These readers have available semantic cues that signal the ineffectiveness of the substitution; nevertheless, they reject semantic information, relying more heavily on syntactic and graphophonic cues.

There are, however, repeated substitutions in which readers ultimately make use of the semantic system. In these instances meaning tends to be ambiguous, allowing for semantically acceptable alternative responses. For example, in Chapter 4 we discuss "Bill Evers and the Tigers," a story about boys on a baseball team who meet a professional player who gives them tips on the game. The word *baseball* appears seven times, but only one other clue in the story refers to baseball. It is something more than coincidence, then, when three very different readers (an eight-year-old girl, an eleven-year-old bilingual boy, and a 23-year-old man) all read *basketball* for *baseball* the first six times this word appeared. These readers stopped to assess their choices when, eight lines from the end of the story, they encountered the sentence *Then, just when Bill Evers was showing Ben the right way to hold his bat, a newspaperman came.* On coming to the word *bat,* two of the readers paused and turned back through the text to hunt for the word *baseball* because they knew bats related to baseball. All three went on to read *baseball* in its next (and final) text appearance.

In a story about a pet bird in a space station, a dozen or more students ranging in ages from seven to fourteen read *cardinal* for *canary* each of the six times the word appeared. Their only semantic cue that *cardinal* might not be appropriate was one early reference to the bird's yellow color.

When reading "Sheep Dog," (discussed in Chapter 2) a story about a dog's efforts to save a flock of sheep from coyote attacks, some middle school students read *wolf* for *coyote.* Within the context of this story there were no semantic cues disruptive to these readers' concept of *wolf.*

In books for young children, animals are often the major characters. Their gender, in many cases, is irrelevant to the story. With neutral names such as Kitten Jones, Pepper, or Yellow Bird, the only reason for assigning gender may be to be consistent with the masculine or feminine pronoun.

Kitten had been playing in the rose vines.

he
Now she walked over to the camera.

Pepper saw Jimmy ride to a house and stop.

She
He saw Jack stop, too.

Such miscues are less likely to occur if the pronoun refers to a person who has already been introduced with appropriate cues about gender. Similar semantic circumstances can exist for *she* and *he* and for the titles *Mr., Mrs., Miss,* and *Ms.*

A text will usually have pronoun cues available to the reader in distinguishing *Mr.* from *Mrs., Miss,* and *Ms.* Frequently, *Mrs., Miss,* and *Ms.* are semantically ambiguous, especially when no reference or significance is placed on the character's relationships within a cultural community:

Miss
One morning old Mrs. Duck said, "What a good day for a walk!"

Mr.
We want to surprise Miss Bear.

In semantically ambiguous texts, many young readers fall back on their personal experiences. If their pet is female, Kitten Jones and Pepper are likely to be female. In the case of *wolf* for *coyote*, background knowledge or the reader's schema about the world combined with the semantics of the story was stronger than graphophonic concerns.

Our language is filled with lexical items that look alike, but their meaning and grammatical function are changed on the basis of changed context.

The *bear* went over the mountain.
Bear with me for one more minute.

I *saw* what you did.
We will cut the wood with a *saw*.

Old Mrs. *Duck* went for a walk.
Duck when someone throws something at you.

In some instances there is both a meaning and a pronunciation change:

I will *lead* you home.
Lead is a heavy metal.

Araminta *read* from the sampler on the wall.
He will *read* when he wants to.

Language users accept these uses of homonyms as a natural part of language use. However, in a few rare instances, a reader develops a strong specific-meaning relationship that overrides considerations of both syntax and meaning. For example, *Happy Birthday* is a phrase that some readers find so semantically powerful that they are apt to produce miscues such as:

Birthday
He is called Happy‸Joe.

happy
On his‸birthday Franklin woke up early.

Another semantically-related repeated substitution is closely tied to instructional procedures stressing word-level vocabulary development that makes use of repetition. In contrived texts, for the sake of vocabulary practice, particular words are repeated a number of times. While the instructional intent is to make such items "sight words" (*here* and *come* in the following example) for the reader, the actual result can be to build a strong relationship between them. The reader may then produce the following repeated substitutions:

Come
Here is my blue airplane.

Here
Come and look in here.

Here
Come with me.

Here
"Come out here," said Jimmy.

Repeated substitutions with high graphophonic similarity may make little use of the semantic and syntactic cueing systems.

it
Look at my toy train.
See it go.

it
Look at my little train go.

brown
Here I go down.
Come, Sue.

brown, brown, brown
Come down, down, down.

Such miscues represent a very small portion of repeated substitutions and are produced almost exclusively by young learners reading linguistically impoverished materials. Older readers who have significant problems with reading rarely make miscues of this type in authentic reading materials. Over time, readers of all levels of proficiency become more sensitive to the constraints of language cues. This sensitivity allows readers to make higher quality reading predictions, to disconfirm unacceptable predictions, and then to self-correct.

Strategy Lesson Experience

Initiating: A student's specific repeated associations depend on the reader's unique encounters with print. It will be necessary to decide whether the repeated substitution miscues that will be the focus in the lesson (those disruptive to meaning construction) are easily found in a published text or if special material needs to be written similar to the ones that are included in this strategy lesson. To establish context for one word that is repeatedly miscued, present the reader with a text that includes only one word in the associated pair; for example, *bought* in "I Had a Party!" (page 209) and *through* in "The Trip around Cape Horn" (page 209). In both of these stories the first occurrence of the associated word is preceded by strong semantic support. A reader should be able to predict appropriately on the basis of context.

My mom gave me a dollar and said I could buy some candy.
I went to the store.
I _____ lots of candy.

Today, ships have powerful engines that can move them even _____ the roughest seas.

The particular meaning established for the item should be maintained throughout the first text. Later, additional texts (See "Camping" (page 211) and "The Argument" (page 211)) that contain both words in the repeated substitution will be read.

I Had a Party!

I had a party!
My Mom said I could buy
everything for the party.
I went to the store,
I bought lots of candy,
and cookies galore.

I bought fancy napkins,
I bought paper cups,
I bought Alka-Seltzer,
For those with hiccups.

I bought a big cake
And pink lemonade,
I got out my money,
and the grocer was paid!

I bought all these goodies,
and took them on home,
"Happy Birthday to me."
(That's the end of this poem.)

(VALERIE GELFAT)

The Trip around Cape Horn

It is hard to understand what it was like to take a trip on the great wooden sailing ships of the past. Today, ships have powerful engines that can move them through even the roughest seas. A long time ago, ships were made of wood and had only the wind blowing against canvas sails to push them through the water.

In those days, one of the hardest trips to make was the trip around the southern tip of South America from the Atlantic Ocean to the Pacific Ocean. This trip around Cape Horn was called "Rounding the Cape," and it was very dangerous. Many ships were lost at sea and on the rocks. And many people died. But the ships had to get through. Today, ships don't have to go anywhere near Cape Horn to get from the Atlantic to the Pacific or from the Pacific to the Atlantic. Today, ships sail peacefully through the Panama Canal. But in the days of the sailing ships, it was another story.

First, a ship would try to cross from the Atlantic to the Pacific around the Cape itself. At the place where the cool waters of the Atlantic Ocean meet the ice-cold waters of the Antarctic Ocean, there would be cold weather and fog and very high waves. If the people on the ships looked to the north they would see the low hills of Tierra del Fuego, the southern tip of South America. If they looked to the south, they would see open ocean. Beyond the open ocean to the south was Antarctica, covered with snow and ice all year around.

As the ships tried to sail west toward the Pacific Ocean, they might meet terrible storms. These storms pushed the ocean waves higher and higher, until they were as tall as the masts of the ships. Imagine looking up at a wave taller than the highest mast of the ship! When such waves hit a ship, they rolled it back and forth in a terrible way. There was wind and rain and snow and sleet. Sometimes, the weather was so bad that ships had to turn back.

Ships that turned back because of weather could try another route: the dangerous trip through the waters and rocks of the narrow Strait of Magellan. The sailors who passed through the strait saw the wrecks of ships that had crashed on the rocks. And if a ship made it through to the very end of the Strait of Magellan, it had to pass the point where the waters of the Atlantic Ocean met the waters of the Pacific Ocean. Can you imagine the kinds of waves a ship sailed through? At the end of the Strait of Magellan, the giant waves of the Pacific rolling in toward the east meet the choppy waters of the Atlantic moving toward the west. A wooden sailing ship caught in this kind of water would be in for a rough time. It was so rough that captains would order their sailors to tie themselves to the ship. All openings on the ship would be closed. Then, the ship would head into the waves. Many ships never made it through the danger.

But if a ship was lucky enough to pass that dangerous spot, and reach the Pacific Ocean without sinking, the waves would get smaller until the ocean was peaceful again. Then, as the ship sailed northward, the sun would shine, the water would be blue and peaceful again, and everyone could relax. You can be sure that those who lived through a "passage around the Horn" had a story to tell when they reached San Francisco or Hawaii.

(BARRY SHERMAN)

Additional strategy lesson materials include both words of the associated pair, with a suitable text distance between them, and with semantic and syntactic support for both words. For example, in "Camping," *brought* is introduced first, with both semantic and syntactic support:

Camp at last! Rusty had very carefully packed every item he needed. He *brought*. . . .

Bought is then introduced in the second paragraph, preceded by appropriate semantic cues:

He had to buy only two things . . .
At the store he *bought* . . .

Camping

Camp at last! Rusty had very carefully packed everything he needed. He brought things he knew would make camp life comfortable and interesting. He brought his old sleeping bag. It was warm and just right for the cold nights when all the kids backpacked into the mountains. He brought his guitar. Last year, Rusty was Mr. Popularity because he could play so well. He always played at the evening camp fires. He brought scuba-diving equipment, his flashlight, a couple of paperback books, and a big box of cookies.

Rusty had carefully looked over the list the camp sent him to see that he had everything needed. He had to buy only two things. He had left the batteries in his flashlight last year and the acid had ruined it. At the store he bought a good flashlight and enough batteries to last all summer.

Two days before leaving for camp Rusty bought something he had worked for over three years to buy. He bought, with his hard-earned money, a lap-top computer!

Lots of kids brought sleeping bags, flashlights, and scuba equipment. Some even brought guitars, but there was only one lap-top.

(DOROTHY WATSON)

Give the students in the strategy-lesson group a copy of "The Argument." Invite them to read the story and then with the aid of a transparency discuss and mark the syntactic and semantic constraints intended to aid in the prediction of *thought* and *through*.

The Argument

Richard and Sean were through with their bath. They both stood wrapped up in towels feeling very clean. They were leaning over the edge of the bathtub, watching the water flowing down the drain.

"I wonder where the water goes," Richard said.

"If I was the size of a small mouse," said Sean, "I would put on a mask and an oxygen tank and jump down the drain. Then I could take a ride through the pipes and find out where that water is going."

The two boys walked into the kitchen. And Richard got the cookies, while Sean poured the milk.

"Well," Richard said, "if I was a mosquito, I'd fly right into your body, through your nose, and I'd bite you on the inside of your head!"

"Oh, yeah?" Sean said. "Well, if I was a germ, I'd hide in your milk, and you'd drink me and I'd go swimming through all your blood vessels and poison you on the way!"

"You would, would you?" Richard demanded, looking at his milk fearfully. "Well, if I was a—if I was a—" Richard thought and thought, but he couldn't think of anything smaller than a germ. "You just wait!" he shouted as he ran out of the kitchen and into the living room.

"Momma," he asked, "what's smaller than a germ?"

"Hmmm," Momma said, "everything on earth is made of tiny, tiny things called molecules. If the molecules are very close together, the thing is hard like a rock. If the molecules are farther apart, the thing is liquid like milk. And if the molecules are very far apart, the thing is a gas like the air. Molecules are so small you can't even see them when you look with a microscope."

Richard wrinkled up his nose and thought about what his mother had said. Then he asked, "What do molecules do?"

"What do they do?" his mother said. "Well, they move around. Sometimes they bump into each other and float off in another direction."

Richard laughed and ran back to the kitchen. "If I was a molecule," he shouted, "I'd float right through your body and bump into everything, and you couldn't even see me!"

"If you were a molecule," Sean said seriously, "I don't think I'd feel you."

Richard yawned just as their father came in and said it was time for bed. He picked up both boys at the same time and carried them into their bedroom. He tossed Richard into the top bunk and dropped Sean into the bottom bunk. And he turned off the light as he left.

"If I was a beam of light," said Sean in a very sleepy voice, "I'd peep through the keyhole and watch you sleeping."

Richard didn't say anything, because he was fast asleep.

(DEBRA GOODMAN)

Transacting: Until now, this lesson has focused the reader's attention on using context to build meaning. Now, the learner's attention is drawn to the troublesome pairs of associated words or phrases, never losing sight of the need to construct meaning.

Invite the students to review their Reader-Selected Miscues (RSM) (see page 46). If there are examples of repeated substitutions ask the readers to share them. Encourage students to describe and categorize the miscues. Talk about the quality of the miscues. Help students consider which miscues are supportive of their meaning construction, and which are disruptive and why. Does the substitution move the reader along in the text without losing meaning? When should the reader make a special effort to correct the miscue? If the miscue warrants attention, investigate why the substitution might have been made.

Because certain function words are frequently substituted for each other and because they serve a basic structural role in language, the discussion might start with them. Using RSM, help students understand the role of function words and understand that when the function word fits the reader's concepts the miscue is likely to be of high quality. High-quality miscues are those that move the reader along in the construction of meaning.

Investigate the RSM to discover how the three language systems contribute to the miscue. Talk with students about why they think the miscues were made. Was it the result of instruction, text information, or of the reader's strategies? Was more than one factor involved?

RSM and RMA (see page 46) discussions should involve the reader's previous instruction. If students report that they have been told to "slow down and look at each word carefully," discuss the role of syntax and semantics in the role of speed in constructing meaning.

Some of the most powerful lessons occur when students listen to each other, tell about their earlier reading instruction, and then talk about the credibility of such advice. For example, readers have been told to read *look* by searching for the two *o's*, to read *there* by memorizing the initial *th*, and to read *monkey* by remembering that the *y* looks like the monkey's tail. This advice may work until the reader meets *book*, *three*, and *Monday*, at which time associations with *look*, *there*, and *monkey* might mislead them. Students need to know that some of their repeated miscues often indicate that they paid too much attention to the graphic similarity between the two words at the exclusion of semantic information. The reader who has a repeated substitution between *book* and *look*, for example, is not in need of more practice with the sounds related to *b* and *l*, nor is the reader failing to attend to initial consonants. Finally, students must understand that they should question all instruction, even if it is given with the best intentions.

To emphasize the need to use all the cueing systems, the teacher might draw analogies to situations in which people make non-linguistic identifications. For example, a medium-priced car may closely follow the body lines of a luxury model and we can't distinguish them as they pass us on the highway. Or, just by looking, we can't tell which is the stick of butter and which is the margarine. When we meet such close similarities we don't just keep staring at the items, we gather additional information. We do not expect a single cueing source to carry the weight of decision making when more immediately applicable and significant cues are available from other sources. There are easier ways to determine differences than to focus on the minimal distinctions available within a single system.

Some readers take a slightly more expanded view of text by attending to short sequences of words rather than being limited to graphophonic information at the word level only. They consider the word in relationship to the immediate, preceding, and following text. It is as if they shifted from one pinpoint of information to a series of keyhole views of the sentence, seeing it section by section as they shift their focus.

This slightly increased focus provides for the inclusion of some limited use of grammatical and semantic cues and self-corrections. But the view is seldom broad enough to pick up syntactic alternatives; therefore, substitutions result in many partially acceptable structures. Of course, even this perspective is much too narrow to include semantic relationships. Such substitutions might include *for the school* for *from the school*, *when guests came* for *then guests come*, or *but then who would* for *but then who could*.

The reader's minimal use of syntactic and semantic information can also be caused by the reading material. The reader may be forced to rely on graphic cues and snatches of syntactic structure if the material has hard-to-predict or inauthentic structures or deals with information irrelevant to or beyond the knowledge and understanding of the reader. Encourage students to talk candidly about their reading.

Applying: The effects of repeated-substitution strategy lessons will be felt gradually over an extended period of time. Continue to observe the occurrences of repeated substitutions found in science, math, social studies, and other materials. Encourage students to bring their miscues to strategy lesson discussions. Talk about the major factors that led to the miscues. Discuss the difference between graphically similar miscues that have very different meanings (*look* and *nook*, *run* and *rip*, *house* and *horse*, *pond* and *pony*) and miscues whose meanings are similar (*country* and *county*, *house* and *home*, *morning* and *day*, *job* and *work*, *alligator* and *crocodile*). Interested students might interview their parents and friends to find out if they make repeated-substitution miscues.

Expanding: Encourage students to write their own stories or articles for strategy lessons using their own repeated substitutions. In the writing they will expand their awareness of how the substitutions are differentiated in context. Students can read each others' compositions and observe how they respond to the repeated substitutions.

6

Focus on the Graphophonic Cueing System

GENERAL RATIONALE

The graphophonic cueing system refers to three related kinds of information: 1) phonological; 2) orthographic; and 3) phonic (K. Goodman 1993). Phonology is the sound system of a language. Orthography deals with spelling, punctuation, and other components of a written language. The relationships between the phonological and orthographic systems of a language are referred to as phonics.

The graphophonic system works integrally with the semantic and syntactic systems as readers produce concepts and ideas—the big picture. The graphophonic system includes the smallest and most observable unit of language, the *grapheme*. A grapheme is a letter or letter combination that combines with other graphemes to form *spelling patterns*. These graphemic patterns represent *phonemic patterns*.

When teachers plan their instructional practices, the role of graphophonic cues in reading becomes an issue. In designing any strategy lesson, but particularly one that focuses on graphophonic cues, it is important first to consider what students already know. Concerning orthographic and phonological knowledge, all of us, including youngsters, are bombarded with print found on billboards, street signs, posters, labels, and clothing, as well as print found in books, letters, notes, and newspapers. As print takes on meaning and as it becomes interesting to them, children begin to pay attention to the print produced by others and begin to generate their own marks. In the example on page 216, five-year-old Christy recorded print messages that surrounded her as she waited for her dad in Wal-Mart.

At birth, infants coo and babble using a variety of phonemes found in different languages. By age three or four, youngsters have sorted out, through use, most of the sounds of their own language. Christy's print message shows us that just as children are familiar with oral language, they are familiar with written language before they step into our classrooms. For the most part, the young linguists who walk into our schools are proficient language users; we need not spend time teaching them what they already know. Rather, *our first responsibility is to find out what our students do know about both written and oral language.* Children's book handling and environmental print experiences, as well as their spelling inventions, help us understand their perceptions and attitudes toward written language, how it works, and what functions it serves. By observing what children notice, read, and comment on as they walk through their school and neighborhood, we become aware of and then document their responses to environmental print (Y. Goodman et al. 1989). Once we learn what children's strengths are, we can build on their knowledge in order to plan and

"Ms. Wundram, I went to Wal-Mart
with my daddy. This is what I read
that I wanted."

MEXICO EECROCOMEXICO
RLAISKOOLRA INBOWBITEEASTER
MICKEYMOUSE!! IDONTFRTL
CAUTIONCHILDRENGONOFOISS555
ONE WALSE RVAICERUDO PH 55
BEDKOOMRO A LSGEN OFA
BABYLANDKANSASS 771 M
TISSUESSAMARFLADYCASERW
FISHERPRICEPARKING RAMS
IV Decenter R WONDERTOUCH
UNEHANES EGHSTART)
HADDMORAMETRAMNEKE
ERTECNDSMAGMLB
RKCS EGGSTOMMYPAGHLO
IXSNOOORXOPENO LTAD
TK!PLELEEMRLORENZFAITID
J00 SOVEBROOKSAMMODDPEY
MADEINTAIWANKANSASCV
WP E AN WHITEDGIEA015Y
HURCHADLOOM
SCX520FOG F12 N2O
26 N1 91 51 1 5 22
53 95 #!!!<!5 5

Christy

organize expanding reading and writing experiences, thus helping them become even more proficient language users.

If they are immersed in print over an extensive amount of time, young readers learn, within the total discourse, to sample graphophonic cues and to predict meaning and structure within common sentence patterns. For example, if readers sample the letter *T* in a short word at the beginning of a sentence, they will more than likely predict either *The* or *They*. If they sample *Z*, they will likely predict a proper noun. Proficient readers confirm their predictions by sampling additional text which includes more syntactic and semantic cues. Learners do so more easily when they are regularly involved with print that has something to say to them as thinkers. Through ongoing evaluation of students' *reading*, teachers become aware of readers' growth in their understanding of spelling patterns, spacing between words, relationships between upper- and lowercase letters, ways letters appear in print (A, a, **A, a,** *A, a*), and punctuation marks. Ongoing evaluation of their *writing* also reveals children's growing knowledge of spacing, punctuation, letter formation, and spelling inventions.

In this chapter, we consider strategy lessons that focus on spelling patterns and other written cues that are a part of the orthographic conventions of language. These cues include a variety of lower- and uppercase letter forms and their embellishments, punctuation marks, spaces between words and other text organizers, and highlighting with italics, underlines, and boldface. Rarely do these orthographic features correspond directly to features of oral language. As in the example below, the hyphenated word at the end of a line of text and some punctuation marks such as commas and quotation marks have no oral representations:

> The cattle gradually moved across the plain to-
> ward the river as they grazed.

> "I am not, after all, the greatest thing in the world," he said.

The hyphen separating *toward* is a result of a printing convention, not a meaning-bearing mark that is reflected in speech. The commas separating *after all* from the rest of the sentence are the author's signal that the speaker interrupted the flow of thought to add information to his speech. This interruption is not simply a pause in a string of words; it is a complex syntactically meaningful message that establishes a pompous tone. The quotation marks are indicators of speech. Depending on the reader's interpretation of the text and on his or her tendency toward dramatic expression, the tone may or may not be reflected in the oral reading of the sentence; dramatic expression is rarely an issue in silent reading.

While reading, learners use their eyes and brains. Their eyes view the print, while their brains tell them which written symbols to attend to or perceive. Not all available graphic cues are utilized by any one reader because to do so hinders efficiency. To predict something meaningful, proficient readers select minimal graphic cues based on their past experiences with written language. Using only the graphophonic information they need, proficient readers are able to sample, infer, predict, and confirm meaningful text. The initial word segment and configuration (word length and shape) are quickly sampled within the syntactic and semantic context of the material already read and are used for predicting. For example, in a story about a child visiting a zoo, the word *elephant* appears in the sentence: *At the zoo, we fed peanuts to the elephant.* The reader attends to *el* at the beginning of the word plus its length. Within the total context of the sentence in the story about the zoo visit, the word *elephant* is read.

The medial part of a word becomes a significant graphic cue as readers use confirming strategies. When a prediction is not semantically and syntactically acceptable to readers, they are likely to reconsider the available graphophonic cues by sampling the text again, using additional visible cues to predict alternative structures that will fit semantically and syntactically with the text.

The following two examples show the sampling, predicting, and confirming role of graphophonic information.

> ©
>   *hoped*
> He hopped down from the truck.

> © *rain*
>   *r-r*
> Penny rushed up the front steps . . .

It was on the basis of the sentence contexts . . . *down from the truck* and . . . *up the front steps* that the first predictions were disconfirmed, and the reader sampled the text again to gain new information to result in acceptable self-corrections.

The ways in which readers perceive the importance of graphic symbols are a result of the complex context of their literacy experiences, including the instruction in reading they receive, the demonstrations of those around them (family members, teachers, and peers), and the materials used and valued in the learning process.

STUDENTS WHO NEED TO FOCUS ON THE GRAPHOPHONIC SYSTEM

Through miscue analysis, kidwatching, and students' own evaluations of their reading, we can determine if there is a need to develop a strategy lesson that focuses on the graphophonic system.

Graphic similarity scores from RMI coding are helpful but must be used with insights about the reader's use of graphophonic cues in relation to semantic and syntactic cues. For example, a score of 80–100% on *high graphic similarity* could indicate that a reader is attending to surface features of the text at the expense both of constructing meaning and of making the reading sound like language. For example:

while
Last night I read your letter to my whale.

It is always necessary to consider the syntactic and semantic acceptability of the reading and any meaning change caused by the miscues when considering graphophonic information.

In Reading Miscue Analysis Procedure III (see Chapter 3, pages 38–39), questions are asked about syntactic acceptability, semantic acceptability, and meaning change that result from readers' miscues. A question is also asked about the graphic similarity between the expected response and the reader's response (miscue) at the word substitution level. In other miscue analysis procedures found in *Reading Miscue Inventory: Alternative Procedures* (Y. Goodman et al. 1987), teachers/researchers also ask questions about sound similarity. Miscue research has shown that graphic similarity scores are often slightly higher than sound similarity scores; therefore, some information about sound similarity can be inferred from the graphic score (K. Goodman & Burke 1973).

John's miscues on a story taken from a fourth-grade basal text resulted in the following RMI Procedure III scores. John is a fourth grader.

Syntactic Acceptability	Y 55%	N 45%	
Semantic Acceptability	Y 45%	N 55%	
Meaning Change	N 50%	P 4%	Y 46%
Graphic Similarity	**H 75%**	**S 13%**	**N 12%**

John's word substitution miscues included the following:

	(H)	*(H)*	*(H)*
	home	*pond*	*$hearly*
Text:	horse	pony	hardly

(*(H)* indicates high graphic similarity between the miscue and the text. $ indicates a nonword.)

John's classmate, Kevin, read the same text. Kevin's miscues resulted in a high (H) graphic similarity score of 55% as compared to John's score of 75%. Kevin's reading, on the other hand, resulted in syntactically and semantically acceptable sentences 89% and 87% of the time, respectively, compared to John's scores of 55% and 45%.

Syntactic Acceptability	Y 89%	N 11%	
Semantic Acceptability	Y 87%	N 13%	
Meaning Change	N 89%	S 4%	Y 7%
Graphic Similarity	**H 55%**	**S 21%**	**N 24%**

Kevin's word substitution miscues included the following:

	⑤	⑤	Ⓝ	Ⓝ
	kids	*dad*	*lake*	*a*
Text:	children	father	pond	the

(Ⓝ indicates no graphic similarity and ⑤ indicates some graphic similarity between the miscue and text.) Forty-five percent of Kevin's substitutions showed *no* or *some* graphic similarity but resulted in sentences that are fully acceptable semantically and syntactically. Although John's miscues resulted in high graphic similarity (75%), many sentences resulted in no syntactic acceptability (45%) and even more sentences that are semantically unacceptable (55%). Therefore, his high score in graphic similarity suggests too strong a reliance on surface text features to the detriment of a concern for meaningful reading.

Before being too quick to address individual miscues with direct phonics instruction, the teacher should evaluate the overall pattern and nature of the miscues. The section under each strategy lesson on "Evaluation: Who Will Benefit" sheds additional light on such evaluation. ("Strategy Lesson: Documenting Problems With Print" on page 221 provides a way to determine the need for strategy lessons that focus on graphophonic cues.)

As is true of syntactic and semantic strategy lessons, the order of graphophonic strategy lessons is flexible; no one lesson necessarily precedes or follows another. Through miscue analysis and discussion, the student provides the evaluative information that helps the teacher decide which lessons are suitable and the order of their use in reading instruction. Keep in mind that the lessons are exemplars. Teachers should feel free to adapt them to suit the needs of their students.

The following student behaviors indicate a possible need for strategy lessons that integrate the use of sampling, inferring, predicting, and confirming graphophonic cues:

- Readers who insist on accuracy in pronunciation and, as a result, make multiple attempts to read a syllable or word. As a result of prolonged sounding out, such readers may lose meaning and momentum. These readers believe that every word is equally important and that reading means correctly pronouncing each word; often, they do not show concern for constructing meaning.

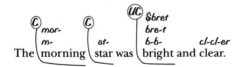

The morning star was bright and clear.

- Readers who read so slowly that they lose interest or become discouraged. These readers may have long pauses before attempting unknown or unfamiliar text items, especially on multisyllabic words.

It was an unconstitutional act and the citizens knew it.

- Readers who repeatedly omit the text item or substitute nonwords (marked $) that have high graphic similarity.

Joe (waded) in and came eye to eye with the legendary 'gator.

- Readers who abandon correct responses (marked ⒶⒸ). In the example below, the student read *waded* first and then abandoned it for *wooded*. At the end of the sentence, he read *alligator* and then settled for a nonword substitution that sounded like *gavor*.

ⒶⒸ   \$gavor

    wooded   *alligator*

Joe \waded in and came eye to eye with the legendary 'gator.

- Readers who avoid reading materials in which unfamiliar format and print variations are found. Such variations might include eye dialect (spelling based on dialect-influenced pronunciation such as *liberry* for *library*), foreign language terms, print or font variations, tables, graphs, or texts with columns.
- Readers who are unsure of prefixes, suffixes, and inflectional endings. These readers may stare, point, or attempt to sound out parts of the word.

        ⌐ 8 sec. pause   ⓊⒸ   cross-ed

                                                cross

He was (unsure) of his footing as he \crossed the levy.

- Readers who demonstrate little difference between reading words on a list and reading words in a supportive context. These students are often identified as "word-for-word readers." Such a label should be avoided as it is likely to mask how readers are using syntactic and semantic information.

Although there is no set order of lessons, it may be useful to begin with the first of the following lessons to determine whether lessons that focus on the graphophonic system are even warranted.

STRATEGY LESSON: DOCUMENTING PROBLEMS WITH PRINT

Evaluation: Who Will Benefit

This strategy lesson will benefit students who:

- have a recurring problem with a particular word or letter pattern.

This lesson helps both the reader and teacher determine the degree to which such a problem exists. For example, if the teacher believes a reader has a pattern of substituting *was* for *saw* or frequently miscues on a word containing an *ea* digraph or the double *p* consonant, it is necessary to determine the linguistic contexts in which such patterns occur and to document whether the reader miscues on every occurrence of the item or only on a few of them in a specific context.

Specific Rationale

Young readers naturally build a linguistic relationship between the graphic patterns they encounter in print and the sound system of their language. As writers, this relationship is reflected in their invented spellings. As readers, children become aware of which spelling patterns are more likely than others to appear in written language; specifically, they are able to predict the most common consonant and vowel patterns in English. Because this knowledge is integrated with the syntactic and semantic cueing systems, readers can often select the most efficient graphic cues, such as initial consonants or past tense markers, when predicting a word or phrase. However, there are times when readers predict an unacceptable structure based on what they have just read. For example, in the text below, David expected Little Bear to "see the star" that was introduced and described in the previous sentence.

Little Bear thought the star was the most beautiful thing

he had ever seen. He ⓒ*saw* ⌐was alive⌐ with the excitement of . . .

Given the sentence prior to his prediction of *saw*, David's substitution is understandable. Nevertheless, he immediately used his knowledge of syntax to disconfirm his prediction and to self-correct; *He saw alive* does not sound like language.

Students may appear to be poor readers when they are asked to read inauthentic materials (worksheets, flash cards, or text that has been tampered with, for example). Although Amy scored very low on a worksheet in which she was to identify the three sounds represented by *ea,* she could read words with *ea* patterns within the context of a written text that related to her background experiences.

Amy's Worksheet

The vowel digraph *ea* has three sounds: long e, short e, and long a. If a word is unfamiliar, try each of the three sounds. You should then recognize the word. Show the sound of *ea* on the line after each word. Show the sound of a short e with an unmarked e.

-15 (-41)   KEY: EACH __ē__   HEAD __e__   GREAT __ā__

1. TREATMENT __ē__
2. STEADIER __a__ ✓
3. STEALTHY _____ ✓
4. TEAK __ā__ ✓
5. GREATEST __ā__
6. WREATH __ē__
7. DEALT __e__
8. CONGEAL __ē__
9. SHEATH _____ ✓
10. CREASED __ā__ ✓
11. MEASLES __ē__
12. BEACON __ā__ ✓
13. BREAKNECK __ā__
14. HEATHEN __e__ ✓
15. HEAVENLY __e__
16. EASEL __ē__
17. SWEAT __ē__ ✓
18. UNHEALTHY __e__
19. SEASONING __ē__
20. CHESAPEAKE _____ ✓
21. STREAMLINED __ē__
22. TREACHERY __ē__ ✓
23. DEFEATED __ē__
24. PHEASANTS __ē__ ✓

25. CREAKING __ē__
26. JEALOUSY _____ ✓
27. APPEAL __e__ ✓
28. DECREASE __ē__
29. BEEFSTEAK __e__ ✓
30. PEASANT __e__
31. PEACEABLE __e__ ✓
32. REVEAL _____ *finish your work! (-41)*
33. WEAPON _____
34. CLEANSING _____
35. BEAGLE _____
36. SNEAKERS _____
37. FEATHERY _____
38. FEAT _____
39. FLEA _____
40. MEANWHILE _____
41. CEASE _____
42. HEAVILY _____
43. PEALED _____
44. WEASEL _____
45. DREAD _____
46. EATABLE _____
47. INCREASING _____
48. DEALER _____

49. TREACHEROUS _____
50. HEADQUARTERS _____
51. CLEANLINESS _____
52. MEANT _____
53. UNDERNEATH _____
54. BREAKTHROUGH _____
55. REPEAL _____
56. STREAKED _____
57. WEATHERED _____
58. MEANTIME _____
59. EAGERNESS _____
60. EAVES _____
61. THREATENED _____
62. LEASED _____
63. LEASH _____
64. BREAKWATER _____
65. DEAFEN _____
66. EASTERN _____
67. RETREATING _____
68. BLEACHERS _____
69. DEATHLESS _____
70. HEADACHE _____
71. LEAKY _____
72. SNEAKY _____

Strategy Lesson Experience

Initiating: Using reading material relevant and interesting for the student, find other instances of the identified word or letter pattern. In David's reading, for example, there are five other occurrences of *was* and two occurrences of *saw* that he read conventionally. David doesn't have a pattern of saw/was "confusion," since it only occurred once out of six possibilities. The text influenced his response.

Amy's teacher was moving into a whole language curriculum but wanted her students to do worksheets to "be sure all the skills were covered." She was, however, willing to use two whole language opportunities to gain additional evaluative information. First, she discovered in Amy's journal several instances in which she spelled conventionally words with the *ea* pattern. Second, the teacher wrote the following story to determine if Amy had problems with the *ea* construction in a complete text that was meaningful to her. As an alternative, she might have used a few pages from the book Amy was reading, if it included words with the *ea* pattern. To check her responses to a range of *ea* occurrences, it is important for Amy to read a complete passage. A worksheet does not provide information about the influence of other cueing systems.

Amy's Reading

When hunting season comes Uncle Bill is almost as eager to head for the woods

as Babe and Bingo are. Babe and Bingo are beautiful beagles, but Uncle Bill calls

them eager beavers when it comes to pheasant hunting.

When Uncle Bill releases those dogs from their steady leash, you should see

them streak across the meadow at break-neck speed. They can really work up

a sweat!

Aunt Joan dreads hunting season. Babe and Bingo's steady stream of barking

is deafening and gives her headaches. She can't bear to think of one feather on a

bird being harmed. Uncle Bill gives the pheasants to a neighbor. Babe and Bingo howl.

(Dorothy Watson)

Transacting: Amy's and David's teachers talked with their students about the miscue phenomenon. David was praised for making a reasonable prediction and for self-correcting when his substitutions didn't sound like language. Amy's teacher considered alternatives to worksheets in order to determine Amy's use of graphophonic information. Documenting Amy's reading and writing and checking for patterns that signaled her use of the graphophonic cue *ea* was a most promising alternative experience.

Applying and Expanding: If, after considering miscues within an entire story, the teacher and student discover a persistent problem with specific graphophonic features in context, a *brief* discussion is warranted. While looking at specific miscues, talk about the importance of constructing meaning by using all the language cueing systems. Students must not be led to believe that sounding out words or knowing phonics rules is the most important or the only cueing system to use or that such use is equivalent to reading.

If teachers decide, after this strategy lesson, that there are graphophonic features that need attention, the following lessons may be explored.

STRATEGY LESSON: FOCUS ON COMMON SPELLING PATTERNS THROUGH PREDICTABLE LANGUAGE

Evaluation: Who Will Benefit

This strategy lesson will benefit students who:

- are so insecure in their reading that they characteristically take few linguistic risks, stare at the text, jab at words, glance around the page or at the teacher for help, mumble (sound out) under their breath, and generally show that they are uncomfortable; or
- are having trouble using common spelling patterns to gain pattern familiarity and confidence in their reading.

Specific Rationale

Proficient readers do not utilize all the information in the graphic field because to do so would be inefficient. Efficient readers *sample* only enough information to make a meaningful *prediction*.

Certain language forms are highly predictable and, therefore, more accessible to the reader. Predictable language involves expected patterns at the graphophonic, syntactic, and semantic levels. Although patterns found in poetry and songs are perceived as highly predictable language, predictability is an aspect of all authentic materials. Predictability is especially high when the picture and the text are mutually supportive as in *Rosie's Walk* (Hutchins 1968), when words and phrases are immediately repeated as in *Each Peach Pear Plum* (Ahlberg & Ahlberg 1978) and *I Was Walking Down the Road* (Barchas 1975), when cumulative language is used as in *The Napping House* (Wood & Wood 1984) and *This Is the House Where Jack Lives* (Heilbroner 1962), when responses are made as in *Whose Mouse Are You?* (Kraus 1970) and *Where Does the Sun Go at Night?* (Ginsburg 1981), when repeated portions appear throughout the text as in *It Didn't Frighten Me* (Goss & Harste 1981) and *Lizard's Song* (Shannon 1981), when the text is rhythmic as in *Jamberry* (Degen 1983), and when text is interlocking as in *When the Elephant Walks* (Kasza 1990). For a discussion of these categories and additional examples see *Raising Readers: Helping Your Child to Literacy* (Bialostok 1992). Predictable language texts used in this lesson are traditionally thought of as material for young readers *but work well with students of all ages*. However, it is always important to select materials that are suitable to the interest, age, and development of the reader.

Strategy Lesson Experience

Initiating: Invite students to explore a highly predictable text in which certain letters are covered by a self-adhesive note or in some way blacked out. (An overhead transparency placed over the text provides a surface on which text can be marked out with a transparency pen.) Predictable big books are especially appropriate because their size makes them suitable for use with a group and the print is large enough to cover with self-adhesive notes. Provide additional support by leaving the first verse or a few lines intact. To determine how easily students can construct meaningful sentences even when some of the text is missing, consider the following:

This is the house that Jack built.
This is the malt
That lay in the house that Jack built.

This is th_ rat
That ate the malt
That l_y in the h__se that J__k built.

Th_s is the c_t
That kill_d the r__
That ate th_ malt
Th_t l__ in the h____ th_t J___ b__lt.

Explore with students their concepts of *predictability*. As they begin to understand the intentions and writing style of the author, as in *The House That Jack Built*, students will depend less on graphic cues and more on the meaning and structure of language. These supportive systems, in concert with sampled graphic information, will equip readers to make appropriate predictions about every feature of the text.

Select a poem, a song, or a story that contains the graphophonic pattern that appears to cause problems. For example, a second-grade teacher had miscue evidence that in several contexts Rita and a few other students were not utilizing the *ck* pattern. She brought the small group together to read David McCord's poem "The Pickety Fence," a complete text that includes the *ck* pattern. The teacher asked the children to feel the rhythm and enjoy the sound of the language as she read the poem. One of the children copied the poem in large letters and placed it on a chart for future group reading.

The Pickety Fence

The pickety fence
The pickety fence
Give it a lick, it's
A clickety fence
Give it a lick it's
A lickety fence
Give it a lick
Give it a lick
Give it a lick
With a pickety stick
Pickety
Pickety
Pickety
Pick.

(DAVID MCCORD 1984)

Transacting: The children read the poem with their teacher (assisted reading) and then read it in small groups in as many combinations as possible: for example, only boys, only girls, only those wearing jeans, and only those who like pickles. Finally, they read it silently and individually. Primarily, the children had fun with the sounds and cadence. The teacher briefly talked with them about the *ck* pattern, pointing it out in the poem and in other material they were reading. The poem was added to a room collection of poetry that the second graders loved. Some of the children copied it into their personal poetry books. A group of children added illustrations to the chart.

 Rita's teacher later introduced the response book *The Chick and the Duckling* (Ginsburg 1972).

The Chick and the Duckling

A duckling hatched out of its shell.
"I am out," said the duckling.
"Me too," said the chick.
"I am going for a walk," said the duckling.
"Me too," said the chick.
"I am walking," said the duckling.
"Me too," said the chick.

The children divided into two groups and took turns choral reading the parts of either the chick or the duckling. Following the reading, they talked briefly about how it was the job of quotation marks to highlight the dialogue and let readers know exactly what they were to say as they became the chick or the duckling. After enjoying the book, the children and teacher explored the *ck, sh,* and *ch* patterns found in the text. Discussion of these features of text took less than five minutes.

Applying: If more discussion is needed, the children might investigate other occurrences of *ck,* determining for each word the graphic pattern that represents the /k/ phoneme. Through their inquiry, students may discover that they cannot find the *ck* pattern at the beginning of words. This may motivate interested learners to make "a search for *ck*" and to record the data on a chart or to write an information book about their language research. Class or individual books become resources that students can add to as the year progresses and as their interest in language grows. However, searching for a lot of patterns would surely kill enthusiasm and appeal. Reserve the personal language book (see page 112) or the class language book (see page 112) for issues of interest.

Expanding: Predicting occurs in reading not only because of recognizable spelling patterns but because of other powerful cues. Invite the students to go on a special journey. This inquiry excursion can be called *sidewalk safari, sign tour,* or *billboard cruise.* Before the outing, select texts such as *STOP, Martin Luther King, Jr. School, BOYS, Pepsi, pizza, STUDENT OF THE WEEK, EXIT,* and other signs and labels the students see daily and ask why these signs might be easy to read. Start on the safari after talking about what clues (such as the place in which the signs are found) help people read. The purpose of the expedition is to find words and phrases in school, in the community, or on a field trip that students can read or want to read. As the explorers read and record the discovered texts, remind them that they are readers using written language and context to create meaning. Explore all the cues that help make sense of the print form. In addition to spelling patterns, discuss the purpose of the print, where it is found, who reads it, and other visual information that provides clues to its meaning, such as logo, color, or script. The students might want to record their findings on charts, on audio or videotapes, and in class and individual books. Add to these records as the safaris continue throughout the year.

Readings for Expanding This Strategy Lesson

Cameron, Alice. *The Cat Sat on the Mat.* Boston, MA: Houghton Mifflin, 1994.
     A story game for children to predict by looking through a peephole to guess where the cat will be next.

Elting, Mary and Michael Folsom. *Q Is for Duck.* New York, NY: Clarion, 1980.
   While learning some facts about animals, the reader is challenged to guess
   why *A* is for zoo, *B* is for dog, and so on.

Hutchins, Pat. *Rosie's Walk.* New York, NY: Macmillan, 1968.
   Rosie the hen is pursued by a fox, but she innocently eludes him at every
   turn. Also available in big book format.

STRATEGY LESSON: FOCUS ON UNFAMILIAR PATTERNS THROUGH LANGUAGE EXPERIENCE

Evaluation: Who Will Benefit

Students often assume that their reading problems lie within themselves; they have trouble because they are not doing what their teachers told them to do or because they lack some necessary skill or talent. Such readers often believe they can't handle words with unfamiliar graphophonic patterns. Further, they are hesitant to take linguistic risks and to abandon previous instructional experiences that focus their attention and efforts on sounding out small units of language. This strategy lesson and those that follow will free readers from an inefficient and inordinate focus on graphophonic features.

Specific Rationale

Through language experience, attention can be drawn to how meaning is constructed by integrating all the cueing systems. *Language experience* is a strategy appropriate for learners of all ages and abilities: 1) adults who have limited experiences with writing; 2) students new to the English language; 3) students labeled reading or learning disabled who believe they are nonreaders and nonwriters; and 4) youngsters tentatively exploring reading. (For information on the history, theory, and practice of language experience see Roach Van Allen (1976), Roach Van Allen and Claryce Allen (1982), and Robert J. Tierney, J.E. Readence, and E.K. Dishner (1990).)

Language experience incorporates the learner's experience, thought, and language in the creation of a text. The teacher, in the role of scribe, transcribes the student's oral language into written expression, thereby making use of the learner's abilities, interests, and competencies. Through language experience, language comes alive in front of students' eyes as they attend to features of written language that do and do not match oral forms. The learners become aware of names, words, and expressions that they know orally but may not have perceived in written form. Written conventions, such as quotations, commas, and periods, that students may not have paid attention to in their reading now become important in the process of communication.

Strategy Lesson Experience

Language experience involves a six-step process.

Initiating, Step 1: Each language experience lesson begins with an attention-getting, meaningful event. Recent experiences are often the most fruitful because they are the experiences students want to talk and write about.

The effectiveness of an experience is determined, not necessarily by its uniqueness, but by the intensity of the intellectual and emotional attention it draws and the interest it holds for the student. Throughout the lesson, students focus on the experience itself rather than on reading instruction. This encourages readers to handle print—writing it or reading it—on the basis of meaning and intention.

Transacting, Step 2: It is important to establish a reason for recording an experience. While the teacher's purpose in recording the learners' narratives may be to create a vehicle for learning to read, students need to have more personal purposes for turning talk into print. Writing narrative from their own lives can be motivated by both unusual and commonplace experiences, such as:

- Reports of class experiences: histories of class trips; accounts of science and math experiments; planning a class party; taking a sidewalk safari; how-to materials on growing plants, raising guppies, and making windmills; resource papers about rocks, stamps, baseball, dinosaurs, political parties, and topics from world news;
- Accounts of absorbing community events: the celebration of Earth Day, a visit by a famous person, and school fund raisers;
- Position papers on topics important to students: gun control, recycling, cafeteria food, and smoking;
- Individual and group stories: fiction and nonfiction for the class or school library, including stories, plays, and songs to be presented to other students, parents, and friends;
- News articles: for class or school newspapers or community newsletters and newspapers; and
- Letters: to families, community members, or a favorite author.

By composing from experience, teachers help students value writing as a means of self-expression and as a way of preserving important circumstances and occurrences in their lives. When students choose their own topics to discuss and write about, they will not think of language experience strategy lessons as primarily a form of reading instruction.

Step 3:   It is now time to organize, evaluate, and wonder about the experience. When learners are invited to explore all aspects of an event through talk, they have the opportunity to relive the experience. Through small group or whole class discussion, students become aware of their classmates' lives and of their opinions and values. Uninterrupted talk makes it possible for students mentally and verbally to revisit, roam, reorganize, and highlight parts of the experience.

As the discussion progresses, the teacher and students raise questions designed to bring out significant points not yet considered, suggest unexplored alternatives, and facilitate organization of the piece. As the experience is explored, students select ideas that are consequential and discard those that are repetitive or irrelevant. In doing this, the talk is elevated from a loosely related series of descriptions to a cohesive narrative. When the group members feel they have explored the essentials of the experience and there is a workable format, dictating and recording begin.

Step 4:   The teacher or another capable scribe takes dictation from the author or authors and records the experience on the chalkboard, on an overhead transparency, or on paper. The following procedures ensure valuing language, including the students' own language preferences:

a. Observe standard English spelling conventions. English has standard spelling patterns, regardless of oral dialect.
b. Use standard punctuation forms.
c. Use the students' word choices and grammar. If the student says, "Me and Kate learned Jeff his science stuff," this should be recorded as dictated. If a student asks about "the correctness" of the language, a brief discussion explores different ways to write about the experience, but the authors decide on the final form to use. If the topic of language variation is interesting to the pupils, it can be discussed more fully at another time, so as not to interrupt the flow of the writing. (In preparation for a strategy lesson on language preference, the teacher might suggest that students explore how particular language forms are used in different contexts. See "Strategy Lesson: Eye Dialect," page 237.)

Step 5:   The entire narrative is read aloud without interruption before the close of the session. This reading allows students to edit any writing they find awkward, inappropriate, or inaccurate within the context of the whole. It also allows teachers to catch any inadvertent changes they may have made in recording the learners' language.

Step 6:   Language experience narratives that students select as their favorites are often made into books to add to the class library. Kids love to read each others' books. Authors can become illustrators and put the books together.

Applying: Language experience stories or personal accounts are important in helping learners focus their thoughts, clarify their perceptions, and organize for action.

Reports, reflections, and summaries written by the class through the language experience strategy lesson may serve their purpose for a day or so and then be discarded. Seeing work erased from the board or tossed into the wastebasket frees students to take risks, to share "off-the-top-of-their-head" thinking, and to value written language for the purpose of organizing ideas. When their texts are discarded, students come to understand that written language is not always a permanent record.

Single-use language experience materials can be written to:

- plan a class party. What activities should we have? What refreshments should there be? Who will plan the program?
- review and evaluate the day's activities. What did we accomplish? Did anything unusual or exciting happen?
- compose messages to take home.
- predict the author's position prior to reading a text or trade book. What topics might be covered concerning the development of a railroad system in America? What *wild things* will we meet in *Where the Wild Things Are* (Sendak 1963)?
- organize by thinking and writing. Compose schedules and outlines (including questions) for interviewing classmates, family members, or community members for a special project.

Expanding: Encourage students to serve as a scribe for the language-experience story of a study partner, a younger student, a parent, or a research group. When acting as a scribe, writers should understand that whenever they need to invent spelling (see Chapter 2) in order to keep the writing going, it is acceptable to do so. Editing is left for a later time when publication is the result.

Readings for Expanding This Strategy Lesson

Hepworth, Cathi. *Antics.* New York, NY: G.P. Putnam's Sons, 1992.
    Alphabetical entries from *A* to *Z* all have an "ant" somewhere in the word: There's *E* for Enchanter, *P* for Pantaloons, *S* for Santa, and *Y* for your Ant Yetta.

Jonas, Ann. *Aardvarks, Disembark!* New York, NY: Greenwillow, 1990.
    After the flood, Noah calls out of the ark a variety of little-known animals, many of which are now endangered.

STRATEGY LESSON: MAKING MEANING WITHOUT GRAPHOPHONIC CUES (SELECTED DELETIONS)

Evaluation: Who Will Benefit

This strategy lesson will benefit readers who:

- overuse the graphophonic cueing system by producing nonwords and making multiple attempts at sounding out words;
- refuse to continue reading; or
- abandon semantically acceptable substitutions in favor of nonwords or words that are not acceptable semantically but have a high graphic similarity to the text.

Paying attention to sound/letter relationships while ignoring available syntactic and semantic cues can result in miscues such as:

The boys walked around the *$cure-v* ⓐⓒ curve in the road.

This student first read *curve*, then abandoned the expected response (ⓐⓒ) in favor of a nonword *$cure-v*. When asked why he made the change, the reader said that because the word ended in *e*, it had to have a long *u* sound. Not only did this reader treat graphophonic relationships as a simple one-to-one correspondence (a single sound for a single letter or letter sequence), but he also let a simple prescriptive application of a phonics rule override his knowledge of syntax and semantics. He chose to apply a spelling pattern rule rather than retain a meaningful sentence.

Specific Rationale

Tests and didactic instructional materials frequently require students to demonstrate their use of the graphophonic system in isolation from the other language systems; that is, students are asked to respond to words out of context through worksheets, flash cards, and word lists. Readers differ in the ways they handle words in isolation as opposed to words in context, as the examples below demonstrate and as reading miscue research studies report (K. Goodman & Burke 1973).

When asked to read isolated words on a word list (first column), an eight-year-old gave the following responses to four of the words (second column). However, the student read each of the words as expected or produced high-quality, acceptable miscues when they occurred in the meaningful context of a story (third column).

Listed Word	Oral Response	Oral Response in Context
there	$thore	<u>there</u> were many windows . . .
pieces	prizes	Some <u>pieces</u> were painted. *(pictures)*
sail	smile	. . . boats <u>sail</u> on its waters.
blue	blue	. . . with a <u>blue</u> door. *(little)*

Correctly reading a word on a list does not guarantee that the reader will predict the word in context (as in the case of *blue*). Even if the student pronounces the listed word correctly, there can be no assurance that meaning is constructed. Nor will a reader miscue in the same way when reading a list or in context (as with *pieces*).

When reading a list, readers have few choices: 1) sounding out the word; 2) applying a phonics rule; or 3) responding with a previously memorized word that the word resembles. When the focus is mainly on graphophonic cues, a reader's miscues often result in either nonwords ($caward for *carried*, $hayve for *have*, $intelkual for *intellectual*) or look-alike words (*some* for *same*.)

Attempts at sounding out a syllable or word may produce a broken-record effect, interrupting the flow of meaning construction and seldom producing the expected text. Here are examples of multiple attempts at single words made within the context of a complete story. They are read from bottom to top and numbered in the order produced. (1. represents the reader's first attempt, 2. represents the second, and so on.)

4. s-	*4.* $soowthing	
3. $sinwhys	*3.* sou-	*3.* $diferations
2. $sinwile	*2.* smoothing	*2.* dif-
1. sin	*1.* smooth	*1.* differs
sinewy	soothing	definitions

When readers treat reading in context as if it were merely a word recognition task, they focus on graphophonic cues. Some readers omit words they believe they do not know, thinking they are not supposed to use meaning and syntactic cues to help them predict. When readers fail to take advantage of the syntactic and semantic cueing system, they do not learn to sample the graphophonic system or to use it to confirm predictions. This strategy lesson demonstrates the power of the semantic and syntactic cueing systems and the place of graphophonics in the construction and confirmation of meaning.

Strategy Lesson Experience

Initiating: Invite students to read the following note written on the board or on an overhead transparency:

Brng hm sm hmbrgr nd rlls.

Encourage discussion about whether it was easy or difficult to read the sentence. Were there any alternative ways of reading some of the words? The only ambiguity in this sentence is whether *hm* represents *him* or *home*. Help students see that the ambiguity can be cleared up with pragmatic information; that is, is the note a reminder to take *him* some food or is it meant to remind someone to bring food *home*.

Students may be interested in learning that languages such as Hebrew and Arabic do not normally represent vowel sounds in the written language system. The reader uses the available consonants, syntax, and context to know which words are appropriate.

Discuss the necessity of reading *meanings*, not letters, syllables, or even words. Reading is constructing meaning, not sounding out text. Explore the pragmatics (how meaning relates to the specific social context), the role of semantics, and the necessity of syntax in constructing meaning. The discussion needs to focus on the relationship of graphophonics to the other cueing systems (see Chapters 4 and 5).

How do students think proficient readers use graphophonic information? The first segment of a word, with emphasis on the initial letter, is the graphophonic cue attended to by most readers and the one most frequently used by efficient readers. Proficient readers sample from the first segment and use predicting strategies based on their inferred knowledge of the text. Such readers sample from all the cues, including graphophonics, to confirm their predictions.

In this strategy lesson, students are asked to read material in which graphic cues are omitted. These omissions give readers the opportunity to trust and value their knowledge of the pragmatic, semantic, and syntactic cueing systems as support for their use of graphophonics.

Transacting: *Selected deletions* within predictable text involve not only the removal of letters but also the omission of highly predictable words from a story that is within the reader's conceptualization. The student is asked to insert *any* semantically acceptable words or phrases in the blank slots. (See "Cooperative Controlled Cloze" in Chapter 5.)

An assortment of one- or two-page fiction or nonfiction complete texts that are of interest to the reader and are highly predictable is most helpful in this strategy lesson. It is helpful to have a collection of material that includes nursery rhymes, folktales, songs, storybooks, and any materials the learners have heard or read and liked to use for selected deletion purposes. Examine each story for predictable syntax and meanings that are based on reader experience. The most predictable of the items are deleted and replaced by a line or space. More support is provided if the length of the line is the same as the length of the deleted word. However, if the student doesn't need such support, the lengths of all the blanks can be the same, usually five or six spaces.

> Once upon a time there were three little pigs. One day the three little pigs left home. Each little pig wanted to build a _____. The first little pig made a house of _____. The second little pig made a house of _____. The third little pig made a house of _____.

The predictability of these examples comes from the reader's familiarity with the syntax and semantics of stories they have heard many times.

The basis for predictability of material may also be related to familiar concepts, relationships, story line, straightforward sentence structure, and familiar lexical items. For example:

Tree Animals

One reason it is interesting to observe trees is because they are the homes for animals.

Some of the animals that live in trees can fly and have feathers. These animals use sticks and twigs to build their nests. We all know them as _____.

Another animal likes to live in tree holes. These furry animals frolic around hunting and eating nuts. Many of us have _____ in trees right in our own backyards.

Some animals are so small that they can live on the leaves of the tree. They eat the leaves for food. When birds spot these _____ they eat them for a fine meal.

Such materials may be typed on an overhead transparency or duplicated for each participating student. Explain to the students that they will be reading about things they are familiar with, and when they come to a blank, they are to fill in a word that makes sense to them.

To encourage students to take risks and to trust their knowledge of a familiar story or their knowledge of the contextual cues of an unfamiliar story, move along at a comfortable pace through the reading. Alternate familiar stories with less familiar texts. Make no corrections and give no help. Remind students, if necessary, that they can guess or skip the unknown word or phrase. This lesson needs to be lively and short. If students are taking linguistic risks by making sensible predictions based on all the language cues, there is no need to continue with more materials.

Following each selection, encourage students to talk about their reading and about any problems they are experiencing. The following questions and comments help learners think about the strategies they are using:

1. How did you know what to put in the blanks?
   Reexamine the material. Help students discover that the material can be sorted on the basis of stories they are familiar with (nursery rhymes, folktales, and so on) and stories that are unfamiliar but contain known concepts. Help students realize that it is a strength when they use their own language, knowledge, and experiences as they read.
2. Did you give more than one answer for any blank?
   The structure of these materials may permit alternative responses. How many responses are synonyms? How many are semantically acceptable even though meaning changes? Help students discover which syntactic and semantic cues they used in arriving at their choices.

Applying: Students may work with a tape recorder individually or in pairs as a reader-listener team. With a partner or in a small group, one student reads the text aloud, pausing at each blank as the listener does the writing. If after a brief pause the listener does not produce a filler, the reader continues. The partner or group members should not interrupt the process to discuss the merits of the choices. Help students understand that there is no one acceptable response. In a discussion following the reading, the participants talk about their choices and justify their decisions.

The student who chooses to work alone reads the text aloud into a tape recorder. Encourage readers to fill in the blanks quickly rather than to follow past advice such as "slow down and get each word." By moving along at a good pace, students begin to break away from ponderous reading. By accepting the first response that comes to their minds they are more likely to take semantic and syntactic cues into consideration. When the selection is completed, the reader plays back the tape to evaluate choices and to try other alternatives. The student can discuss these choices with the teacher during an individual conference or with other students who have listened to the tape.

Expanding: Content area materials provide good passages for this lesson. From materials that students are using for study or research, delete a few highly predictable text items that are closely related to the major concepts. Copy the text on an overhead transparency and invite students to talk about the possibilities for filling the slots. What provides the best cues? Does the text give information? Can students provide knowledge from their own background? How much does the learner rely on graphophonics? On the transparency, write in all the likely answers. At the close of the lesson, show the transparency again, adding answers that are now possible and deleting any that students now know are not feasible substitutions. Big books are also helpful for expanding this lesson. Use self-adhesive notes to cover up words or phrases.

Readings for Expanding This Strategy Lesson

Anno, Mitsuma. *Anno's Journey*. New York, NY: Philomel, 1982.
    Through illustrations the author records his journey through Northern Europe and his impressions of the land, the people at work and play, and their art, architecture, folklore, and fairy tales.

Baker, Jeannie. *Window.* New York, NY: Greenwillow, 1991.
> From the window of his room, readers view the events and changes in a young boy's life and in his environment from babyhood to adulthood through wordless scenes.

Geisert, Arthur. *Oink.* Boston, MA: Houghton Mifflin, 1991.
> When their mother falls asleep, the baby pigs sneak away, get into big trouble, and must be rescued.

Geisert, Arthur. *Oink Oink.* Boston, MA: Houghton Mifflin, 1993.
> Eight piglets wander off while their mother is still asleep and enjoy a feast in a cornfield before she brings them home again. The story is told with one word.

Ginsburg, Mirra. *The Chick and the Duckling.* New York, NY: Macmillan, 1972.
> The chick imitates everything the duckling does until he goes swimming. The pictures expand the text and provide opportunities for prediction.

Ginsburg, Mirra. *Across the Stream.* New York, NY: Morrow, 1982.
> A hen and her chicks escape from a fox with the aid of a mother duck and her babies.

Kraus, Robert. *Whose Mouse Are You?* New York, NY: Mulberry, 1987.
> A lonely mouse daydreams about rescuing his parents and sister.

Kraus, Robert. *Come Out and Play, Little Mouse.* New York, NY: Penguin, 1990.
> Each day the cat tries to tempt the little mouse, but the mouse is too smart to listen.

Martin, Bill Jr. *Brown Bear, Brown Bear, What Do You See?* New York, NY: Henry Holt, 1991.
> This classic picture book describes different animals as an unseen narrator asks and then answers a question in a repetitive chant.

Novak, Matt. *Elmer Blunt's Open House.* New York, NY: Orchard, 1992.
> Some animals and a robber explore Elmer's house when he mistakenly leaves the door open.

Schories, Pat. *Mouse Around.* New York, NY: Farrar, Straus & Giroux, 1991.
> In this wordless picture book, an adventurous young mouse finds its way home after falling out of the nest.

Tafuri, Nancy. *Have You Seen My Duckling?* New York, NY: Morrow, 1984.
> Mother Duck is missing one of her ducklings, so she visits all her neighbors inquiring "Have you seen my duckling?"

Tafuri, Nancy. *Jungle Walk.* New York, NY: Greenwillow, 1988.
> A little boy falls asleep after reading a book about animals in a jungle, and then he meets them all in his dream.

Ward, Lynd. *The Silver Pony.* Boston, MA: Houghton Mifflin, 1973.
> A lonely boy, with the help of a winged horse, is able to escape from the isolated world of his mid-western farm and, through a series of adventures, comes to know the larger realism of the world outside.

Williams, Sue. *I Went Walking.* San Diego, CA: Harcourt, Brace, Jovanovich, 1989.
> A boy repeats, "I went walking." He's asked, "What did you see?" His answers tell of encounters with animal friends. Also available in big book format.

STRATEGY LESSON: SYNONYM SUBSTITUTION

Evaluation: Who Will Benefit

This strategy lesson will benefit students who:

- are afraid to take cognitive and linguistic risks; or
- sometimes make an exceptionally good substitution and then regress in the text, abandoning their high-quality miscue, preferring a graphophonic match.

Specific Rationale

See "Strategy Lesson: Making Meaning Without Graphophonic Cues (Selected Deletions)" in this chapter and "Strategy Lesson: Cooperative Controlled Cloze" in Chapter 5.

Strategy Lesson Experience

Initiating: Using a text that students are relatively familiar with, underline words and phrases for which other words may be easily substituted. Each reader will need a copy of the text. For a group of students, an overhead transparency is useful.

Invite students to read the passage through silently, taking note of the underlined items. Invite one student to begin the oral reading, which should continue at a steady pace without interruption. Another option would be to have several readers take turns reading sections. When readers come to underlined items, they don't say what is written; instead, they substitute something that makes sense to them. Encourage students to focus on moving ahead past any problems.

Transacting: After the reading, discuss the interesting alternatives that were read. The point of the experience is to show readers that they need more than graphophonic information to construct meaning.

Applying: The passage may be made available to individuals or partners in a learning center. Materials include the typed or original version of the story with the selected synonyms underlined, a tape recorder, and directions. A student reads the story into the tape recorder, substitutes anything that makes sense for the underlined words or phrases, listens to the tape with a partner, and discusses the cues that helped in making the substitutions.

If a picture book is used, ask the student to use the pictures, not the written text, to tell a story. This tape-recorded story is then compared with the writing. The reader begins to see that meaning can be inferred from information other than print, that the story must connect with the illustrations, that the reading must sound like something an author has written, and that it must make sense.

Expanding: Make a transparency of selected social studies, science, math, and other content area materials. Underline selected concept-laden words and phrases. Place a blank transparency over the transparency of the text and invite students to substitute synonyms for the underlined selections. Write the synonyms on the blank transparency. If working individually or in pairs, a blank transparency can be placed directly on a book or resource material and the students can use a marker to write in their substitutions.

STRATEGY LESSON: EYE DIALECT

Evaluation: Who Will Benefit

This strategy lesson will benefit readers who:

- have trouble when authors use nonstandard spelling to represent a speaker's dialect, such as *fer* for *for* or *wuz* for *was;*
- do not like to read certain books, comics, or magazines because they have too many "funny" words; or
- stop at a word or phrase written in nonconventional spelling and sound it out differently each time, often producing nonwords rather than substituting a high-quality synonym.

Specific Rationale

When authors want to indicate socioeconomic class, regional vernacular, or national origins of their characters, they often change the spelling of particular words so that readers can quickly recognize the characters' uniqueness. The use of nonstandard spelling to represent a particular way a person speaks is called *eye dialect.* With few exceptions, eye dialect is confined to dialogue and includes:

- the representation of informal language or forms of English not usually considered of high social status.
    He was gonna go home.
    They are runnin' fas'.
- the representation of the English of people who speak English as their second language.
    Zat iz a sweet leedle shild.

Readers need to understand that the same strategies they successfully use to predict common graphophonic cues can also be used to predict uncommon spelling patterns.

Proficient readers who have experience in hearing stories and reading texts that include eye dialect will be able to predict such patterns. To comprehend uncommon patterns, proficient readers often:

- are knowledgeable about the cues that alert them to foreign language influences or eye dialect that appear in the material;
- predict the words or phrases that are different from common spelling patterns; and
- decide whether eye dialect words or phrases are significant to the meaning of the story.

If the words or phrases are significant to constructing meaning and if appropriate cues are available, proficient readers make efforts to understand them.

The strategies used by proficient readers to understand eye dialect involve predicting the uncommon spelling pattern and predicting meaning, based on both the totality of the text and on the reader's own background of linguistic experiences. Some readers, however, do not know that eye dialect can appear in written material, so they sound out the text rather than predict the semantic possibilities; in doing so, they risk an unfamiliar rendition. Sometimes readers are surprised to discover that professionally authored materials contain words and phrases used in their oral language, even those words often corrected by adults. These lessons help readers:

- predict materials in which eye dialect is likely to occur;
- predict eye dialect through its uncommon spelling patterns as well as through the use of apostrophes, quotation marks, italics, and other printer's conventions; and
- focus on constructing meaning.

Strategy Lesson Experience

Initiating: Familiar cartoons and songs that make use of eye dialect set the stage for a comfortable and enjoyable learning experience. Students see regional dialect represented in comics such as "Snuffy Smith" and "Andy Capp." A *baby talk* dialect is represented in "The Family Circus" and "The Ryatts." Current popular music, especially rap, and folk songs such as "She'll Be Comin' Roun' the Mountain" and "Papa's Gonna Buy You a Mockin' Bird" reflect regional and ethnic dialects.

Select a song with eye dialect that is familiar to the students or use "She'll Be Comin' Roun' the Mountain," below. Distribute copies of the song or make an overhead transparency. Invite students to sing along with you or ask a capable student to lead the singing.

The words in parentheses on the song sheet are spoken at the end of the first, second, and last lines of each verse and are accompanied with motions (described below).

SHE'LL BE COMIN' ROUN' THE MOUNTAIN

2. She'll be drivin' six white horses when she comes.
   (Whoa, Bill; Toot, toot)

3. An' we'll all go out and meet her when she comes.
   (Hi, Babe; Whoa, Bill; Toot, Toot)

4. An' we'll kill the ol' red rooster when she comes.
   (Ek, Ek; Hi, Babe; Whoa, Bill; Toot, toot)

5. We'll all have chik'n an' dumplins when she comes.
   (Yum, yum; Ek, ek; Hi, Babe; Whoa, Bill; Toot, toot)

6. She'll havta sleep with gramma when she comes.
   (Snore, snore; Yum, yum; Ek, ek; Hi, Babe; Whoa, Bill; Toot, toot)

(ADAPTED AND ARRANGED BY YETTA GOODMAN AND KELLY SMITH)

WORDS	MOTIONS
1. toot, toot!	Pull a train whistle.
2. whoa, Bill!	Pull back the reins as you ride.
3. Hi, Babe!	Wave.
4. ek, ek!	Hand across your neck.
5. yum, yum!	Rub stomach.
6. snore, snore!	Close eyes and lay head on hand.

Transacting: After singing, students might study the lyrics for a few minutes and then comment on the language used. Examine cartoons that have similar eye dialect. Invite students to find instances in which the words in the song lyrics and those in the cartoon are the same or have similar features. After an exploratory discussion, the following questions may be useful:

1. What is happening in the cartoon? Ask students to explain in their own language what each character is saying. You may want to invite them to reflect on their reasoning by asking: "What makes you think so?" and "How has the author shown you that?"
2. What is the author trying to tell about the characters in the cartoon or the song? After the students discuss general characteristics, help them focus on the author's use of eye dialect. Does the dialect provide readers with information about the characters?
3. In what ways are the print of the song and that of the cartoon similar? When students talk first about characters, action, events, and even a theme, it is a good indication that they are constructing meaning. After responding favorably to such comments, it may be time to focus attention on the use of apostrophes, italics, and nonstandard spellings, that is, on the attempts by authors to represent the relationship between written language and oral language.
4. When you notice eye dialect, what strategies can you use? Help students focus on the necessity of gaining a general understanding of what the characters are saying rather than focusing on the author's spelling.

"Hambone" provides an invitation to continue the discussion on the relationship between a particular type of print and meaning.

HAMBONE

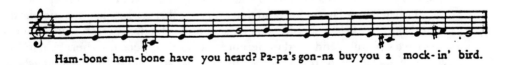

Ham-bone ham-bone have you heard? Pa-pa's gon-na buy you a mock-in' bird.

Hambone

If that mockin' bird don't sing,
Papa's gonna buy you a diamon' ring.

If that diamon' ring don't shine,
Papa's gonna buy you a bottle of wine.

If that bottle of wine gets broke,
Papa's gonna buy you a billy goat.

If that billy goat run away,
Papa's gonna buy you a Chevrolet.

If that Chevrolet don't run,
Papa's gonna buy you a BB gun.

If that BB gun won't shoot,
Papa's gonna buy you a baseball suit.

If that baseball suit don't fit,
Papa's gonna say "Ah, shoot! I quit!"

(ADAPTED AND ARRANGED BY YETTA GOODMAN)

Applying: Interested students might make a collection and then display books, poems, stories, and songs that contain eye dialect. See readings at the end of this lesson.

Students might organize a chart or class notebook, similar to the one below, to record examples. Help learners develop criteria for the kinds of eye dialect they want to categorize. Encourage work in groups of two or three to stimulate exploratory discussion. Students may want to ask family members for examples of their use of dialect.

Examples of Eye Dialect

Source	Text	Author's Purpose	Our Meaning
Comic book	"Da boys n' da hood"	To establish characterization	the boys in the neighborhood
Sports section of the newspaper	"It ain't easy," the coach said.	Use of authentic language	It is not easy to make that play.

Periodically, call attention to the collection. What does the language mean? What is the author trying to say about the characters? If students ask, "What does this say?" encourage them to discover the meaning through context. Ask if they have discovered new purposes for eye dialect or new places where it is found. Provide newspapers, books, magazines, and environmental print for students to search for interesting examples.

As students consider their examples, they need to know that blatant linguistic stereotyping is often found in cartoons and comic books. Authors sometimes use eye dialect in ways that indicate the low educational or social status of speakers, perpetuating the notion that certain groups of speakers are careless or sloppy. Through their study, students can determine authors' opinions, values, and prejudices.

Learners need to understand that every speaker is a speaker of a specific dialect and that every dialect should be respected and valued. A person's pronunciations, sentence structure, and word preferences depend as much on where that individual grew up and learned to talk as they do on educational background. Teachers can help students understand the relationship between oral and written language and can help them gain an accurate picture of how people talk. Such language study can promote sensitivity to the value and beauty of all forms of language and can encourage students to become critical of language or illustrations that stereotype or diminish a group of speakers. Students will come to understand that dialect is an expression of the sensitivity, creativity, and humanity of people.

Expanding: Invite students to use eye dialect to express their own language (such as *gonna, hafta,* and *wachamacalit*) in their writing, thereby using this form for an authentic purpose. Such stories could be shared with other students, teachers, and parents.

Students enjoy investigating the dialects of people on television or radio—actors, announcers, disc jockeys, people in commercials, and politicians. The use of tape-recorded examples collected by students provides opportunities for repeated listening and discussions; the decisions students make about language should be based on accurate and authentic information.

Explore the idea that even though people pronounce words in different ways, written language does not reflect phonological differences unless eye dialect is used. In other words, the spelling of American English is standard despite dialect differences.

Students might: 1) examine collections of folk songs brought from home or the library; 2) compare the same songs found in different books to see if eye dialect is used in the same way in each version; and 3) compare different uncommon spelling patterns used in versions of the same song. Students might look for additional renditions of "She'll Be Comin' Roun' the Mountain," "Hambone," or other songs, noting how each version presents the lyrics.

Teachers usually prefer to read aloud dialects they are familiar with and can reproduce without giving the impression that they are making fun of the characters. To add variety, use recordings of poets, authors, and actors reading various literary selections in authentic dialects. Invite parents and other community members who are comfortable with such materials to read aloud to the students. Help students make a collection of such material.

Readings for Expanding This Strategy Lesson

Books for Primary Grades

Aliki. *Hush Little Baby*. Englewood Cliffs, NJ: Prentice Hall, 1975.
> A traditional children's lullaby with eye dialect in picture-storybook format.

Appelli, Kathi. *Bayou Lullaby*. New York, NY: Morrow, 1995.
> The author spins a lilting lullaby with Cajun words that soothe.

Isaacs, Anne. *Swamp Angel*. New York, NY: Dutton, 1994.
> A new folk-tale heroine, Swamp Angel, wrestles a bear to supply food for settlers in Tennessee. The grammar, eye dialect, and vocabulary represent the period during which they were used.

McKissack, Patricia C. *Flossie and the Fox*. New York, NY: Dial, 1986.
> A wily fox, notorious for stealing eggs, meets his match when he encounters a bold little girl in the woods who insists upon proof that he is a fox before she will be frightened. Each character uses his or her own dialect.

McKissack, Patricia C. *Mirandy and Brother Wind*. New York, NY: Knopf, 1988.
> To win first prize in the Junior Cakewalk, Mirandy tries to capture the wind for her partner. The characters' dialects are represented in print.

Thomasie, Tynia. *Feliciana Feydra LeRoux*. Boston, MA: Little, Brown, 1995.
> Even though Feliciana is her grandfather's favorite, he refuses to allow her to go alligator hunting with him, so one night she sneaks out and surreptitiously joins the hunt anyway. Cajun dialects are represented.

Turner, Glennette Tiley. *Running for Our Lives*. New York, NY: Holiday House, 1994.
> The story of a family escaping from slavery in the U.S. to gain freedom in Canada using the underground railway. The author uses eye dialect in the narrative and in the dialogue of certain characters.

Van Laan, Nancy. *Possum Come a-Knockin'*. New York, NY: Knopf, 1990.
> A finger-snapping rhythmic poem/story that lends itself to choral reading and readers' theater. When possum come a-knockin', the whole family is busy with their personal pastimes and family chores.

Books for Older Readers

Wigginton, Eliot, editor. *The Foxfire Books*. 9 volumes. Garden City, NY: Doubleday/
Anchor Press, 1971–1986.

> Each volume focuses on different aspects of life in the Appalachians. Volume 1 provides information on chimney building, soapmaking, preserving vegetables, and other activities. Volume 2 includes ghost stories as well as information on midwifery and burial customs, among others. The volumes provide insight into a people who are part of the cultural heritage of the United States. High school students did most of the writing.

STRATEGY LESSON: FOREIGN WORDS AND PHRASES

Evaluation: Who Will Benefit

This strategy lesson will benefit readers who:

- do not easily or accurately predict unfamiliar spelling patterns found in foreign words and phrases;
- read names such as *Sven* as *seven* or *seeven;* or
- say they do not like to read certain books because there are too many foreign or "funny looking" words in them.

This strategy lesson helps readers:

- broaden their experiences by reading material that includes foreign language words and phrases;
- use context surrounding the foreign expression; and
- understand that texts contain *tentative unknowns* that may not be immediately understood but that may become clear as the reading continues and as contextual meaning is built.

Specific Rationale

Because they have little experience reading foreign language patterns, some readers treat these as if they were English phrases. Inexperienced readers are likely to be overly concerned with pronunciation and unaware that exact pronunciation is often not necessary in constructing meaning. Sometimes even proficient readers revert to sounding out strategies when they meet foreign language units, allowing this to interfere with their usual ability to use the syntactic and semantic cueing systems.

In the following lessons, *foreign language* refers to any second language embedded within the dominant language of the text.

Authors use foreign-language words or phrases to:

- provide cues to the background of a character, develop the setting, present an expression that is generally recognizable in the foreign language, and establish a mood.

   Maria said, "*Vámanos,* we really must hurry."
- convey meaning and subtleties of meaning for which, in the author's opinion, there is no adequate equivalent term in the dominant language.

   It is *oeuvre* of life, not death.
- provide emphasis or status to the setting or to the characters in the story.

   He saved the *pièce de résistance* for last.

Italics, underlining, or quotation marks are sometimes used as a cue to help readers predict a foreign expression, but even when some print variation is used, the reader must build meaning through the syntactic and semantic cueing systems. Proficient readers handle such foreign language units in a variety of ways, depending on their knowledge of the language. Those who are familiar with the word or phrase as a foreign language will treat the unit as if it were part of the language of the text. Proficient readers who do not have such knowledge can comprehend if the author provides necessary context cues. If the expression is insignificant, proficient readers often ignore it, with minimal or no loss of meaning.

If the author has erroneously assumed that the reader's background includes knowledge of the foreign language, even proficient readers may lose meaning. It is helpful to remind students that writers don't communicate perfectly with their audience and that readers must compensate for that.

Strategy Lesson Experience

Initiating: Invite students to read "Open House" silently.

Open House

The students in Ms. Peters' fifth-grade class had been busy getting their room ready for Open House. Tonight was a very special time for everyone in Room 15. Ms. Peters wanted the parents to see how hard their children had worked and how much they had improved since the beginning of the school year.

The boys and girls were excited and eager to show their parents their beautiful room. They also wanted everyone to meet their favorite teacher, Ms. Peters, who had a way of getting them excited about learning new and interesting things. Ms. Peters was special because she knew how to make learning fun.

Many of the parents had not met Ms. Peters. They hoped she would like them as much as she liked their children. Some of the parents spoke Spanish; others spoke Vietnamese, Italian, or French. When all the parents spoke English, it sounded different from Ms. Peters' English, and the parents sounded different from each other.

It was seven o'clock, and Ms. Peters was at the classroom door waiting for the parents and students.

Teresa was the first to arrive with her mother.

"Buenos noches," Ms. Peters said to Mrs. Orcaza. "Welcome to our classroom."

Ms. Peters turned to Teresa and said, "Teresa, that's a very pretty dress."

Mrs. Orcaza smiled when Ms. Peters said, "Bonita, muy bonita," pointing to Teresa's dress.

"Sí," said Mrs. Orcaza proudly. "She made the dress herself."

Ms. Peters saw the other parents arriving. She turned to Teresa and said, "Show your mother all the stories you've written and the books you've made. I'll be with you as soon as I greet the other parents."

Transacting: Encourage students to talk about the story. If they point out the use of Spanish, ask them to consider why the author chose to use that language. Discuss what they did when they came to the Spanish words and phrases. The following questions may help students develop their understanding of a second language within a predominately first-language text:

1. In what ways does the story seem unusual or unfamiliar to you or different from other stories you have read? Continue to encourage discussion until someone comments on the foreign words or phrases. Without asking for pronunciation of the terms, write the words on the board.
2. What makes these words unusual? What clues are there that help us know these are not English words? Students may notice unusual spellings, as in *buenos* or *muy,* or the use of accent marks. When working with other materi-

als, answers may also include the use of question marks in unfamiliar places; italics, boldface, or underlining; diacritical markings such as tildes, apostrophes, and accent marks; nonalphabetic Chinese and Japanese characters, among others; different alphabetic letters such as Greek and Russian letters; and other nonalphabetic symbols.

3. How can we find out what these unusual words or phrases mean? Ask students to remember what they did to understand the foreign-language expressions in "Open House." Help them realize that they can best discover meaning by predicting and making connections to ongoing events. Invite students to reread quickly "Open House," examining the English language context that provides clues to the meaning of the foreign language units. Ask any students who know Spanish to explain how the context of the story provides clues to meaning. Explore the idea that knowing the general meaning is more important than knowing the exact word-for-word translation or pronunciation.

4. What can you do if the foreign language cannot be understood through context? Students might suggest that they ask someone who speaks the language, check the dictionary, or ask a teacher. Continue to explore what they would do if an expert or a dictionary were not available. Emphasize that it is acceptable to continue reading without being able to pronounce the unfamiliar words or phrases. If a word or phrase is significant, they will discover its meaning as they continue reading, since the author will probably provide additional information. If the author does not do so, the students may then have to postpone understanding this word or phrase until they read it in some other context. The intention is to produce independent readers who are concerned with comprehension and who are aware that in certain situations there are limitations to what can be understood from their reading.

5. Does anyone know which languages are represented by the words or phrases listed on the board? Ask students to explore the story for clues to the language source. Learners who are especially interested in languages might be encouraged to do further research (see the *Expanding* section).

6. In what materials or stories are you likely to find foreign-language expressions? Have you read any stories or other materials that contain such language units? This discussion should help students explore other types of materials in which they might find foreign-language words and phrases, such as menus, recipes, and advertisements. Some students may want to collect examples.

7. Why do authors use foreign language in their writings? Would there ever be a time when we might want to use such terms in our own writings?

8. When is it important to know how to pronounce foreign-language words and phrases? It is only when the language is read orally that knowing the pronunciation becomes useful. Consider that some speakers of the foreign language might be offended if words are mispronounced, sensing that others are making fun of their language. Students should be aware that in some cases the only accurate sources of pronunciation are speakers of that language, but even native speakers may present a variety of pronunciations. When an important foreign name or place is in the news, ask students to listen to radio and television commentators to discover variability in pronunciations.

Applying: The following two texts ("A Letter from Brazil" and "The Map") may help students read materials that include foreign language words and phrases. After students have read them, help them discuss the stories by using questions similar to those listed under *Transacting*. Emphasize that:

- it is unnecessary to be able to pronounce foreign language expressions to understand them;
- context provides cues to the meaning and origin of unfamiliar foreign language units; and
- it is often necessary to read the entire story, article, or poem before meaning can be constructed.

Many of the questions used in the *Transacting* phase of this lesson can be used again to establish these principles.

Invite students to keep an individual list of foreign-language words that can be recorded on a class chart or in a class language book. Ask students to write any clues that help them understand the meaning, mood, origin, and purpose of the foreign-language unit.

Discovering Foreign Language in English Texts

Sentence with Foreign-Language Words or Phrases	Which Language?	Where Found?	Meaning	Cues to the Language and Meaning
She thought about char sui bao, her favorite food	Chinese	Louise, E. *I Hate English.* New York: Scholastic, 1989.	some kind of food	the part after the Chinese
I will bring the tou bob!!	A language from West Africa	Haley, A. *Roots.* New York: Dell, Publishing Co. 1976.	scary white monster	It says something in later sentences

A Letter from Brazil

March 28

Dear Jim,

I am sorry that I did not write to you last month. You're my only pen pal from the USA, and I should write to you at least once every two weeks. Now that you are back home, I don't get a chance to speak English anymore. Do you get to speak Portuguese? If you don't write to me and I don't write to you, you may forget the Portuguese you learned when you were here in Brazil, and I will forget English. We can't let that happen.

You asked in your last letter if there have been any changes in our town since you left. You should know that things change slowly in a little Brazilian seashore town. You can be pretty sure that everything here is *como siempre*. If you came back tomorrow, you would recognize everything. Sr. Santos still sits outside his grocery store all afternoon, smoking thin *bahiano* cigars. The flowers in all the little gardens still smell sweet. The sea rolls in toward the shore, making big waves on our white sand beaches. And the *palmeiras*—the beautiful coconut palm trees—wave in the ocean breezes. Yes, everything is the same.

But a few new things happen, *amigo*. We had a terrible time two weeks ago. We were all very frightened. It was terrible—*terrível mesmo*!

It started two weeks ago, when my father and uncle went fishing early in the morning, as they do every morning. Do you remember our fishing boats, our *jangadas*? Most of the men of our town are fishermen. Each day they sail out to sea on *jangadas.* A *jangada* is like a big raft. It is made of big logs of balsa wood, a wood that is so light that it floats on water easily. The logs are tied together, and each *jangada* has one sail. Usually, our fishermen start out together in the morning and return at sunset. When you see all the white sails coming into the harbor, it is *bonito*—a beautiful sight. Two weeks ago, on Monday, the fishermen sailed out as always. I watched until they disappeared from sight. Oh, how I wished I could be with them. All during school vacation, I sailed on the *jangada* with my father and uncle. But now I have to go to school. *Que pena!* It is a real pity.

That night I walked down to the beach to watch the fishermen come home. One by one the boats pulled up to shore. But my father's *jangada* did not come back. Old Tomás put his arm around my shoulder and said, "Come, Carlos. We will walk to your house together. I want to talk to your mother."

We didn't say a word to each other, but inside I was very, very scared. Maybe you remember the old saying among the fishermen, that sooner or later the Goddess of the Sea, *Yemanjá*, takes a *jangada* down to the bottom of the ocean. Every day the fishermen go out to sea, but every once in a while someone doesn't return. This time I was afraid that *Yemanjá* had taken my father and uncle.

When we got to my house, old Tomás said to my mother, "Today we had a storm at sea. It was one of those quick storms that come from nowhere and disappear as quickly as they come. Your *jangada* was separated from us when the mast broke. The last time we saw it, the boat was drifting farther out to sea. We could not move fast enough to catch it. Your husband is lost at sea. I am afraid that *Yemanjá* has claimed another victim."

My aunt and two brothers and sisters began to cry when they heard about the storm. I wanted to cry, too, but I am the oldest boy, and I must learn to act like a man. But I tell you, *amigo,* it is hard not to cry when you learn that your father is lost at sea.

My mother did not cry. I could see that she was holding her feelings inside herself, but she did not cry. Instead, she said, "Tomás, we thank you for coming to us, even though your news is sad. It is very possible that the cruel sea has taken my husband. We are in God's hands, and what must be, must be. But I feel in my heart that my husband is not dead. So we will wait."

My mother and I sat on the beach all night, waiting. We were both very sad. We waited and waited. Ten days passed. It was impossible that they were still alive, but my mother would not give up hope. She said that she knew they were still alive. Every morning, before dawn, she would leave our house and walk down to the beach. It was still dark outside, but I would wake up and follow her. I knew she was hoping against hope.

Yesterday, we saw a big *helicóptero* flying toward us from the sea. It came closer and closer until it reached the beach. Then it began to come down for a landing. None of us had ever seen a *helicóptero* before, even from far away. All of a sudden, here was one close up. I forgot my sadness for a minute. On the side of the *helicóptero* were words that said it belonged to the Brazilian Air Force—the *Força Aeréa do Brasil.* After a few minutes a door opened and out came my father and my uncle! Can you imagine! They had been drifting at sea for more than ten days until they were picked up by a ship heading for Africa. The ship radioed the *Força Aeréa* and they sent a *helicóptero* to get my father and uncle. We were so happy to see them. And my mother, who didn't cry when we all thought they were lost at sea, suddenly started to cry when she saw my father. She didn't stop crying for a long time.

That night, the whole town got together for a big *festa* in honor of my father and uncle. We had all kinds of good food. You would have loved it. The next day, everything was back to normal. I went back to school. My father and uncle began to build a new *jangada*.

I'd better say *adeus* now because I want to mail this letter today. I hope you remember to write soon.

Your friend,
Carlos

(Barry Sherman)

The following story contains both foreign language phrases and eye dialect. Invite students to discuss the differences between the two forms.

The Map

"I hope the bus gets here soon," Mary said. "I don't want to be late for school. Mr. Roberts started a great story yesterday. He said he would finish it first thing this morning, if we all got there on time."

As Mary and Beth stood waiting, they saw a family walking toward them, all dressed up. They looked as if they were going somewhere special on a holiday. There was a father, a mother, and two small children.

The man came up to them and said, "*Guten Tag.*"

The two girls looked at each other. They did not understand the language the man spoke, but Beth took a chance and said, "Good morning. Can we help you?"

"Ve vant go to town. Vich bus ve take?"

Mary said, "This is a school bus stop, not a city bus stop."

The man shook his head and replied, "*Ich versteh nicht.* . . . I speak not very vell English. Ve vant a bus to go to town."

Beth turned to Mary. "I don't think he understands you. Try again."

"This bus does not go downtown. I'll show you how to go."

Mary took paper and pencil from her school bag. Beth began drawing a map on the paper, talking and pointing at the same time.

"We are here on Royale Street."

"Royale Street," the man said nodding.

Beth nodded, too, and continued to draw.

"You go one block north in that direction to Fifteenth Street."

She pointed and the man nodded his head.

"At the corner you cross the street and walk two blocks past Superior Road to Johnson Road."

She looked at the man's face. He was looking at her map closely and seemed to understand.

"Then cross over Johnson and take the Number Forty-Four bus there. It will say Central Station on the front."

She handed over the map just as the school bus arrived.

When the man saw the bus, he said, "Oh, *school* bus." He smiled and said something to his family. Beth and Mary thought they knew what the words meant even though they didn't know the language. They smiled at the family.

As Beth and Mary got on the bus, the man said, "Tank you, very much, girls. Tank you." He waved at the girls and so did all his family.

The girls waved back. The beginning of a good day.

(YETTA GOODMAN)

Expanding: Students may want to expand the story "Open House" with a description of Ms. Peters greeting other parents who speak a language other than English. This experience is especially appropriate if there are classmates whose first language is other than the predominant one. Encourage students to interview people who speak other languages or to do some library research to find appropriate greetings. The pupils might act out their stories after they have written additional episodes.

Suggest that students act out "The Map," then discuss the problems of traveling in foreign countries. If it seems appropriate, they might write a handbook called "How to Help Non-English Speakers," or "How to Help Non-Spanish Speakers," or any variation, depending on the community.

After some discussion about when it is appropriate to include non-English words and phrases, students may want to add some to their own writings. Their stories may be shared with others and kept in a collection of such materials to be used with other classes.

If students want to experiment with pronouncing foreign words or phrases, suggest that they interview and tape-record proficient speakers of the language to get acceptable pronunciations. Students will find that all speakers of a given language do not have the same pronunciations.

Students may categorize the various foreign language expressions as they read, discovering familiar spelling patterns that help them predict which language is being represented.

There are many foreign language words and phrases found in the study of history, geography, and the development of societies. Help students build concepts related to place names and origins of the names of people. Such meaning-making strategies are more important than a focus on precise pronunciation. (See "Strategy Lesson: Nouns as Names for People" and "Strategy Lesson: Nouns as Place Names" in Chapter 5.)

Scientific names of plants and animals are usually derived from Latin and Greek. When students read materials that have scientific terms, help them use reading strategies similar to those used with foreign language words or phrases. The remaining text, including illustrations, should provide clues to what is being described. Often, common names are also provided. Many scientific terms are concepts for which learners must build meaning. Students could also begin to discover that some scientific terms have bound morphemic endings, such as *-ology* or *-ium*, that can provide clues to the meanings of words. (See "Strategy Lesson: Developing Meaning Through Context" in Chapter 4.)

Abuela, the beautiful book written by Arthur Dorros (1991) and illustrated by Elisa Kleven, will help readers understand how meaning is constructed through story and illustration. The words in Spanish are understood because of the author's and illustrator's contributions combined with the readers' willingness to use their own background information and to take some linguistic risks.

Readings for Expanding This Strategy Lesson

Books for Primary Grades

Conrad, Pam. *Animal Lingo.* New York, NY: HarperCollins, 1995.
>   This beautifully illustrated book provides the words different languages use for a variety of animal sounds.

Feder, Jane. *Table * Chair * Bear: A Book in Many Languages.* New York, NY: Houghton Mifflin, 1995.
>   Common objects found in a child's room are labeled in thirteen different languages, including Spanish, Vietnamese, Japanese, and French.

Johnston, Tony. *The Iguana Brothers.* New York, NY: Scholastic, 1995.
>   As Dom and Tom, the Iguana Brothers, eat flowers and pretend to be dinosaurs, they discover they can be best friends.

Kessler, Cristina. *One Night.* New York, NY: Philomel, 1995.
> When one of his goats gives birth, Muhamad spends the night alone in the desert and thus becomes a man in the eyes of his family.

Kuklin, Susan. *Kodomo.* New York, NY: G.P. Putnam's Sons, 1995.
> The customs and spirit of Japan are portrayed as the author-photographer visits with seven children living in Hiroshima and Kyoto.

Markel, Michelle. *Gracias, Rosa.* Morton Grove, IL: Albert Whitman & Co., 1995.
> At first, a young girl does not like her new babysitter, Rosa, but after getting to know her and learning some of her language and customs, she is sad when Rosa returns to her family in Guatemala.

Rattigan, Jama. *Dumpling Soup.* Boston, MA: Little, Brown, 1993.
> A young Hawaiian girl and her family, representing different ethnic groups, make traditional food for their New Year's celebration.

Soto, Gary. *Chato's Kitchen.* New York, NY: G.P. Putnam's Sons, 1995.
> To get the "ratoncitos," little mice who have moved into the barrio, to come to his house, Chato, the cat, prepares all kinds of good food: fajitas, frijoles, salsa, enchiladas, and more.

Books for Older Readers

Avi. *The Fighting Ground.* New York, NY: HarperCollins, 1987.
> Thirteen-year-old Jonathan learns what it means to be a soldier during the Revolutionary War. The text provides examples of both French and German words and their meanings.

Lindgren, Astrid. *The Tomten.* New York, NY: Coward, McCann & Geoghegan, 1968.
> The simple tale of a strange but gentle creature who comes out only at night, talks to animals in Tomten language, and is never seen by human beings.

STRATEGY LESSON: PRINT VARIATIONS

Evaluation: Who Will Benefit

This strategy lesson will benefit readers who:

- consider changes in print to be an insurmountable interruption; or
- do not use appropriate intonation when they encounter print variations during oral reading.

Students with limited experiences in reading materials with print variations are usually unfamiliar with the wide range of print forms and unaware of the purposes of such variations.

Specific Rationale

There are print conventions that writers and publishers use to cue readers to greater understanding of writers' meanings and purposes. Such conventions include varying typeface or fonts as *italics* or **boldface,** placing words and phrases in "quotation marks" or ALL CAPITAL LETTERS, and underlining text. A graphic display may convey meaning; for example, the word *gigantic* is printed in very large, bold letters or the word *fat* is produced in round pudgy letters. Children actually experiment with such graphic representations in their own writing. It is an important feature in graffiti. Authors use varied graphic conventions to:

- indicate emphasis.
  Her dad said, "Don't you ever, *ever* let me catch you smoking."
  Nothing, **absolutely nothing,** would stop her from dancing.
- show a change in the mood or tone of a story or of a character.
  The storm got worse and WORSE.
  His voice got softer and his whole body began to *shake* .
- indicate titles of publications.
  She read *Les Miserables* three times.
  Read "The Importance of Talk" in *Language Arts.*
- indicate an overused or unusual statement.
  She "was no better than she ought to be."
  He was "as strong as an ox."
- indicate that a word or a phrase is being referred to as a unit in itself.
  "Mess" is a four-letter word.
  He asked Linda how to spell *beautiful.*
- identify eye dialect or foreign language words or phrases (see preceding strategy lessons).
  " *'Enry, pahk the cah,*" commanded the passenger.
  The young man added politely, "*S'il vous plaît.*"

This strategy lesson helps students understand that authors' and publishers' purposes for using print variations are to enhance readers' understanding of text.

Strategy Lesson Experience

Initiating: If readers appear to have trouble with print variations, ask the following questions in a conference:

1. Why did the author capitalize, underline, use quotation marks, change the print font, and so on?
2. How does the change in print help you understand what the author is saying?

Encourage students to look for print variations in everything they read: newpapers and content area materials, advertisements, letters, and so on. Invite them to keep a personal or class record of the print examples found over a period of two weeks or so. List the variations, including a significant segment of the language context; next to each, indicate their interpretation of the author's meaning and the author's purpose.

Collection of Print Variations

Source	Print Variation	Author's Meaning and Purpose
The Stinky Cheese Man (Scieszka & Smith, 1992)	print size, shapes, colors change	to make fun of folktales

Invite students to explore the meaning and purpose of print variations in poetry and cartoons. Readers may find that big books (enlarged texts) are excellent sources of print variations.

Transacting: Help students classify the reasons authors use print variations. Although the categories may be similar to those listed in the "Specific Rationale," do not provide students with categories; suggestions should emerge from discussion. Students' examples might be collected and duplicated. To discover new or different reasons authors use print variations, students might work as a group sorting or categorizing the combined examples and adding to them over time.

Applying: Students may want to record different print variations or those that they do not understand. In a small-group discussion or in an individual conference with the teacher, students can explore print variations: their uniqueness, the problems they cause, what they mean, and why a particular author uses them.

Expanding: Encourage students to use print variations in their own writings and to discuss reasons for their use. Discuss what happens when such forms are overused in a story or article. Explore the variations that support meaning and those that might disrupt meaning. As students compose, encourage them to explore print variations available on the computer.

Art activities can convey the idea that written language has aesthetic quality and may be examined as an art form. Students may draw a word or name in cursive writing, then copy its mirror image and fill it in with crayons or a watercolor wash. They may sketch words or phrases in such a way that the meaning of the unit is conveyed graphically. The word *cracked* may be written to look as if it is actually cracked, and *tall* may be written vertically across two or more spaces to represent height. Discuss the artistic qualities of the scripts of languages such as Chinese and Arabic, the illuminated letters at the beginnings of old manuscripts, and the characters on Chinese chops (signature seals).

Concrete poetry often utilizes print variations as well as taking on the "concrete" form of the theme or topic of the poetry, such as when a poem about a frog is formatted in the shape of a frog. Students may be interested in collecting and creating such poetry. Encourage students to create appropriate visual expressions of the poem's content.

Readings for Expanding This Strategy Lesson

Books for Primary Grades

Carle, Eric. *The Secret Birthday Message.* New York, NY: Harper, 1972.
    The title provides a good summary statement for this exciting picture book. Carle uses an unusual format that matches the story line and the

artistic work. Pages are cut appropriately to look like rocks and doors. Peepholes are used to find surprises.

Falwell, Cathryn. *The Letter Jesters*. New York, NY: Houghton Mifflin, 1994.
A celebration of the variety of sizes and styles of letters. Hundreds of typefaces are shown with many variations.

Scieszka, Jon and Lane Smith. *The Stinky Cheese Man and Other Fairly Stupid Tales*. New York, NY: Viking, 1992.
The author and illustrator have fun retelling well-known tales with their own twists, such as "The Really Ugly Duckling." The narrator interacts with the print. The author/illustrator take liberty with the format and order of the book and the use of print.

Sendak, Maurice. *In the Night Kitchen*. New York, NY: Harper & Row, 1970.
Max has a nightmare that involves the night kitchen, the Milky Way, and other adventures before he wakes up. Max loses his pajamas through his adventures. Although the print is always in caps, its style and shape change from page to page. It occurs horizontally, vertically, in speech balloons, in varied sizes of rectangles, and on buildings.

Books for Older Readers

Brunhoff, Jean du. *The Story of Babar*. New York, NY: Random House, 1984.
The first of the well-loved series about an elephant family. The story is in cursive script.

STRATEGY LESSON: FORMAT VARIATIONS

Evaluation: Who Will Benefit

This strategy lesson will benefit students who:

- frequently lose their place while reading newspaper columns;
- are unsure where to read when the print goes across two pages of a text; or
- ignore graphs and keys in nonfiction material that support comprehension of the text.

Specific Rationale

Written material comes in a wide variety of formats. Publishers use a format to convey meaning, to make the material easier to read, or to overcome limitations of space or cost. Poetry, recipes, mathematical equations, and science experiments are formatted in conventional ways because they are best understood when organized in those ways. Editors lay out newspapers and magazines in multiple columns to make their publication readable and to create space for advertising and graphics.

Other format variations include cutlines under pictures and print that wraps around maps, pictures, and graphs. Tables of contents, indices, dedications, and other parts of books follow layout conventions that differ from the main text format. Other format variations include lists, newspaper headlines, telephone directories, television program guides, the ingredients lists on food containers, traffic signs, cartoons, advertisements, guarantees, deeds, tickets, posters, and menus. This short list indicates opportunities for students to investigate a great variety of reading materials.

Strategy Lesson Experience

Initiating: Students may need to be encouraged to share problems that arise when reading new material. As part of a conference, you might ask, "Was there anything about the way the story/text was arranged that caused you difficulty?"

Help students broaden their reading experiences by providing opportunities to read materials involving new formats. Because they have repeatedly seen print variations on cereal boxes, candy wrappers, television captions, posters, games, and toys, readers have background experiences to build on, and a lesson could be started by discussing such familiar print settings. The use of materials included in the Materials/Functions Grid, Figure 2–3 in Chapter 2, will expand students' contacts with a variety of formats.

Transacting: If students and teachers collect an assortment of formats, they can explore similarities, differences, and functions. Encourage students to include those formats that give them the most difficulty.

The following questions may be helpful:

1. In what ways are these formats similar? Students may tell how cartoon formats are like a page of ads, how a science resource is like an encyclopedia, or how recipes are similar to directions for putting together a bike.
2. How are these formats different, and why are they different? Students should discover that the content and the purpose of the text dictates the format.
3. Do we do anything differently when we read materials in unusual formats? Help students discover, for example, that some materials may be read faster than others and that some print can even be ignored depending on the reader's background and purpose. In reading newspaper articles, one need only read the first paragraph to get an overview of a story and then decide

whether to read the rest of the article. In the case of recipes, pattern instructions, and other directions, it is sometimes important to read everything through once in order to know what the outcome will be and what ingredients or materials are required; the reader then rereads and follows the directions step by step and may even reread periodically to check that all has been done correctly.

4. When a picture or graph accompanies the reading, at what point is it best to read the caption related to it? Why is it important to do so? Are special strategies needed for this task? Since very little research has been done to discover the different ways in which reading strategies are used for various formats, invite students to examine what they do, and then discuss effective and efficient strategies.

5. What problems do you have with formats? Help students understand that the difficulty may lie in their lack of familiarity with a particular type of reading material or with the author's purpose.

6. As a reader of text in an unfamiliar format, what do you need to know? Why do you need to know it? How will you get the information you need?

7. As an author, how will you decide how to arrange material in a particular format? How might this arrangement aid a reader? What problems could this arrangement cause the reader?

Applying: Most students love Joanna Cole's books about the adventures of children on the magic school bus (*The Magic School Bus at the Waterworks* (1986), *The Magic School Bus Inside the Earth* (1987), *The Magic School Bus Inside the Human Body* (1989), *The Magic School Bus Lost in the Solar System* (1990), and others). Invite learners to read the books independently; then with a partner, list the print (see "Strategy Lesson: Print Variations," page 252) and format variations. Discuss with a partner or in a group why the author decided to use a particular format to express certain information.

In Cole's books, do readers use the same strategies for reading the cartoon sections as for reading the reports, the environmental print, the author's text, and the resource information? What strategies support the reader's search for meaning within each format?

Help students find other materials that provide opportunities to try their strategies. Many books use formats suitable for radio scripts, memos, letters, diaries, comic books, and recorded telephone conversations.

Expanding: The teacher, perhaps with the help of parents and students, may set up a store to encourage primary students to use print as they simulate shopping. Older students can use recipes, the print on containers, and the print on measuring cups and spoons to prepare a class treat or to set up a restaurant. Students might travel to see outside-the-classroom examples of different print formats, such as metered gas pumps and air pressure gauges at service stations; scales, appointment lists, medical records, blood pressure gauges, and prescription pads at doctors' offices; stamps, postage meters, and scales at post offices; and tape measures and patterns at tailor shops.

As students explore new types of reading materials, discuss print and format variations. The following questions may help readers understand the pragmatics of visual information:

1. For whom did the author intend the material?
2. What purpose did the author have in writing it?
3. Why would a learner read this material?
4. In what different ways might different students read the same material? Why?
5. Why is the material organized as it is?

Nonfiction materials provide a particularly wide and diverse collection of format variations. For each kind of material (see Materials/Functions Grid, Figure 2–3 in Chapter 2), students might record the specific problems they face, indicating why particular materials present a problem, why the author chose the format, and how reading strategies are used in each situation.

Readings for Expanding This Strategy Lesson

Books for Primary Grades

Brumpton, Keith. *Rudley Cabot in the Quest for the Golden Carrot*. New York, NY: Delacorte, 1994.

A carrot-crunching, paw-biting comic strip about rabbits in space.

Cummings, Pat. *Petey Moroni's Camp Runamok Diary*. New York, NY: Bradbury, 1992.

A diary kept during camp unravels the mystery of a food-snatching raccoon.

Hergé. *The Adventures of TinTin*. Boston, MA: Little, Brown, 1991.

TinTin's adventures are portrayed in comic strip format.

Meddaugh, Susan. *Martha Speaks*. Boston, MA: Houghton Mifflin, 1992.

Problems arise when Martha, the family dog, learns to speak after eating alphabet soup.

Smith-Baranzini, Marlene and Howard Egger-Bovet. *USKids History: Book of the New American Nation*. Boston, MA: Little, Brown, 1995.

History is more than facts and figures about a time long past. It is stories about real people who live and learn, hope and dream, and triumph and fail. This book brings these stories to life by providing vividly written accounts, dramatic readings, plays, poems, songs, speeches, and illustrations.

Williams, Vera B. *Stringbean's Trip to the Shining Sea*. New York, NY: Greenwillow, 1988.

Stringbean describes his trip to the west coast in a series of postcards.

Williams, Vera B. *Scooter*. New York, NY: Greenwillow, 1993.

With her scooter, Elana discovers that a big city has many opportunities for adventure and making friends of all kinds. Each chapter starts with an overview that does not necessarily match the table of contents.

Books for Older Readers

Avi. *City of Light, City of Dark*. New York, NY: Orchard, 1993.

Using a comic-book novel format, Avi writes an urban folktale in which the characters race to save the metropolis from destruction.

Cushman, Karen. *Catherine, Called Birdy*. New York, NY: Harper Trophy, 1994.

The diary of Catherine, a young girl growing up in 1290 in England.

Feiffer, Jules. *The Man in the Ceiling*. New York, NY: HarperCollins, 1993.

The story of a boy cartoonist who learns to deal with failure and complex family relationships. This book is filled with pathos and humor.

STRATEGY LESSON: MAKING OUR OWN MARKS; READING OUR OWN WRITING

Evaluation: Who Will Benefit

This strategy lesson will benefit students who:

- need to see the relationship between the writing an author constructs and the meaning they construct as readers; or
- are unaware that they use graphophonic knowledge when they invent spellings or other visible linguistic features.

Specific Rationale

The phenomenon of writers using their personal knowledge about language to create their own spellings is called *invented spelling*. (To show that students can move to standard spelling, some teachers refer to invented spelling as *temporary* or *developmental* spelling.) The term *invented spelling* reflects the constructive and inventive process of language learning and shows the ownership, knowledge, and active participation of the learner (see Chapter 2). When students invent spelling and other visual features, they are performing sophisticated linguistic tasks and reveal through their inventions their knowledge of the graphophonic system.

Invented spelling is accepted and valued in whole language classrooms because it frees writers to express their feelings and intellect without interrupting their flow of ideas, making students more willing, efficient, and prolific writers. It is also a strategy all writers use in their first draft writing.

In this lesson, invented spelling is considered for a different purpose. We want children to understand that authors can create or invent spelling, punctuation, and other visual features to convey meaning. Just as professional writers do, student writers decide what they want to express and then use all they know about the way words look, sound, and are produced in the mouth in order to create spelling.

Strategy Lesson Experience

Initiating: Learners' interest in invented spelling is enhanced by investigating other students' writings. Invite students to examine examples of invented spelling.

The first piece on page 259 was composed by Pom, a kindergartner. Pom drew the picture and wrote the caption when she returned from Disneyland. Encourage discussion about what the invented spelling represents ("I took the picture at Disneyland."). What cues did the students use to decide what Pom wrote? Why did Pom choose these particular letters?

Transacting: To make the concept of invented spelling relevant and pertinent, ask students to select three or four pieces they have written since the beginning of the year. If they have stories that they wrote when they were younger, encourage them to bring these to class.

With the students, examine the pieces and determine which were written earlier and which were written recently. To focus on development, find examples such as the evolution of the spelling of a word. Mary investigated her spelling of "puppy": first she wrote only a single *p;* later she used *pp;* then a vowel appeared, *pep* or *pup;* later *e* was added as a final marker, *pupe;* and finally conventional spelling appeared. The point to be made is that invented spellings are important because they are chosen by the author to represent something meaningful, and as they change over time, they show that the writers have greater knowledge about the graphophonic system.

The children's writing can also be examined for invented punctuation marks or other graphic symbols. Students often put a dot between words ("so they won't slide

together"), draw a line in the text where a paragraph might appear, or try to provide meaning through a drawing and letters as Steve, at age five, does below, when he writes the word *Eskimo*.

Older students can examine the inventions they use over time, determining which are stable and which they change each time they write them. The purpose is to show how all writers use the phenomenon of invention in their spelling and how spelling strategies change over time as experience with writing grows.

Applying: Students see their ideas come alive by using books without words. Invite pupils to examine pictures from a wordless book that have been transferred to overhead-projector transparencies. After the learners have studied the first picture, urge them to write their own text on paper or on the chalkboard. If the students agree, discuss their work with others in the class. Invite the authors to read their pieces. What reasons do students give for selecting the letters used to represent their meaning? Did the letters represent the most prominent sounds? Were those the letters the students remember seeing in the word when it appeared in other texts? Did they copy the word from something in the room? How were decisions about spelling patterns made? One student author may share his or her entire text on overhead transparencies. This may take more than one session; it may be appropriate to ask a small group of interested learners to work together after the initial lesson and discuss their findings later with the teacher or the class.

Expanding: Relate these activities to the topics students are studying and writing about in science, math, or social studies. In groups of four or five, students might select the topic area they're most interested in and then make a list of words and phrases relevant to that topic. Provide colored markers and large chart paper. The students may suggest or write their own invented spellings for the selected words and make a chart of all their inventions. Each group announces its topic and then shares its chart. Encourage comments and questions: Can we read the spellings? What helped us read the words? Did they guess at the conventional spellings? What cues or knowledge did they use to make their guesses? How did knowing the topic help? Why did the group members choose to spell the words that way? Was there any agreement or disagreement on the way words were spelled? This lesson may become part of each theme cycle. (See Wilde (1992) and spelling strategies in K. Goodman et al. (1992).)

Discuss why invented spelling is helpful. Talk about what they have learned about the graphophonic system of language and how, in concert with the other systems of language, it helps them read conventional and invented spelling.

Selected Bibliography for Teachers/Researchers

These selected references on language and thought and their relationship to the reading process are recommended for teachers/researchers to supplement the references and information presented in this book.

Reading and Reading Strategies

Gilles, Carol, Bixby, Mary, Crowley, Paul, Crenshaw, Shirley R., et al. 1988. *Whole Language Strategies for Secondary Students.* Katonah, NY: Richard C. Owen Publishers, Inc.

Goodman, Kenneth S. 1982. *Language and Literacy: The Selected Writings of Kenneth S. Goodman, Volume 1: Process, Theory, Research.* Ed. Frederick V. Gollasch. Boston, MA and London, England: Routledge and Kegan Paul. Available in the Office of Language and Literacy, College of Education, University of Arizona, Tucson, AZ 85721.

Goodman, Kenneth S. 1982. *Language and Literacy: The Selected Writings of Kenneth S. Goodman, Volume II: Reading, Language, and the Classroom Teacher.* Ed. Frederick V. Gollasch. Boston, MA and London, England: Routledge and Kegan Paul. Available in the Office of Language and Literacy, College of Education, University of Arizona, Tucson, AZ 85721.

Goodman, Kenneth S. 1993. *Phonics Phacts.* Portsmouth, NH: Heinemann.

Goodman, Kenneth S. In press. *On Reading.* Portsmouth, NH: Heinemann.

Goodman, Yetta M. and Wilde, Sandra, eds. In press. *Notes from a Kidwatcher: Selected Writings of Yetta Goodman.* Portsmouth, NH: Heinemann.

Read, Charles. 1975. *Children's Categorization of Speech Sounds in English.* Urbana, IL: ERIC Clearinghouse and National Council of Teachers of English.

Read, Charles. 1986. *Children's Creative Spelling.* Boston, MA: Routledge and Kegan Paul.

Rosenblatt, Louise M. 1994. *The Reader, the Text, the Poem.* Carbondale, IL: Southern Illinois University Press.

Smith, Frank. 1973. *Psycholinguistics and Reading.* New York, NY: Holt, Rinehart & Winston.

Smith, Frank. 1975. *Comprehension and Learning.* Katonah, NY: Richard C. Owen Publishers, Inc.

Smith, Frank. 1978. *Understanding Reading.* New York, NY: Holt, Rinehart & Winston.

Smith, Frank. 1979. *Reading Without Nonsense.* New York, NY: Teachers College, Columbia University.

Spencer, Margaret Meek. 1988. *How Texts Teach What Readers Learn.* Stroud, UK: Thimble Press.

Watson, Dorothy. 1987. *Ideas and Insights: Language Arts in the Elementary School.* Urbana, IL: National Council of Teachers of English.

Reading Curriculum

Atwell, Nancie. 1987. *In the Middle: Writing, Reading, and Learning with Adolescents.* Portsmouth, NH: Heinemann.

Britton, James. 1993. *Language and Learning.* Portsmouth, NH: Boynton/Cook, Heinemann.

Cullinan, Beatrice E. 1987. *Children's Literature in the Reading Program.* Newark, DE: International Reading Association.

Goodman, Kenneth S. 1986. *What's Whole in Whole Language.* Ontario, Canada: Scholastic.

Goodman, Kenneth S., Goodman, Yetta M., and Flores, Barbara. 1979. *Reading in the Bilingual Classroom: Literacy and Biliteracy.* Rosslyn, VA: National Clearinghouse for Bilingual Education.

Goodman, Kenneth S., Smith, E. Brooks, Meredith, Robert, and Goodman, Yetta M. 1987. *Language and Thinking in School: A Whole Language Curriculum.* 3d ed. Katonah, NY: Richard C. Owen Publishers, Inc.

Goodman, Yetta M., Watson, Dorothy, and Burke, Carolyn. 1987. *Reading Miscue Inventory: Alternative Procedures.* Katonah, NY: Richard C. Owen Publishers, Inc.

Hart-Hewns, Linda and Wells, Jan. 1990. *Real Books for Reading.* Portsmouth, NH: Heinemann.

Martens, Prisca, Goodman, Yetta M., and Flurkey, Alan. 1995. "Miscue Analysis for Classroom Teachers." *Primary Voices*, Volume 3, issue 4.

Moffett, James. 1968. *Teaching the Universe of Discourse.* Boston, MA: Houghton Mifflin.

Moffett, James. 1973. *A Student-Centered Language Arts Curriculum, Grades K–12: A Handbook for Teachers.* Boston, MA: Houghton Mifflin.

Mooney, Margaret. 1988. *Developing Life-long Readers.* Wellington, New Zealand: Learning Media, Ministry of Education.

Mooney, Margaret. 1990. *Reading To, With, and By Children.* Katonah, NY: Richard C. Owen Publishers, Inc.

Peterson, Ralph. 1992. *Life in a Crowded Place.* Portsmouth, NH: Heinemann.

Peterson, Ralph and Eeds, Maryann. 1990. *Grand Conversations.* New York, NY: Scholastic.

Pierce, Kathryn Mitchell and Gilles, Carol. 1993. *Cycles of Meaning: Exploring the Potential of Talk in Learning Communities.* Portsmouth, NH: Heinemann.

Short, Kathy G. and Burke, Carolyn. 1991. *Creating Curriculum.* Portsmouth, NH: Heinemann.

Short, Kathy G., Harste, Jerome C., and Burke, Carolyn. 1995. *Creating Classrooms for Authors and Inquirers.* Portsmouth, NH: Heinemann.

Watson, Dorothy and Wilde, Sandra, eds. In press. *Supporting Whole Language Teachers: Selected Writings of Dorothy Watson.* Portsmouth, NH: Heinemann.

Weaver, Constance. 1990. *Understanding Whole Language.* Portsmouth, NH: Heinemann.

Weaver, Constance. 1994. *Reading Process and Practice.* Portsmouth, NH: Heinemann.

Wilde, Sandra. 1992. *You Kan Red This: Spelling and Punctuation for Whole Language Classrooms, K–6.* Portsmouth, NH: Heinemann.

Reading Strategies Lessons

Allen, Roach Van. 1976. *Language Experiences in Communication.* Boston, MA: Houghton Mifflin.

Brown, Hazel and Cambourne, Brian. 1989. *Read and Retell.* Portsmouth, NH: Heinemann.

Freeman, Yvonne S. and Freeman, David E. 1992. *Whole Language for Second Language Learners.* Portsmouth, NH: Heinemann.

Gilles, Carol, Bixby, Mary, Crowley, Paul, Crenshaw, Shirley R., et al. 1988. *Whole Language Strategies for Secondary Students.* Katonah, NY: Richard C. Owen Publishers, Inc.

Goodman, Kenneth S., Bird, Lois B., and Goodman, Yetta M. 1991. *The Whole Language Catalog.* Santa Rosa, CA: American School Publishers.

Goodman, Kenneth S., Bird, Lois B., and Goodman, Yetta M. 1992. *The Whole Language Catalog Supplement on Authentic Assessment.* Santa Rosa, CA: American School Publishers.

Huck, Charlotte, Hepler, Susan, and Hickman, Janet. 1993. *Children's Literature in the Elementary School.* New York, NY: Holt, Rinehart & Winston.

Martin, Bill Jr. 1972, 1974. *Teacher's Editions: Sounds of Language Readers.* New York, NY: Holt, Rinehart & Winston.

Tierney, Robert, Readence, John, and Dishner, Ernest. 1990. *Reading Strategies and Practices: A Compendium.* Boston, MA: Allyn & Bacon.

(See professional journals such as *Language Arts* and *English Journal*, and books published by National Council of Teachers of English, Urbana, Illinois; *The Reading Teacher* and *Journal of Reading*, published by International Reading Association, Newark, Delaware; both organizations have book lists for various ages and subject matter. Also see *Horn Book* for critiques of books written for children and youth.)

Selected Miscue Research

Allen, David and Watson, Dorothy. 1977. *Research Findings in Miscue Analysis.* Urbana, IL: National Council of Teachers of English.

Altwerger, Bess and Goodman, Kenneth S. 1981. *Studying Test Difficulty Through Miscue Analysis. A Research Report. Occasional Paper #3.* Tucson, AZ: University of Arizona, Program in Language and Literacy.

Brown, Joel, Goodman, Kenneth S., and Marek, Ann. 1994. *Annotated Chronological Miscue Analysis Bibliography. Occasional Paper #16.* Tucson, AZ: University of Arizona, Program in Language and Literacy.

Goodman, Kenneth S. 1983. *Text Features as They Relate to Miscues: Determiners. A Research Report. Occasional Paper #8.* Tucson, AZ: University of Arizona, Program in Language and Literacy.

Goodman, Kenneth S. and Bird, Lois B. 1982. *The Working of Texts: Intra-Text Word Frequency. A Research Report. Occasional Paper #6.* Tucson, AZ: University of Arizona, Program in Language and Literacy.

Goodman, Kenneth S. and Burke, Carolyn. 1968. *Studies of Children's Behavior while Reading Orally.* Washington, DC: U.S. Dept. of Health, Education, and Welfare, Office of Education, Project No. S425.

Goodman, Kenneth S. and Burke, Carolyn. 1973. *Theoretically Based Studies of Patterns of Miscues in Oral Reading Performance.* Washington, DC: U.S. Dept. of Health, Education, and Welfare, Office of Education, Project No. 9-0375.

Goodman, Kenneth S. and Gespass, Suzanne. 1983. *Text Features as They Relate to Miscues: Research Report.* Tucson, AZ: University of Arizona, Program in Language and Literacy.

Goodman, Kenneth S. and Gollasch, Frederick V. 1981. *Word Level Omissions in Reading: Deliberate and Non-deliberate. A Research Report. Occasional Paper #2.* Tucson, AZ: University of Arizona, Program in Language and Literacy.

Goodman, Kenneth S. and Goodman, Yetta M. 1978. *Final Report Project NIE-C-00-3-0087: Reading of American Children Whose Language is a Stable Rural Dialect of English or Language other than English.* Washington, DC: National Institute of Education.

Goodman, Yetta M. and Marek, Ann. 1985. *Retrospective Miscue Analysis. Occasional Paper #19.* Tucson, AZ: University of Arizona, Program in Language and Literacy.

Goodman, Yetta M. and Marek, Ann. 1996. *Retrospective Miscue Analysis: Revaluing Readers and Reading.* Katonah, NY: Richard C. Owen Publishers, Inc.

Long, Patricia C. 1985. *The Effectiveness of Reading Miscue Instruments. A Research Report. Occasional Paper #13.* Tucson, AZ: University of Arizona, Program in Language and Literacy.

Watson, Dorothy J. 1973. *A Psycholinguistic Description of the Oral Reading Miscues Generated by Selected Readers Prior to and Following Exposure to a Saturated Book Program.* Unpublished dissertation. Detroit, MI: Wayne State University.

Williams, Geoffrey, Jack, David, and Goodman, Kenneth S. 1985. *Revaluing Troubled Readers. Two Papers. Occasional Paper #15.* Tucson, AZ: University of Arizona, Program in Language and Literacy.

Woodley, John W. 1984. *Perception in a Psycholinguistic Model of the Reading Process. A Research Report. Occasional Paper #11.* Tucson, AZ: University of Arizona, Program for Language and Literacy.

References

Ahlberg, Janet and Ahlberg, Allen. 1978. *Each Peach Pear Plum.* New York, NY: Viking.

Allen, Paul D. and Watson, Dorothy J. 1976. *Findings of Research in Miscue Analysis: Classroom Implications.* Urbana, IL: ERIC Clearinghouse on Reading and Communication Skills and National Council of Teachers of English.

Allen, Roach Van. 1976. *Language Experiences in Communication.* Boston, MA: Houghton Mifflin.

Allen, Roach Van and Allen, Claryce. 1982. *Language Experience Activities.* Boston, MA: Houghton Mifflin.

Bank Street College of Education. 1972. "Bill Evers and the Tigers." In Y. Goodman and C. Burke, eds., *Readings for Taping: Reading Miscue Inventory.* New York, NY: Macmillan.

Barchas, Sarah. 1975. *I Was Walking Down the Road.* New York, NY: Scholastic.

Barnes, Douglas. 1992. *From Communication to Curriculum.* Portsmouth, NH: Heinemann.

Bialostok, Steve. 1992. *Raising Readers: Helping your Child to Literacy.* Winnipeg, Manitoba, Canada: Peguis.

Charlip, Remy. 1972. *What Good Luck, What Bad Luck.* New York, NY: Scholastic.

Cole, Joanna. 1986. *The Magic School Bus at the Waterworks.* New York, NY: Scholastic.

Cole, Joanna. 1987. *The Magic School Bus Inside the Earth.* New York, NY: Scholastic.

Cole, Joanna. 1989. *The Magic School Bus Inside the Human Body.* New York, NY: Scholastic.

Cole, Joanna. 1990. *The Magic School Bus Lost in the Solar System.* New York, NY: Scholastic.

Dahl, Roald. 1982. *The BFG.* New York, NY: Farrar, Straus & Giroux.

Davis, Peter, ed. 1970. *The American Heritage Dictionary of the English Language.* New York, NY: Dell.

Degen, Bruce. 1983. *Jamberry.* New York, NY: Harper & Row.

Dorros, Arthur. 1991. *Abuela.* New York, NY: Dutton.

Flexner, Stuart Berg and Hauck, Leonore Crary. 1987. *The Random House Dictionary of the English Language.* New York, NY: Random House.

Fox, Mem. 1987. *Possum Magic.* New York, NY: Macmillan.

Freire, Paulo and Macedo, Donald. 1987. *Literacy: Reading the Word and the World.* South Hadley, MA: Bergin & Garvey.

Gilman, Phoebe. 1989. *Little Blue Ben.* New York, NY: Scholastic.

Ginsburg, Mirra. 1972. *The Chick and the Duckling.* New York, NY: Macmillan.

Ginsburg, Mirra. 1981. *Where Does the Sun Go at Night?* New York, NY: Macmillan.

Goodman, Kenneth S. 1964. "The Linguistics of Reading." *Elementary School Journal,* Volume 64, number 8, pp. 355–361.

Goodman, Kenneth S. 1989. "Whole-Language Research: Foundations and Development." *Elementary School Journal,* Volume 90, number 2, pp. 207–221.

Goodman, Kenneth S. 1993. *Phonics Phacts.* Portsmouth, NH: Heinemann.

Goodman, Kenneth S. 1994. "Reading, Writing, and Written Texts: A Transactional Socio-psycholinguistic View." In R. B. Ruddell, M. R. Ruddell, and H. Singer, eds., *Theoretical*

Models and Processes of Reading, pp. 1093–1130. Newark, DE: International Reading Association.

Goodman, Kenneth S., Bird, Lois, and Goodman, Yetta M. 1991. *The Whole Language Catalog.* Santa Rosa, CA: American School Publishers.

Goodman, Kenneth S., Bird, Lois, and Goodman, Yetta M. 1992. *The Whole Language Catalog Supplement on Authentic Assessment.* Santa Rosa, CA: American School Publishers.

Goodman, Kenneth S. and Burke, Carolyn. 1973. *Theoretically Based Studies of Patterns of Miscues in Oral Reading Performance.* (Grant No. OEG-0-90320375-4269). Washington, DC: U.S. Dept. of Health, Education, and Welfare, Office of Education, Project No. 9-0375.

Goodman, Kenneth S. and Gespass, Suzanne. 1983. *Text Features as They Relate to Miscues: Pronouns. Occasional Paper #7.* Tucson, AZ: University of Arizona, Program in Language and Literacy.

Goodman, Kenneth S. and Goodman, Yetta M. 1978. *Final Report Project NIE-C-00-3-0087: Reading of American Children Whose Language Is a Stable Rural Dialect of English or a Language Other than English.* Washington, DC: National Institute of Education.

Goodman, Kenneth S., Smith, E. Brooks, Meredith, Robert, and Goodman, Yetta M. 1987. *Language and Thinking in School: A Whole Language Curriculum.* Katonah, NY: Richard C. Owen Publishers, Inc.

Goodman, Yetta M. 1985. "Observing Children in the Classroom." In A. Jaggar and M. T. Smith-Burke, eds., *Observing the Language Learner,* pp. 9–18. Newark, DE and Urbana, IL: Co-published by the International Reading Association and the National Council of Teachers of English.

Goodman, Yetta M. 1989. "Roots of the Whole-Language Movement." *Elementary School Journal,* Volume 90, number 2, pp. 113–127.

Goodman, Yetta M. 1991. "Informal Methods of Evaluation." In J. Flood, J. M. Jensen, D. Lapp, and J. R. Squire, eds., *Handbook of Research on Teaching the English Language Arts,* pp. 502–509. New York, NY: Macmillan.

Goodman, Yetta M., Altwerger, Bess, and Marek, Ann. 1989. *Print Awareness in Preschool Children. Occasional Paper #4.* Tucson, AZ: University of Arizona, Program in Language and Literacy.

Goodman, Yetta M. and Marek, Ann. 1989. *Retrospective Miscue Analysis. Occasional Paper #19.* Tucson, AZ: University of Arizona, Program in Language and Literacy.

Goodman, Yetta M. and Marek, Ann. 1996. *Retrospective Miscue Analysis: Revaluing Readers and Reading.* Katonah, NY: Richard C. Owen Publishers, Inc.

Goodman, Yetta M. and Watson, Dorothy J. 1977. "A Comprehension-Centered Reading Program." *Language Arts,* Volume 54, number 8, pp. 868–879.

Goodman, Yetta M., Watson, Dorothy J., and Burke, Carolyn L. 1987. *Reading Miscue Inventory: Alternative Procedures.* Katonah, NY: Richard C. Owen Publishers, Inc.

Goodwin, Doris K. 1987. *The Fitzgeralds and the Kennedys.* New York, NY: Simon & Schuster.

Goss, Janet and Harste, Jerome. 1981. *It Didn't Frighten Me.* St. Petersburg, FL: Willowisp/School Book Fairs.

Haley, Alex. 1976. *Roots.* New York, NY: Dell.

Heath, Shirley Brice. 1983. *Ways with Words: Language, Life, and Work in Communities and Classrooms.* New York, NY: Cambridge University Press.

Heilbroner, Joan. 1962. *This Is the House Where Jack Lives.* New York, NY: Harper & Row.

Houston, Gloria. 1988. *Littlejim.* New York, NY: Philomel.

Hurwitz, Johanna. 1989. *Much Ado about Aldo.* New York, NY: Morrow.

Hutchins, Pat. 1968. *Rosie's Walk.* New York, NY: Macmillan.

Johnston, Tony. 1992. *The Quilt Story.* New York, NY: Putnam.

Kasza, Keiko. 1990. *When the Elephant Walks.* New York, NY: Putnam.

Kelly, Earl. 1955. "Teaching Current Issues in the Schools." In R. Ellsworth and O. Sands, eds., *Twenty-sixth Yearbook of the National Council for the Social Studies: Improving the Social Studies Curriculum.* Washington, DC: National Council for the Social Studies.

Kipling, Rudyard. 1952. "How the Whale Got His Throat." In *Just So Stories,* pp. 8–11. Garden City, NY: Doubleday.

Kraus, Robert. 1970. *whose mouse are you?.* New York, NY: Macmillan.

Kurusa. 1985. *The Streets Are Free.* New York, NY: Annick Press.

Levine, Ellen. 1989. *I Hate English.* New York, NY: Scholastic.

Lobel, Arnold. 1980. *Fables.* New York, NY: Harper & Row.

Lowry, Lois. 1993. *The Giver*. Boston, MA: Houghton Mifflin.

Martin, J. R. and Marx, P. 1992. *Now Everybody Hates Me*. New York, NY: HarperCollins.

McCord, David. 1984. "The Pickety Fence." In J. Cole, ed., *New Treasury of Children's Poetry: Old Favorites and New Discoveries*. Garden City, NY: Doubleday.

Moll, Luis, Amanti, Cathy, Neff, Deborah, and Gonzalez, Norma. 1992. "Funds of Knowledge for Teaching: A Qualitative Approach to Connect Households and Classrooms." *Theory Into Practice*, Volume 31, number 2, pp. 132–141.

Montessori, Maria. 1966. *The Secret of Childhood*. New York, NY: Ballantine Books.

Neisser, Ulric. 1976. *Cognition and Reality*. San Francisco, CA: W. H. Freeman.

Paterson, Katherine. 1991. *Lyddie*. New York, NY: Lodestar Books.

Rapoport, Roger. 1970. "Why We Need a Generation Gap." *Look*, Jan. 13, p. 14.

Redmond, Eugene B. 1993. "Boyz n Search of Their Soular System." In T. Feelings, ed., *Soul Looks Back in Wonder*, p. 4. New York, NY: Dial.

Rhodes, Lynn and Shanklin, Nancy L. 1989. *A Research Base for Whole Language*. Denver, CO: LINK.

Roosevelt, Eleanor. 1961. *Autobiography of Eleanor Roosevelt*. New York, NY: Harper.

Rosenblatt, Louise. 1938. *Literature as Exploration*. New York, NY: Appleton-Century-Crofts.

Rosenblatt, Louise. 1978. *The Reader, the Text, the Poem*. Carbondale, IL: Southern Illinois University Press.

Rosenblatt, Louise. 1983. *Literature as Exploration*. New York, NY: Modern Language Association.

Rosenblatt, Louise. 1994. *The Reader, the Text, the Poem*. Carbondale, IL: Southern Illinois University Press.

Russell, David et al. 1966. "The Stonecutter." In *Roads to Everywhere—The Ginn Basic Readers*. Needham Heights, MA: Silver Burdett Ginn.

Schulberg, Budd. 1968. *The Disenchanted*. New York, NY: Bantam Books.

Scieszka, Jon and Smith, Lane. 1992. *The Stinky Cheese Man*. New York, NY: Viking.

Sendak, Maurice. 1963. *Where the Wild Things Are*. New York, NY: Scholastic.

Shannon, George. 1981. *Lizard's Song*. New York, NY: Greenwillow.

Short, Kathy G. and Pierce, Kathryn M. 1990. *Talking about Books*. Portsmouth, NH: Heinemann.

Soukhanov, Anne H., ed. 1992. *The American Heritage Dictionary of the English Language*. Boston, MA: Houghton Mifflin.

Steig, William. 1988. *Sylvester and the Magic Pebble*. New York, NY: Trumpet Club.

Stephens, Diane. 1990. *Research on Whole Language: Support for a New Curriculum*. Katonah, NY: Richard C. Owen Publishers, Inc.

Taylor, Denny. 1983. *Family Literacy: Young Children Learning to Read and Write*. Portsmouth, NH: Heinemann.

Taylor, Denny. 1993. *From the Child's Point of View*. Portsmouth, NH: Heinemann.

Taylor, Denny and Dorsey-Gaines, Catherine. 1988. *Growing Up Literate: Learning from Inner-City Families*. Portsmouth, NH: Heinemann.

Thoreau, David. 1980. *Walden*. London, England: Folio Society.

Tierney, Robert J., Readence, John E., and Dishner, Ernest K. 1990. *Reading Strategies and Practices: A Compendium*. Boston, MA: Allyn & Bacon.

Verne, Jules. 1965. *A Journey to the Center of the Earth*. New York, NY: Scholastic.

Watson, Dorothy. 1973. "A Psycholinguistic Description of the Oral Reading Miscues Generated by Selected Readers Prior to and Following Exposure to a Saturated Book Program." Ph.D. diss., Wayne State University.

Watson, Dorothy. 1978. "Getting More from Sustained Silent Reading: Reader Selected Miscues." *English Education*, Volume 10, number 2, pp. 75–85.

Watson, Dorothy and Hoge, Sharon. 1996. "Reader-Selected Miscues." In Y. Goodman and A. Marek, eds., *Retrospective Miscue Analysis: Revaluing Readers and Reading*. Katonah, NY: Richard C. Owen Publishers, Inc.

Weisman, JoAnne. 1991. *The Lowell Mill Girls: Life in the Factory*. Lowell, MA: Discovery Enterprises.

"Whale." 1995. *World Book Encyclopedia*. Volume 21, pp. 256–267. Chicago, IL: World Book, Inc.

Wheatley, Nadia and Rawlins, Donna. 1987. *My Place*. Melbourne, Australia: Collins Dove.

Whitmore, Kathryn F. and Crowell, Caryl G. 1992. "Can We Talk? Evaluating Oral Language from the Inside and Outside." In K. S. Goodman, L. B. Bird, and Y. M. Goodman, eds.,

The Whole Language Catalog Supplement on Authentic Assessment, p. 145. Santa Rosa, CA: American School Publishers.

Whitmore, Kathryn F. and Crowell, Caryl G. 1994. *Inventing a Classroom: Life in a Bilingual, Whole Language Learning Community.* York, ME: Stenhouse.

Wilde, Sandra. 1992. *You Kan Red This: Spelling and Punctuation for Whole Language Classrooms, K–6.* Portsmouth, NH: Heinemann.

Wood, Audrey and Wood, Don. 1984. *The Napping House.* San Diego, CA: Harcourt Brace Jovanovich.

Index